H.E. Bates

A bibliographical study

Twentieth Century Writers series No.6

Twentieth Century Writers No. 6

H.E. BATES

A bibliograhical study

PETER EADS

Peter Eads (signature)

St Paul's Bibliographies
Winchester, Hampshire
Omnigraphics
Penobscot Building • Detroit • 1990

First published in Great Britain in 1990
by St Paul's Bibliographies, 1 Step Terrace
Winchester, Hampshire
and in the United States by
Omnigraphics, Penobscot Building, Detroit

British Library Cataloguing Publication Data
Eads, Peter, *1922 -*
H.E. Bates: a bibliographical study
(Twentieth century writers series)
1. Fiction in English. Bates, H.E. (Herbert Ernest)
1905-1974 bibliographies
I. Title II. Series
016 823'914
ISBN 0-906795-76-1

Library of Congress Catalog Card Number 90-4 3504

♾ Printed on long-life paper
Typesetting by Bureau One Ltd, Winchester
Printed in Great Britain by
The Alden Press, Oxford

Contents

Erratum

page 54   The heading for the unpublished item **A 50** should precede *Notes*
which at present appear under **A 49.**

FOR

VERNA

Preface

I have endeavoured to include in this bibliography all of the published work of H.E. Bates, with the exception of reviews he wrote for *Everyman* (14 January-2 July 1932), the *New Clarion* (April 1932-April 1933), *Morning Post* (22 January-24 September 1937) and *John O'London's Weekly* (October 1932-April 1933 and April 1937-December 1940).

I have included a small number of unpublished works, 'The Night Interception Battle 1940-1941' and 'The Battle of the Flying Bomb', two long pamphlets held in the Public Record Office and which I regard as important historical documents bearing on events in the 1939-1945 war. Two plays are also included, 'Carrie and Cleopatra' and 'The Spider Love'. The first was performed at the Torch Theatre in London and became the centre of a publication dispute between Bates and Jonathan Cape; the second, never performed or published, was described by Bates in his autobiography as 'incontestably formidable in its demands on actors', offering that as the probable reason why it was never performed.

In Section A, Books, Plays and Pamphlets, bibliographical information is recorded of all English and the majority of American first publications. I have taken the opportunity to describe as fully as possible all dust jackets. Where available, I have included print quantities, those for the Jonathan Cape publications having been obtained from the Cape archives in the library of Reading University. The lack of precise figures in some cases is due to publishers' records not having been preserved or of their reluctance to provide them. Gerald Pollinger, who remains literary agent to the Bates Estate, took an immense amount of trouble to provide sales figures for many of the publications where print quantities were not available. I should like to record my sincere thanks to him and his staff for their ready and willing help in many directions; nothing has ever been too much trouble for them.

Contents of collections of short stories and essays have been listed in a separate note below each such publication. The history of each short story and essay is fully recorded in Sections B and C and may be easily found by reference to the Index. I am told by many avid collectors that they welcome this method as they do wish to know of first publications. Another valid point is that as early collections have become scarce and expensive it will point collectors in the direction of anthologies and magazines where many of the stories can be found at relatively low cost. It is also hoped that this method will remove all existing doubts concerning publication of the 'Flying Officer X' stories. Much of the confusion has arisen because individuals who have produced short bibliographies of Bates's work have followed *The New Cambridge Bibliography of English Literature* where under the Bates listing it is stated that the American publication of *There's Something in the Air* was the American version of the English publication of *The Greatest People in the World*. Although the stories collected in *There's Something in the Air* did include those in *The Greatest People in the World*, twelve other stories were also collected, six of which were never to appear in an English collection. Further confusion was caused when in 1944 an English collection was published and given the title, *Something in the Air*. However, that publication merely brought together the stories previously collected in *The Greatest People in the World* and *How Sleep the Brave*.

Notes of holograph manuscripts traced in this country are recorded under the entries for the works concerned. Many others which found their way to America are preserved at the Harry Ransom Humanities Research Center at the University of Texas and are not separately noted.

As Bates made many comments on his books in the three volumes of his autobiography, those of most interest have been included in the Notes. Where his comments applied to a short story, novella or essay, a note is appended at the foot of the entry in Sections B and C.

Section D records the published poetry and includes the limited editions of three Christmas cards for 1928, 1930 and 1931 and one privately printed in 1949.

During the early stages of my work I quickly learned that a bibliographer can never hope to succeed without relying heavily on the generosity of countless individuals. I owe my greatest debts to Madge Bates and the late Edmund Kirby for not only allowing me unlimited access to their libraries but for their understanding, encouragement and hospitality. My visits to their homes and books became very special. It was a sad day for me when Edmund Kirby died in December 1988, just weeks away from his hundredth birthday. Only a few months before he had written a few lines which he hoped would provide a short foreword to this bibliography. Whilst they flatter me I am happy that he should be associated with my efforts.

I am also most grateful to Graham Greene for his good wishes and his assessment of Bates as a writer of short stories.

I offer my sincere thanks to the following individuals who have given valuable advice and practical assistance:

Mr Richard Bates; Mr Jonathan Bates; Mr John S. Ward, CBE, RA; Mr Ken Geering; Mr J.L. Carr; Mr Philip Brown, Blackwell's Rare Books; Mr Charles Boxer; Mr and Mrs John Evans; Miss A. Ryder; Mr R.A.R. Wilson, Historical Aviation Service; Mr A.J. Sillem, Bell, Book & Radmall Ltd,; Mr Michael Hosking; Mr P. Howarth; Mr Dennis Morris; Mr Allan Roberts; Mr John Shakles; Mr Brian Cocks; Mr Steve Billingham; Mrs D.I. Angus; Mr Christopher Heppa; Mr Richard Holroyd; Mr and Mrs Terry Townsend; Mr John Welland; Mr John Towensend, Old Hall Bookshop, Brackley; Mr Cyril Smith; Ron and Stephen James, Abington Bookshop, Northampton; Mr Peter Jolliffe; Dr William Peden, University of Missouri-Columbia; Mr John Cutts; Mr Tony Marshall; Professor Dean Baldwin and Charles W. Mann, Pennsylvania State University; Cathy Henderson, University of Texas at Austin; Judy Foster, Park Bookshop, Wellingborough; David J. Veryard, Wootton-Billingham, Northampton; and John Sothern, Higham Ferrers.

I would like to offer special thanks to the following for permission to quote from books or for the illustrations:

BBC Data (BBC Drama Script Library and BBC Written Archives Centre) for a quotation from the *Radio Times* and the reproduction of an Agreement between H.E. Bates and the BBC; Mr Norman Longmate for quotations from his book *The Doodlebugs*, published by Century Hutchinson Ltd; Victor Gollancz Ltd for the title-page of *Through the Woods*; Oxford University Press for part of the Introduction by V.S. Pritchett to *Uncle Silas* (1984); Cambridge University Press for the Dedication in *The Seasons & The Gardener*, Jonathan Cape Ltd for the dust jacket of *The Two Sisters*; and finally to Laurence Pollinger Ltd for extensive extracts from the three volumes of Bates's autobiography.

My thanks are also due to librarians and their staffs, publishers and other institutions for their ready and willing assistance. I would particularly like to mention the following:

Rushden, Kettering and Northampton branches of Northamptonshire Libraries; Mr Michael Bott, University of Reading Library; Zoltan Karolyi, Staatsbibliothek Preussicher Kulturbesitz, Berlin; Mr D.S. Goodes, Walpole Library, King's School, Canterbury; Ms M.E.E.E. Ward, Kent County Library, Folkestone; Mrs M. Smith, Kent County Library, Maidstone; Miss H.M. Young, University of London Library; British Library, London and Colindale; Public Record Office, Kew; Mr Gordon Leith, Royal Air Force Museum; Wing Commander B. Taylor, RAF, and Mr Dennis Bateman, Air Historical Branch, Ministry of Defence; Grizelda Ohannessian, New Directions Publishing, New York; Reed International plc; B.T. Batsford Ltd.; Thomas Nelson and Sons Ltd.; Mr Chris Deering, Wheaton (Pergamon Group); Louise Higham, A. & C. Black; Susan Cowan, Express Newspapers plc; Cheryl Francis, Esso UK plc; The Football Association; Jenny Dereham, Michael Joseph Ltd; Her Majesty's Stationery Office; South Eastern Magazines Ltd; Susan Hindess, International Thomson Publishing Ltd,; Katie Burgess, Longman Group UK Ltd.; Annabel Edwards, Robinson Publishing; Mr R Webb, *Sunday Telegraph*; Sarah Cartledge, IPC Magazines Ltd.; Christopher Hall, *The Countryman*.

Last, but by no means least, I have to express my gratitude to the publishers. Over a long period of time Robert Cross has given me his fullest support and without his kindness and understanding publication would not have been possible. My final sincere thanks must go to Helen Lefroy for her patience and skill in the final preparations, and to Lynne Evans for her expertise in designing the dust jacket.

Forewords

After 60 years of writing and reading I would place H.E. Bates and V.S. Pritchett as the best short-story writers of my time.

GRAHAM GREENE

Antibes, France
6 December 1988

H.E. Bates was a lifelong friend. In his Rushden days we spent much time together, and when he moved to Kent a steady correspondence began, which lasted until his untimely death.

He was a hardworking and prolific writer, and the task facing Peter Eads might well have daunted a less determined man. To him it was a labour of love to trace a large and varied output.

He accepted the challenge and I cannot praise too highly the skill displayed in the search. The results will surprise many admirers of Bates, learning for the first time of books quite unknown to them. Everything Peter did was marked by accuracy and close attention to detail. This record is not likely to be superceded: To Bates' admirers it will be indispensable.

EDMUND E. KIRBY

Barton Seagrave, Northants
1988

H.E. Bates

Herbert Ernest Bates (always H.E. to his family and friends) was born at Rushden, Northamptonshire, on 16 May 1905.

From his local school he won a 'free scholarship' to Kettering Grammar School where in 1919 he was destined to meet Edmund Kirby, a young infantry officer who had been seriously wounded in the Great War and on leaving the army had taken a post as English master at the school. From the moment of their first meeting, Bates, who excelled as an athlete and footballer but who had shown a general indifference towards many of the school's teaching practices, found a new inspiration. His lethargy disappeared and a secret ambition to become a writer suddenly emerged. On many occasions in later life he dated his literary career from that moment and acknowledged the debt he owed to Kirby for the awakening. He dedicated *The Last Bread* and *Thirty Tales* to him and they remained life-long friends.

Bates's first literary success came when his poem 'Armistice Day, November 11th 1920' was printed in the school magazine for December 1920. He later described that event as 'the first of a host of embarrassments of seeing myself in print'.

He qualified by examination, obtaining Third Class Honours, for entrance to Cambridge University, but decided himself not to go, a decision he always maintained he never regretted.

He left school when he was sixteen and a half and obtained a post as a junior reporter with a local newspaper at ten shillings a week. Finding his work and his immediate employer equally distasteful he quickly realised that journalism of that sort would not provide easy stepping-stones towards becoming a successful writer. He then obtained work as a clerk in the warehouse of a local leather and grindery factory with a salary of one pound a week. The move was a fortunate one for he found time there to write. Being left alone in the office he somehow managed to dispose of his official work by nine-thirty in the morning and then was able to concentrate on his own work. In fact, every word of *The Two Sisters* was written in the office.

Following the benefits of his employer's time in the writing, the path towards publication was not easy. The manuscript had been in the hands of nine publishers before it was read by Edward Garnett for Jonathan Cape. As with Kirby earlier, Bates's work had again fallen into the right hands, for Garnett had an undisputed reputation for discovering talented writers. *The Two Sisters* was published when

Bates was just twenty-one and the tutelage, encouragement and guidance he was later to receive from Garnett beyond measure. The two became close friends and the acceptance of *The Two Sisters* by Cape was the start of an association which was to last for twenty years. The partnership with Garnett was truly a great one and was acknowleged by Bates in detail when his book, *Edward Garnett: A Memoir* was published by Max Parrish in 1950.

Bates married Marjorie Helen Cox (Madge) at Rushden in July 1931; immediately he and his wife left Northamptonshire to live at Little Chart in the heart of the Kent countryside. There they converted an old granary into a most comfortable home and with a great appetite for gardening Bates created a wonderful garden from what had been a wilderness.

With his reputation as a novelist and short-story writer established he scored two notable successes as a writer of country matters when *Through The Woods* (1936) and *Down The River* (1937) were published by Gollancz. Both books were beautifully illustrated with wood engravings by Agnes Miller Parker and they received general acclamation.

His writing of short fiction continued to impress and the annual inclusion of one or more of his stories in Edward J. O'Brien's 'Best Short Stories' series enhanced Bates's reputation as one of the greatest short-story writers of this century. Many of his books were published in America and at home the 'Uncle Silas' stories were an immediate success.

When war was declared on Germany in 1939, Bates had a wife and four children to support. Many publishers' premises were destroyed during the bombing of London and life for authors became precarious. While waiting for some appointment in which he could best use his skills as a writer for the benefit of the country he compiled *The Modern Short Story: A Critical Survey.* Published in 1941, the book remains today a valuable work of reference for students of the short story.

In the autumn of 1941 Bates was commissioned in the Royal Air Force and given the task of writing stories about the men who were striving at great odds for supremacy in the skies. His commission was literally a roving one for he was able to visit Royal Air Force Stations without hindrance and there observe and talk to the men who fought the war in the air. His stories, written under the pseudonym of 'Flying Officer X' were a phenomenal success, both in this country and in America. The first stories appeared in the *News Chronicle* and when published in collections by Jonathan Cape they sold in hundreds of thousands. Certainly no other writer during the years of war received the acclaim given to Bates. Despite such overwhelming success he made little or no financial gain, for it was argued that as a Crown servant he was not entitled to receive royalties from the huge sales. That situation combined with other matters brought about disagreements with Jonathan Cape and in 1943 Laurence Pollinger became his agent and Michael Joseph his publisher. These fresh associations were given an auspicious start with the publication of *Fair Stood the Wind for France.* The book became an immediate best-seller and was hailed my many critics as the best war-time novel to have been written by a British author.

Following his success as 'Flying Officer X', Bates was promoted to Squadron Leader and continued to write official pamphlets at the Air Ministry. Two of the most important, 'The Night Interception Battle 1940-1941' and 'The Battle of the Flying Bomb' were, for diplomatic and security reasons, never published and remain in their typed state in the Public Record Office.

During this time his own books had not been neglected; *In The Heart Of The Country* (1942), *The Bride Comes to Evensford* (1943) and *O More Than Happy Countryman* (1943) were all published during the war years.

His last overseas assignment for the Air Ministry was in the Far East. Experiences and observations in India and Burma resulted in the publication between 1947 and 1950 of three more best-sellers, *The Purple Plain, The Jacaranda Tree* and *The Scarlet Sword.*

The post-war years saw Bates riding a huge wave of success and when he came to write his autobiography he could faithfully describe that period as The World in Ripeness.

During those years his output was enormous and some critics argued that he had written too much. He astounded some by writing the Larkin novels. The first, *The Darling Buds of May,* was an immediate favourite with the public and despite being censured by some serious critics as a book of nonsense, its popular appeal was repeated in successive years with *A Breath of French Air* and *When the Green Woods Laugh.*

Bates wrote three volumes of autobiography, *The Vanished World* (1969), *The Blossoming World* (1971) and *The World in Ripeness* (1972), each with masterly illustrations by John Ward.

Bates was created CBE in June 1973 and died in January 1974. A service of Thanksgiving for his life and work was held at the Church of St Bride, Fleet Street, London, on 22 April 1974; Sir Bernard Miles read a lesson and Sir Robert Lusty gave an address.

An obituary notice in *The Times* paid tribute to his work: 'he was without an equal in England in the kind of story he had made his own and stood in the direct line of succession of fiction-writers of the English countryside that includes George Eliot, Hardy and D.H. Lawrence.'

Bates was a determined, resolute man who in a literary sense was self-educated; he was a lover of family life, the countryside and his garden.

Since his death critical studies of his work have been made in America and in this country. Without doubt there will be more to come for Bates's versatility has presented the student with a vast and intriguing choice.

THROUGH
the WOODS

The English Woodland—April to April

By

H. E. BATES

With 73 Engravings on Wood
By AGNES MILLER PARKER

VICTOR GOLLANCZ LTD COVENT GARDEN
1 9 3 6

A 27

A
Books, plays, pamphlets

A 1   LOYALTY - A Play in one act   1926

The play (script not available) was first broadcast from the BBC studio at Bournemouth on 20 January and 3 February 1926 and later from London, Aberdeen, Newcastle and Cardiff.

The London (National) broadcast was at 8.45 p.m. on Tuesday, 6 April 1926. From the *Radio Times* (2 April 1926):

"Loyalty", a fanciful fragment by H.E. Bates
Producer HOWARD ROSE
Aunt Matilda MIRIAM FERRIS
Mrs. Peach MABEL CONSTANDUROS
Mr. Peach HENRY OSCAR
David Their Son MICHAEL HOGAN
June, A Girl PHYLLIS PANTING

The time is a Saturday afternoon, about 3 o'clock. The scene a stiff, though comfortably-furnished room in a provincial house. Victorian prints of the Boer War, Queen Victoria, and the Prince Consort adorn the flowery-papered walls. A fire is burning in a big black, shining grate. Rain is splashing on the windows through which comes a greyish light, showing a table completely laid for tea. A kettle is already on the fire. Aunt Matilda speaks.

The play was produced on stage in the author's home town of Rushden, Northants, on Thursday and Saturday 3 and 5 March 1926. It had been previously advertised: 'HAVE WE TALENT IN RUSHDEN?' The BBC chose "Loyalty" (by our prominent author H.E. Bates) for several Broadcasts. You now have a chance of witnessing "Loyalty" at the Co-operative Hall Thursday and Saturday 3 & 5 March. Admission 2/- 1/6 reserved 1/- and 6d unreserved.'

On 4 March 1926 the *Rushden Echo* printed the following review:
'A better first night than most authors experience was the lot yesterday of Rushden's young man of letters, Mr. H.E. Bates. His short play "Loyalty" which

MEMORANDUM OF AGREEMENT made this Eighth day of January Nineteen
Hundred and Twenty-six between THE BRITISH BROADCASTING COMPANY
LIMITED, London, W.C.2. (hereinafter termed the Manager) of the
one part and MR. H. E. BATES of 15, Essex Road, Rushden
(hereinafter termed the Author) of the other part WHEREBY it is
mutually agreed between the parties as follows:-

1.   The Manager shall pay to the Author the sum of Ten Guineas
(£10.10.0.) upon the signing of this Agreement which sum shall
not be recoverable in any event.

2.   In consideration of the payment by the Manager of the above
mentioned sum of Ten Guineas (£10.10.0.) the Author grants to
the Manager the sole license to broadcast the play entitled
"LOYALTY" in the British Isles and in Northern Ireland and he
grants to the Manager no other rights whatever.

3.   The name of the Author shall be broadcast as the Author of
the said play at every broadcasting performance of the play and
it shall appear on all programmes and Press announcements issued
by the Manager.

4.   The Author guarantees that the play is an original work and is
in no way whatever a violation of any copyright belonging to any
other person or persons and he agrees to keep indemnified the
Manager from all sorts and all manner of claims and proceedings
taken against and expenses that may be incurred by the Manager
on the ground that the work is such violation of copyright.

    AS WITNESS the hands of the parties.

had been broadcast from a number of radio stations, was produced on the stage for the first time, and it had a good reception from a fairly large audience ....

' "Loyalty" is not wholly comedy or drama, but a little of both. It is a general skit on those who make a fuss about seeing Royalty, but there would be a little in it if it were not for the intrusion of June. She is the charm of it. She saves it from being a mere farce. She introduces the feeling of youth calling to youth, and the point of the play appears to be that this call is of far greater moment to the universe than the passing of transitory Royal Personages. On the stage this play was more successful than many had expected from their impression of its radio performances. There are a few of those expletives which I suppose modern young authors cannot be without, but on the whole it is a good theme presented in good taste. There is no attack on Royalty at all, but only a pitying exposure of those poor souls who treasure a moment's glimpse of "The Queen" as a great event in life.

'At the end Mr. H.E. Bates was called for and expressed himself as greatly in debt to the performers. He put in a plea for the development of the spoken drama in town and district.'

A 2   THE LAST BREAD   1926

THE LAST BREAD | A PLAY IN ONE ACT BY | H.E. BATES | (publisher's device) | THE LABOUR PUBLISHING COMPANY LIMITED | 38 GREAT ORMOND STREET LONDON W.C.1

Collation: One gathering only. 20 pp, consisting of half-title, terms for professional performance on verso, pp (i–ii); title-page, notice of publication and printer's imprint on verso, pp (iii–iv); dedication 'TO EDMUND E. KIRBY IN DEEP GRATITUDE'. Introduction by Monica Ewer on verso, pp v–vi; Characters, scene and time, verso blank, pp vii–(viii); text, pp 9–18; blank pp (19–20).

Binding: 8vo, $4\frac{4}{5}$ x $7\frac{3}{10}$ins. Buff wrappers printed in blue, inside covers at each end containing advertisements for Plays for the People Series, back cover a whole page advertisement within a rectangular ruled frame for Play Production for Everyone by Monica Ewer. No end papers; all edges cut.

Price: One Shilling net. Published May 1926.
Number of copies printed unknown.

Notes: The advertisement on inside front cover described the play as 'a tragedy of the struggle for existence. Poverty-stricken interior. One man, one woman and a child.'

Monica Ewer's Introduction (p vi): 'This is admittedly a grim little play, but not, I think, grimmer than reality. Of all tragedy that of the age-long struggle for existence is the one in which we are most concerned. We do not need to explore a

THE TWO SISTERS

By

H. E. BATES

WITH A FOREWORD BY EDWARD GARNETT

clash of personalities, drawing-room domestic entanglements, or the introspective melancholy of the idle. Tragedy is always to hand in the most universal and the most comprehensible form. In "The Last Bread" the presentation of the will to survive is shorn of all irrelevancies. We offer it as a simple expression of the most fundamental fact of life.'

The Vanished World (A 107) p 188: 'I was now twenty. As 1925 came to an end I was still unemployed, still on the dole. I had written not only novels, short stories and poems but also plays, mostly one-act plays, into one of which, *The Last Bread*, I had caustically poured some of my bitterness about the post-war twenties, not having read Knut Hamsun's *Hunger* for nothing.'

The Blossoming World (A 110) p 24: 'I had also sent my angry-young-man broadside, *The Last Bread*, to the Labour Publishing Company, run by E.N. and Monica Ewer, and that too had been accepted, though without advance, and was presently to be published at one shilling, thus becoming my first published book, preceding *The Two Sisters* by a month or two.'

A 3   THE TWO SISTERS   1926

A 3a First English edition

THE TWO SISTERS | BY | H.E. BATES | (publisher's device) | With a foreword by | EDWARD GARNETT | JONATHAN CAPE LIMITED | THIRTY BEDFORD SQUARE LONDON

Collation: (A)B-U^8. 320 pp, consisting of half-title, verso blank, pp (1–2); title-page, notice of publication, maker's and printer's imprint, ornament, pp (3–4); dedication 'to MY FATHER AND MOTHER', verso blank, pp (5–6); FOREWORD, pp 7–10; text, pp 11–320.

Binding: 8vo, 5 x 7⅜ins. Maroon cloth; lettered and ruled on spine in gold; publisher's device blind-stamped on back cover; top and fore-edges cut; lower edges uncut; white end papers.

White dust jacket. Front lettered in black with illustration by 'Cole' in blue, black, white and orange, depicting the sisters in foreground of industrial scene at night. Back cover lists 'Some New Jonathan Cape Fiction' in black. Spine lettered in black with publisher's device in blue.

Price: 7s. 6d. net. Published 24 June 1926.

1,500 copies were printed on 19 April 1926 and delivered on 29 May 1926. The type was distributed on 27 June 1927.

Made and printed in Great Britain by Butler & Tanner Ltd, Frome and London. Bound by Nevett.

SHEET NO.1 ·   TITLE. тс.ᴛнε Two Sɪᴀᴛᴇᴀᴀ.
                              ʟⱼ H.ᴇ.Bᴀᴛᴇᴄ.   ACCOUNT NO.1ⴰ.

NUMBER PRINTED	SHEET DELIVERIES	BINDING ORDERS	BINDERS DELIVERIES	BINDERS DELIVERIES	SALES	
PRINTER B.ᴛʜᴇ ₐ Tᴀᴀᴀᴇᴇ		BINDER Nɪᴀʟt				
	Date / Number	Date / Number	Date / Number	Date / Number	Date / Number	
Aₚᵣᵢₗ.₁₉.₁₉₂₆.	29.5.26 / 10.	2.6.16 / 750	2.6.26 / 18	1ᴜ.6.16 / 100	30.6.ᴀᴋ / 26ᴀ	
1500.	29.5.16 / 1,500	2ᴜ.6.16 / 51	21.6.16 / 350	21.6.26 / 150	ᴄᴏˡ.cˡᴇ. / 66	
		22.6.26 / 6	2ᴜ.6.16 / 133	2ᴜ.6.16 / 51	fᴏᴄᴄ / 2ᴜ	
		1.11.1.16 / 250	2ᴜ.6.26 / 6	26.1.26 / 100	31.12.16 / 6•7	
		.7.9.26 / 150	30.8.26 / 50	6.9.26 / 100	ᴄd.cˡᴇ / 223	
			20.9.26 / 100	6.10.16 / 100	ʜᵤ: / 13	
		1-.12.26 / 2ᴜᴜ	25.10.16 / 100	20.12.26 / 50	30.6.17 / 11	
		8.5.28 / 50	1ᴇᴇᴛᴇᴋᴀ / 50	2ᴜ.12.26 / 50	ᴄd cˡᴇ / 7	
			25.11.2ⴰ / 50	.6.5.29 / 25	fᴄᴄ / 2	
			11.6.29 / 15	27.9.29 / 26	31.12.27 / 12	
			11.11.29 / 15	10.11.29 / 2ᴜ	30.6.28 / 12	
			8.1.30 / 25	17.6.30 / 26	ʜᴇ / 2	
			11.ᴜᴜ.ᴀᴜ / 30		31.12.28 / 9	
					ᴄ.ᴄ. / 1	
EXTRAS	DELIVERIES				ʜᵤᵤ / 1	
Description	Date / Number				30.6.29 / 21	
Dᴇ Lₐ ᴍˡₐᵤ ᴜ.6.16					Frᴇᴇ / 1	
ₚᴄᴏᴏ jᴜᵤ	7.6.16 / 1,ᵢᴇᵢ				11.12.29 / .81	
Bᴄ).27.6.17					ᴄ.ᴄ. / ᴜ	
dᵢₛᵗᵣᵢᴄᵤᵗᵤᴜ.					10.6.30 / 6.1	
					ᴏ.ᴄ. / 2	
					fᵣᵉᵉ / 1	
					31.12.30. / 36	
					ᴄᵗₒff / 1	

From Jonathan Cape's sales ledger

Notes: In his Foreword, Edward Garnett wrote: 'A novel of rare poetical order... his achievement is that, whilst identified with his creations, Jenny, Jessie and Michael – the author has known how to detach himself from these figures of eternal youth and show them with all their tumultuous, passionate emotions, in a beautiful mirror. That is remarkable in an author of twenty years.'

The Vanished World (A 107) pp 150–51: 'My next novel, which in fact was to be my first to be published, *The Two Sisters*, had its genesis after this simple fashion: it sprang simply from the sight of a candle, or lamp, burning in a window. I was much given to walking alone at this time, more especially at night, and it was on this stygian, moonless night, I rather fancy in January, that I found myself walking through the tiny hamlet of Farndish, in the neighbourhood of which the Romans indisputably delved for iron. Half way down the village street I passed a biggish, square stone house in one room of which the curtains were not drawn. A light burned inside. I stopped for a moment, stared through the window into a room of a strange and shadowy emptiness and was instantly gripped first by a haunting sense of melancholy and then by the indefinable notion that I had been there, in front of that lamp-lit window before. I went home greatly troubled in imagination. A new genesis had begun.'

p 152 '... *The Two Sisters* was a work solely of imagination; indeed it would not be untrue to say of wild imagination, the rampaging, highly-coloured, not always coherent imagination of youth trying to say something but not knowing quite what it wanted to say.'

p 153 'Every word of *The Two Sisters* was written in the warehouse.'

p 154 '... it was the business of writing *The Two Sisters* in secret and mostly at breakneck speed, and then hiding the MS. away in a disused drawer at night .... I suppose I worked on *The Two Sisters* for a year.'

p 188 '... *The Two Sisters* was now with its tenth publisher. A few days before Christmas 1925, there arrived for me a letter from a firm of publishers, Jonathan Cape. In their letter they expressed a great interest in *The Two Sisters*. They liked it and wished to publish it.'

Manuscripts: An early manuscript was sold by the author to Sir Louis Sterling for £150. In 1954 it was presented by Sir Louis to the University of London Library. It is described in the Sterling Library Catalogue there (SLC V 39): 'The author's holograph manuscript written in ink on one side only of two hundred and eighteen sheets of quarto paper, with numerous corrections. Enclosed in an olive-green buckram folder lettered in gilt. A note by the author on the title page as follows: "This is the earliest draft, much shorter than the final but contains almost all the story, if not all the scenes, from that which the work was set up. The pages are numbered awkwardly and the style is awkward too, but was a product of only a month or two before the other." ' Published in 1926 (v. Part II, No.38).

The final draft manuscript is owned by the Bates family.

Reviews: 'An unusual performance; the story is implied rather than chronicled, the characters of the sisters disclose themselves slowly, incomplete until the last page, the setting becomes vaguely real and does not project itself with the definite violence of stage scenery as so often happens in what set out to be "novels of essentials". Jennie and Tessie and their incredible father live in the mind after the book has been laid aside, as people whose names sharpen the attention to the remembrance of poignant things ... *The Two Sisters* has freshness and great descriptive beauty.' *The Times Literary Supplement*

'A notable creative achievement. Admirably handled and I commend it to the fastidious literary epicure while assuring those who look for interest and excitement that they will not be disappointed.' *Punch*

'A reviewer, on turning the pages of a first novel, shares the hope of the lapidary fondling a strange jewel that 'here is a "find" at once rare and beautiful.

'H.E. Bates, a young English author, commands and justifies this hope with his first novel, *The Two Sisters*. The poetic quality of Mr. Bates's prose, his sensitiveness to his characters, and his flash of beauty herald a writer of charm and distinction. Here is a first novel which has the definite flavour of a new individual, one who, if he chooses the difficult path of art, is destined to go far.'

New York Evening Post

A 3b First American impression

THE TWO | SISTERS | (ornament) | BY H.E. BATES | With a foreword by
| EDWARD GARNETT | (publisher's device) | THE VIKING PRESS | New
York Mcmxxvi (the whole within an ornamental border)

Collation: (A-U⁸) 320 pp, consisting of half-title, verso blank, pp (1–2); title-
page, notices of copyright and manufacture in the United States of America on
verso, pp (3–4); dedication 'to MY FATHER AND MOTHER', verso blank, pp
(5–6); FOREWORD, pp 7–10; text, pp 11–320.

Binding: 8vo, 5 x 7⅜ins. Quarter dark green linen cloth; pale green cloth covers
flecked with dark green; cream paper label lettered and decorated in red on spine;
top edges dyed green; fore and lower edges cut; white end papers.

John & Edward Bumpus Ltd
BOOKSELLERS TO HIS MAJESTY THE KING
350 Oxford Street, London, W1
Telephone: Mayfair 1223

The Booklet enclosed is the work
of a young and brilliant writer.   It was
originally designed to supplement the Map
of Fairyland; but its literary quality is
so considerable that it may worthily be
offered to our friends.   Will you gener-
ously accept it, and with it our sincere
wishes for a Happy Christmas.

JOHN & EDWARD BUMPUS, LTD.

A 4   THE SEEKERS   December 1926

THE SEEKERS | by | H.E. BATES | (design of four stars) | LONDON | JOHN AND EDWARD BUMPUS | 1926

Collation: (A-B)^8 32 pp, consisting of half-title enclosed within a single rule border, verso blank (pp 1–2); title-page enclosed within rule border with four cross rules boxing with a star in each corner, printer's imprint on verso, pp (3–4); 'DEDICATED TO ALL CHILDREN WHO ASK WHY?', verso blank, pp (5–6); text, pp 7–32.

Binding: 8vo, $4\frac{4}{5}$ x $7\frac{4}{5}$ins. Grey paper boards; front cover lettered within a floral border in gold; all edges cut; white end papers. Tissue wrapper.
   Printed for presentation only by R. and R. Clark Limited, Edinburgh. Quantity not known.

Notes: The book was described in the Kettering Grammar School Magazine (No.11, January, 1927) as 'A charming fairy tale which the famous booksellers (Bumpus) sent out as the firm's Christmas card.'
   It was sent with a note from John & Edward Bumpus Ltd.
   The Blossoming World (A 110) pp 39–40: 'Presently I found digs at thirty shillings a week with two old ladies somewhere off the Bayswater Road and John Wilson put me into the Children's Department of the celebrated bookshop in Oxford Street. The old ladies fussed over me with drinks of hot lemon at night as cures for the colds that continually assailed me that autumn and in the bookshop I slightly assuaged my conscience by writing for John Wilson a little children's book, *The Seekers*, which he promptly published and which is today something of a collector's rarity.'

A 5   THE SPRING SONG AND IN   1927
VIEW OF THE FACT THAT
TWO STORIES

A 5a First English edition

THE SPRING SONG | AND | IN VIEW OF THE FACT THAT | TWO STORIES | BY | H.E. BATES | (ornament) | E. ARCHER | 68, RED LION STREET, LONDON, W.C.1. | March, 1927.

Collation: (A)^8 16 pp, consisting of title-page, certificate of limitation and notice of copyright on verso, pp (1–2); text, pp 3–(16). Printer's imprint at foot of p (16).

Binding: 4to, $7\frac{1}{2}$ x $10\frac{1}{10}$ins. Violet and yellow marbled wrappers; lettering and an ornament on front cover in black; top edges unopened; fore and lower edges uncut; white end papers, formed by a double leaf laid under flaps of wrappers at each end; drawing in grey of the author by William Roberts faces title-page.

Issue limited to one hundred copies/privately printed. Numbered and signed by
H.E. Bates. A large paper issue ($8\frac{1}{4}$ x $10\frac{1}{2}$ins.), limited to 25 copies, was produced
simultaneously. Blue wrappers decorated with floral designs in green, white and
blue. White label on front cover, lettering within single rule border in black. In this
issue the frontispiece drawing of the author also carried a facsimile of his signature.

Both issues were printed by Smiths' Printing Co. (London & St. Albans) Ltd.,
22-24 Fetter Lane, E.C.4.

Notes: The book was in fact published by Charles Lahr who kept the Progressive
Bookshop in Red Lion Street, London. Lahr had been interned during World War
I. The press was registered in the maiden name of his wife, Esther Archer.

A 5b American issues March 1927

Two issues were prepared for America, uniform with the English edition. The
small paper issue consisted of 50 copies; the large paper issue of 10 copies. They
bore the imprint THE LANTERN PRESS, | GELBER, LILIENTHAL, INC., |
SAN FRANCISCO, CAL., U.S.A. | 1927.

Their respective certificates of issue stated: PRIVATELY PRINTED FOR
AMERICA. The printer's imprint at the foot of p (16) had the words 'London,
England' added.

A 6   DAY'S END AND OTHER STORIES   1928

A6a First English edition

DAY'S END | and other Stories by | H.E. BATES | (publisher's device) |
JONATHAN CAPE | LONDON

Collation: (A) B-S⁸ 288 pp, consisting of half-title. Also by H.E. Bates on verso,
pp (1-2); title-page, notice of publication and printer's imprint on verso, pp (3-4);
dedication 'To George William Lucas, also a story-teller', verso blank, pp (5-6);
contents, verso blank, pp (7-8); fly title, Day's End, verso blank, pp (9-10); text,
pp 11-286; blank, pp (287-288).

Binding: 8vo, 5 x $7\frac{3}{8}$ins. Green cloth, shot with yellow; lettered on spine in gold;
publisher's device blind-stamped on back cover; all edges cut; white end papers.

Dust jacket lettering in blue. On front cover enclosed within heavy single-rule
border in maroon and two inner double-rule borders in blue and maroon. Publisher's
device on front and spine in maroon.

Price: 7s. 6d. net. Published June 1928.

1,500 copies were printed on 23 March 1928; 500 on 17 May 1928. Printed in
Great Britain by Butler & Tanner Ltd, Frome.

Contents: Day's End - The Baker's Wife - The Birthday - The Shepherd - The
Easter Blessing - The Spring Song - The Mother - Fear - The Dove - The Flame
- The Holiday - Two Candles - The Fuel-Gatherers - The Father - Gone Away -
Harvest - The Barge - The Lesson - The Schoolmistress - Fishing - Never - Nina -
The Voyage - The Idiot - Blossoms

Notes: George William Lucas was the author's maternal grandfather.
The Vanished World (A 107) pp 160–161: The Flame; p 179: The Idiot.

Reviews: '*Day's End* is a book of short stories. They are very good indeed. All
are written in the same vein which would in a lesser writer be described as poignant.
Actually they are studies in diffidence or tenderness described with great reticence
and feeling.' *New Statesman*
          'Splendid short stories by a young man who should be pensioned by the king.'
New Yorker
          'Literary speculators might prudently place their bets on H.E. BATES, whose
Day's End has the same quality of fastidious beauty which distinguished his novel
The Two Sisters. Mr. Bates, like Katherine Mansfield, builds his tales with careful
artistry around a trifling incident, a moment of fleeting, scarcely communicable
emotion .... No epicure can afford to miss his work.' *Forum*
Comment: 'In *Day's End and Other Stories*, his remarkable collection of short
fiction, Bates exhibits remarkable range and polish, especially considering that he
had written all the stories by his twenty-third year. Some of the stories are particularly memorable, comparing favorably with the best from the hundreds Bates
published over his career.' Dennis Vannatta, University of Arkansas at Little Rock,
in *H.E. Bates*, Boston: Twayne Publishers, 1983.

A 6b First American edition 1928

DAY'S END | AND OTHER STORIES | BY H.E. BATES | (publisher's device)
| THE VIKING PRESS | NEW YORK - 1928

Collation: As A 6a.

Binding: Pink cloth with fan designs in deep pink and grey continuous over both
covers and foot of spine; peach label on spine with ornament and lettering in black;
top edges dyed pink; all edges cut; white end papers.
          Dust jacket has mottled hair-line colouring. Front cover lettered and decorated
with five swallows in flight and sunset, all in pale mauve. Publisher's device, note on
the author and imprint on back cover in pale mauve. Spine lettered with decoration
of one swallow in green.

Price: $2.00
Printed in Great Britain by Butler & Tanner Ltd, Frome.

A 7   CATHERINE FOSTER   1929

A 7a First English edition

CATHERINE FOSTER | by | H.E. BATES | (publisher's device) | JONATHAN
CAPE | THIRTY BEDFORD SQUARE | LONDON

Collation: (A)-Q^8 256 pp consisting of half-title, list of books By the same Author
on verso, pp (1–2); title-page, imprint and note of publication on verso, pp (3–4);
dedication 'To EDWARD GARNETT', verso blank, pp (5–6); fly title Catherine
Foster, verso blank, pp (7–8); text, pp 9–256.

Binding: 8vo, 5 x 7$\frac{3}{5}$ins. Grey-green rough cloth with muslin-weave pattern printed in brown; publisher's device blind-stamped on back cover; lettering with an ornament on spine in gold; top and fore-edges cut, lower edges uncut; white end papers.

Dust jacket designed by 'Cole'. White, with illustration on front cover in orange and black; lettered on front cover and spine within ornamental borders in black; advertisement for *Dodsworth* by Sinclair Lewis on back cover within double-rule border in black.

Price: 7s. 6d. net. Published 15 April 1929. 1500 copies of the first impression were printed on 29 January 1929. (An issue of 50 numbered copies, each signed by the author, was simultaneously produced. These were bound in dull grey-green buckram, blocked in gold on spine with the publisher's device blind-stamped on back cover. A few sample copies exist, bound in blue instead of the grey-green eventually chosen.)

500 copies of a second impression were printed on 16 May 1929; bound in smooth grey cloth, lettered on spine in gold.

All issues were printed in Great Britain by Butler & Tanner Ltd, Frome, and bound by Nevett.

Notes: The manuscript was sold by the author to Sir Louis Sterling in 1954. University of London Sterling Catalogue: 'The author's holograph manuscript written in ink on one side only of three hundred and fifty-seven sheets of ruled quarto paper, with corrections and deletions. Bound in olive-green buckram boards, lettered in gilt. Published in 1929.' (v. Part II, No.41)
English and American sales: Extract from a memorandum from Mr. Cape (publisher) to the author, dated 2 December 1930:

	ENGLISH SALES		AMERICAN SALES		TOTAL
	Copies	Royalty	Copies	Royalty	
CATHERINE FOSTER	1335	£59.11s. 2d.	1181	£57.10s. 1d.	£117.2s. 1d.

A 7b First American edition 1929

Catherine Foster | H.E. BATES | (ornament in green) | New York 1929 | THE VIKING PRESS (all within a ruled ornamental border in green)

Collation: (A-U)^8 (viii) + 312 pp, consisting of blank leaf pasted down to form front end-paper, pp (i–ii); half-title, ALSO BY H.E. BATES on verso, pp (iii–iv); title-page, publishing and printing imprints on verso, pp (v–vi); dedication, 'To EDWARD GARNETT', verso blank (vii–viii); fly title, PART ONE, verso blank, pp (1–2); text, pp 3–307; blank p (308); blank pp (309–310); blank leaf pasted down to form back end-paper, pp (311–312).

Binding: 8vo, 5$\frac{1}{8}$ x 7$\frac{1}{2}$ins. Quarter black cloth; green cloth sides; title lettered within an ornamental border in silver on front cover; lettering on spine in silver, the title within an ornamental border in silver; top edges dyed red; fore and lower edges untrimmed; white end papers.

Dust jacket illustrated by DOBIAS. Illustration on front cover depicts a woman in bondage, coloured in green, orange, black and white. All lettering in black.

Price: $2.50
Printed in The United States of America.

A 8   SEVEN TALES AND ALEXANDER   1929

A 8a First English edition

SEVEN TALES AND | ALEXANDER | By H.E. BATES | MCMXXIX | THE SCHOLARTIS PRESS | THIRTY MUSEUM STREET LONDON

Collation: (A)-K^8; L (incorporating M)^{10} (xii) + 168 pp, consisting of blank leaf, pp (i–ii); half-title, verso blank, pp (iii–iv); title-page, certificate of issue and printer's imprint on verso, pp (v–vi); dedication to Constance Garnett, verso blank, pp (vii–viii); Author's Note, verso blank, pp (ix–x); Contents, verso blank, pp (xi–xii); fly title ALEXANDER, verso blank, pp (1–2); text, including sectional fly titles, pp 3 - (167); blank p (168).

Binding: 8vo, $5\frac{3}{8}$ x $8\frac{3}{4}$ins. Quarter blue cloth, lettered along spine in gold; cream paper-board sides; top and fore-edges cut; lower edges uncut; white end papers. (A few copies have been found bound in maroon buckram, top edges gilt, fore and lower edges uncut.)
Cream dust jacket, lettered on front cover and spine in blue.

Price: 7s. 6d. net. Published November 1929. 1,000 copies printed of which 950 were for sale. Copies 1–50 numbered and signed by the author on verso of title-page and bound in saxe-blue silk cloth (price 21s. net).
(A leaf listing books of *Scholartis Fiction* was loosely inserted, the advertisement for *Seven Tales and Alexander* stating that the edition was limited to 900 copies and 50 signed copies,)
Printed by Henderson and Spalding at Sylvan Grove, London, in 12pt Baskerville on Spalding & Hodge Antique de Luxe paper.

Contents: Alexander - The Barber - The Child - A Comic Actor - The Peach Tree : A Fantasy - A Tinker's Donkey - The King Who Lived on Air : A Child's Tale - Lanko's White Mare

Author's Note: 'Of these tales, "Lanko's White Mare" has appeared in the *London Mercury*; "A Tinker's Donkey" in the *Manchester Guardian*; "The Barber" and "A Comic Actor" in the *New Statesman*; and "The Child" in the *Criterion, Now and Then*, and *The Best Short Stories of 1929*. The remaining three stories, including the long title-piece, are here published for the first time. In the others, considerable changes have been made.'

Notes: Dedicated to Constance Garnett, to whom the author inscribed a presentation copy: 'Who by her poetic genius began to influence my life before I lived; to which genius and to her unfailing friendship no less, this book is a tribute.'

The manuscript of *Alexander* was sold by the author to Sir Louis Sterling in 1954. University of London Sterling Catalogue: 'The author's holograph manuscript written in ink on one side only of ninety-seven sheets of ruled quarto paper, with extensive corrections and deletions. There are four chapters, signed and dated "June–July 1929". Published in the same year in a collection entitled *Seven Tales and Alexander*' (v.Part II, No.42).

A 8b First American edition 1930

SEVEN TALES | and | ALEXANDER | By H.E. Bates | (publisher's device) | NEW YORK | THE VIKING PRESS | 1930

Collation: (A-N)^8 (ii) + 206 pp, consisting of blank leaf, pp (i–ii); half-title, ALSO BY H.E. BATES on verso, pp (1–2); title-page, notices of printing and copyright on verso, pp (3–4); dedication to Constance Garnett, verso blank, pp (5–6); AUTHOR'S NOTE, verso blank, pp (7–8); CONTENTS, verso blank, pp (9–10); fly title ALEXANDER, verso blank, pp (11–12); text, including sectional fly titles, pp 13–201, blank, p (202); publisher's imprint, verso blank, pp (203–204); blank pp (205–206).

Binding: 8vo, 5 x 8ins. Quarter cream cloth; pink cloth sides; pink label on spine with lettering and an ornament in blue; top and fore-edges untrimmed, lower edges uncut; white end papers.
       White dust jacket designed by 'LIEBER'; lettered on front cover and spine in blue and red with two ornaments on front cover in red. Reviews of the book on back cover with heading 'Return Tickets to Childhood' in red and blue with publisher's device in red.

Price: $2.00
       Printed in U.S.A.

A 9   THE TREE   1930

BLUE MOON BOOKLETS NO. 3 | (line) | THE TREE | (device) | H.E. BATES | E. LAHR | 68 Red Lion Street | London, W.C.1

Collation: (A)^8 16 pp, consisting of blank leaf not reckoned in pagination, 2 pp; blank page, list of Other Books by H.E. Bates and Blue Moon Booklets on verso, pp (1–2); title-page, verso blank, pp (3–4); text, pp 5–11; printer's imprint, p (12); blank pp (13–14).

Binding: 8vo, 5 x 7ins. Blue wrappers; lettering and a device on front cover in black; all edges cut; no end papers.
       The number issued is not known. Printed by D. White and Son, 25 Richmond Street, London, E.C.1.

Notes: A large paper issue, limited to 100 copies for sale, signed by the author, was produced simultaneously. This was printed on Japanese vellum paper and bound in white wrappers, lettering with a device on front cover in black. The list of Other Books by H.E. Bates and Blue Moon Booklets p (2) was omitted, the certificate of issue with the author's signature appearing there.

A 10   THE HESSIAN PRISONER   1930

THE HESSIAN PRISONER | By H.E. Bates with a line | drawing by JOHN AUSTEN and | a Foreword by EDWARD | GARNETT | Being No. 2 of the Furnival Books | (ornament) | WILLIAM JACKSON (BOOKS) LTD | 18 TOOKS COURT, CHANCERY LANE, LONDON | 1930

Collation: (A-C)^8 48 pp, consisting of blank leaf not reckoned in pagination, 2 pp; blank page, certificate of issue and author's signature on verso, pp (1–2); half-title, list of books By the same Author on verso, pp (3–4); title-page, verso blank, pp (5–6); FOREWORD, pp 7–10; text, pp 11–42; printer's device and imprint, verso blank, pp (43–44); blank, pp (45–46).

Binding: 8vo, 6$\frac{1}{5}$ x 10ins. Red buckram, lettered on front cover and along spine in gold; top edges gilt, fore and lower edges uncut; white end papers. Frontispiece by John Austen is guarded in opposite the title-page, p (5).
    Published February 1930. 550 copies were printed and signed by the author, of which 500 were for sale.
    Printed in London by Charles Whittingham and Griggs (Printers) Ltd, Chiswick Press, Tooks Court, Chancery Lane.

Notes: In his Foreword Edward Garnett judged that *The Hessian Prisoner* 'was not the most striking of the thirty-four short stories he [H.E. Bates] has published'.
    The author was prompted to inscribe a presentation copy of the book to Edward Garnett (see next page).

[handwritten letter]

Edward Garnett,

whose injunctions about this
Tale I did not obey, with
sad results, for which I
hope he forgives me.

Affectionately ours,

H.E. Bates,

Mar 4.   1930.

A 11   CHARLOTTE'S ROW   1931

A 11a First English edition

CHARLOTTE'S ROW | by | H.E. BATES | (vignette) | Jonathan Cape |
Thirty Bedford Square | London.

Collation: (A)-R⁸. 272 pp, consisting of blank leaf, pp (1-2); half-title, a list
of books by H.E. Bates on verso, pp (3-4); title-page, note of publication, publisher's and printer's imprints on verso, pp (5-6); dedication 'TO HENRY JAMES
BYROM', verso blank, pp (7-8); fly title Charlotte's Row, verso blank, pp (9-10);
text, pp 11-271; blank p (272).

Binding: 8vo, 5 x 7½ins. Blue cloth, lettered on spine in gold; publisher's device
blind-stamped on back cover; top and fore-edges cut, lower edges trimmed; white
end papers. (A large number of copies were bound with an advertisement inserted
between pp 270-71.)

White dust jacket, lettered in black. Title-page vignette repeated on front cover in black; advertisement for three books by H.E. Bates on back cover.

Price: 7s.6d. net. Published 30 March 1931.
2,000 copies of the first impression were printed on 30 January 1931.
Another issue of 107 numbered copies (100 for sale only), each signed by the author, was produced simultaneously. This issue was bound in natural niger with marbled boards; top edges gilt, others untrimmed; white end papers.
Second impression of 500 copies printed on 3 June 1931. Third impression of 1040 copies printed on 13 November 1931.
All issues were printed in Great Britain in the City of Oxford at the Alden Press.

Notes: Henry James Byrom was a contemporary of H.E. Bates at Kettering Grammar School, and became a life-long friend.
The title-page vignette was by Ray Garnett (Rachel Alice Garnett, 1891–1940), first wife of David Garnett.
The manuscript was sold by the author to Sir Louis Sterling in 1954. University of London Sterling Catalogue: 'The author's holograph manuscript written in ink on one side only of three hundred and eighty sheets of quarto paper, with interlinear and other corrections. Bound in olive-green buckram boards lettered in gilt. Inscribed on the top title-page as follows: "Planned in 1929 as a short story; completed in 1930 as a novel; rewritten during the autumn of 1931. H.E. Bates. April 15 1931." Published in 1931' (v.Part II, No.43).

A 11b First American issue

CHARLOTTE'S ROW | by | H.E.BATES | (vignette) | LONDON : JONATHAN CAPE 30 BEDFORD SQUARE | NEW YORK : JONATHAN CAPE & HARRISON SMITH

Collation: As A 11a.

Binding: 8vo; 5 x 7⅜ins. Black cloth; publisher's device blind-stamped on front cover; lettering and device on spine in gold; top edges dyed black; fore and lower edges trimmed; white end papers.
Yellow dust jacket. Illustration of a factory on front cover and all lettering in black. Back cover carries an advertisement for *The Birthday* by Samuel Rogers.

Price: $2.00

A 12   A THRESHING DAY   1931

A THRESHING DAY | BY | H.E. BATES | AUTHOR OF | "THE TWO SISTERS," "DAY'S END" | "CATHERINE FOSTER," "SEVEN TALES AND ALEXANDER" | ETC. ETC. | W. AND G. FOYLE, LTD. | "AT THE SIGN OF THE TREFOYLE" | LONDON

Collation: (A)-D⁴ 32 pp, consisting of half-title, certificate of issue and author's signature on verso, pp (1–2); title-page, notice of publication and printer's imprint on verso, pp (3–4); text, pp 5–32.

Binding: 4to, $5\frac{1}{2}$ x $8\frac{7}{10}$ins. Blue canvas; lettered on front cover and along spine in gold; top edges rough trimmed, fore and lower edges uncut; white end papers.
    Published July 1931. The edition was limited to 300 numbered copies, each signed by the author. A large paper issue, limited to 25 copies, printed on Japanese vellum and bound in parchment; each copy signed by the author. Made and printed in Great Britain by Purnell and Sons, Paulton (Somerset) and London.

Notes: The story first appeared as 'A Threshing Day for Esther' in *John O'London's Weekly*, 11 October 1930 (B43.1) and was the title used in later anthologies and collections.

A 13   MRS. ESMOND'S LIFE   1931

Mrs. ESMOND'S | LIFE | by | H.E. BATES | LONDON, 1931 | Privately printed.

Collation: One gathering only (A)^{16}. 32 pp, consisting of blank leaf, not reckoned in pagination, 2 pp; blank page with certificate of issue and author's signature on verso, pp (1–2); title-page contained within a rectangular one-line ruled border, dedication on verso 'TO SHEILA', pp (3–4); text, pp 5–25; blank p (26); publisher's and printer's imprint, verso blank, pp (27–28); blank pp (29–30).

Binding: $4\frac{7}{8}$ x $7\frac{1}{4}$ins. Yellow buckram, lettered on front cover and along spine in gold; top edges gilt, fore and lower edges cut; white end papers. (20 copies of this issue were bound in black buckram; 20 copies of those bound in yellow buckram were surplus for review.)
    A large paper (4to) edition was produced simultaneously, consisting of 50 numbered copies, each signed by the author and containing a page of the original MS. There were a number of changes between the manuscript and the printed version. This issue was bound in apple green buckram, lettered on the spine in gilt with a facsimile of the author's signature gilt-stamped on the front cover; top edges gilt, fore and lower edges untrimmed; white end papers.
    The entire edition was of 370 copies, published by E. Lahr, 68 Red Lion Street, London, W.C.1 and printed by D. White and Son, 25 Richmond Street, London, E.C.1.

Notes: The story was first published as 'Charlotte Esmond' in *The Criterion* (B 44.1).

A 14   THE BLACK BOXER TALES   1932

A 14a First English edition

THE | BLACK BOXER | Tales by | H.E. BATES | (publisher's device) | PHAROS EDITIONS | THIRTY BEDFORD SQUARE | 1932

Collation: (A)-R^8. 272 pp, consisting of half-title, verso blank, pp (1–2); title-page, printer's, paper-maker's and binder's imprint on verso, pp (3–4); Contents, dedication on verso 'TO MY WIFE', pp (5–6); fly title, verso blank, pp (7–8); text, including sectional fly titles, pp 9–272.

Binding: 8vo, $4\frac{7}{8}$ x $7\frac{3}{8}$ins. Lemon cloth; lettered on spine with a star ornament in black; top and fore-edges cut; lower edges untrimmed; white end papers. (A page of advertisements of FIRST PHAROS EDITIONS on recto of an additional leaf bound between pp 270–271.)
    Dust jacket designed by S.B. and white overall. Front cover lettered in green with illustration of boxer in black; publisher's advertisements on back cover in black and green; spine lettered in black with floral design in green.

Price: 7s. 6d. Published 15 February 1932. 1,500 copies were printed in Great Britain in the City of Oxford at The Alden Press on 25 November 1931 on paper made by John Dickinson & Co. Ltd., and bound by A.W. Bain & Co., Ltd.
    A limited edition of 100 copies, each signed by the author, was produced simultaneously. The certificate of limitation and the author's signature in this issue occur on the verso of the half-title. These copies were bound in yellow buckram, with a gilt-lettered black-paper label on spine; top edges gilt, fore and lower edges uncut.
    750 copies of a second impression of the ordinary edition were printed on 4 April 1932. The type was distributed on 9 January 1934.

Contents: The Black Boxer - On The Road - A Love Story - Charlotte Esmond - A Flower Piece - The Mower - The Hessian Prisoner - Death in Spring - Sheep - The Russian Dancer - A Threshing Day for Esther (A head-ornament in black occurs below each of the above titles in the text.)

Reviews: 'His stories challenge comparison with the best of D.H. Lawrence's longer short stories, and to my taste they are more true and more beautiful than most of his short stories.' Compton Mackenzie

A 14b First American impression

THE | BLACK BOXER | Tales by | H.E. BATES | ROBERT O. BALLOU | 347 FIFTH AVENUE | NEW YORK

Collation: As A 14a.

Binding: 8vo, 5 x $7\frac{1}{4}$ins. Quarter mauve cloth; grey cloth sides decorated with designs in orange, mauve and white; lettering and one short rule on spine in gold; top edges dyed black; all edges cut; black end papers with designs of flowers, leaves and mushrooms in white. Cellophane wrapper.
    Printed in Great Britain.

A 15   SALLY GO ROUND THE MOON   1932

SALLY | GO ROUND | THE MOON | by | H.E. BATES | (publisher's device) | THE WHITE OWL PRESS | LONDON | 1932

Collation: (A-O)^4 (gathered in 4s) (viii) + 48 pp, consisting of fly title, First Published, March 1932, verso blank, pp (i–ii); half-title, verso blank, pp (iii–iv); title-page, verso blank, pp (v–vi); dedication, verso blank, pp (vii–viii); fly title, Part I, verso blank, pp (1–2); text, including sectional fly titles, pp (3)–42; three blank leaves, pp (43–48).

Binding: 8vo, $5\frac{1}{2}$ x $8\frac{1}{2}$ins. Half grey canvas, brown paper-board sides; lettered on spine in brown; all edges cut; white end papers.
   First published in March 1932.
   A few publisher's presentation copies of the above issue were produced with the designs used in the large paper issues printed on tops of pp (3); (23); (35).
   Two large paper issues were published, consisting of 150 numbered and signed copies, containing vignette designs on pp (3); (23); (35).
   Copies 1–21 were printed on hand-made paper and bound in yellow vellum; gilt lettered on spine; top edges unopened; fore and lower edges uncut. Provided with slipcases.
   Copies 22–150 were printed on wove paper; half bound buff and grey buckram; lettered on spine in green; top edges green; fore and lower edges untrimmed. White end papers to both issues.

Price: 3s.6d., buckram 21s., vellum 42s.

A 16   A GERMAN IDYLL   1932

A GERMAN IDYLL | BY | H.E. BATES | WITH WOOD ENGRAVINGS BY LYNTON LAMB | PRINTED AND MADE IN GREAT BRITAIN BY | THE GOLDEN COCKEREL PRESS | WALTHAM SAINT LAWRENCE IN BERKSHIRE

Collation: (A)^4 : (B)-D^8 (viii) + 48 pp, consisting of two blank leaves, pp (i–iv); blank page, wood-engraved frontispiece on verso, pp (v–vi); title-page with the lettering incorporated within a design, verso blank, pp (vii–viii); dedication 'TO KARL' within a design, beginning of text on verso, pp (1)–2; text, pp 3–(40); certificate of limitation, verso blank, pp (41–42); three blank leaves, pp (43–48).

Binding: 8vo, $6\frac{1}{5}$ x $9\frac{2}{5}$ins. Half crimson leather; crimson and buff decorated sides with a design of stars incorporating the initials HEB and GCP; lettering on spine in gold; top edges gilt; fore and lower edges uncut; white end papers. Bound by Sangorski and Sutcliffe.
   The edition was limited to 307 copies, produced on hand-made paper, each signed by the author.

Printed and published at The Golden Cockerel Press, Waltham Saint Lawrence, Berkshire, by Robert and Moira Gibbings, assisted by George Churchill, and completed on 26 April 1932. Compositors: A.H. Gibbs and F. Young. Pressman: A.C. Cooper.

Price: 17s. 6d. Published 26 April 1932.

Notes: Wood engravings by Lynton Lamb on pp (vi), (vii), 1, 2, 9, 10, 16, 17, 26, 36 and 40.

The Blossoming World (A 110) pp 54-5: 'Those roads [in Germany], weary though they made me, nevertheless remain with me to this day as something marvellously idyllic. With yellow snapdragons, scarlet poppies, blue chicory, white yarrow, meadowsweet, reddening apples; it was all like some glowing pastoral piece by Renoir or Monet. So idyllic did it seem then, as now, that I wrote a novella about it all, calling it *A German Idyll* ...'

p 117: 'Those were the days, the mid-thirties ... when select Private Presses flourished and there was in the air a certain slight madness about first editions. One result of this was that the Golden Cockerel Press had, in 1935, commissioned me to write a book for them. They had in fact already published two books of mine, *The House with the Apricot* and *A German Idyll*, the latter the long story I had conjured out of that half-crazy visit to Germany ...'

A 17   THE FALLOW LAND   1932

THE FALLOW LAND | BY | H.E. BATES | (Publisher's device) | JONATHAN CAPE | 30 BEDFORD SQUARE | LONDON

Collation: (A)B-U⁸ : X⁴ 328 pp, consisting of blank leaf, pp (1-2); half-title, verso blank, pp (3-4); title page, notice of publication, imprints of publisher, printer, paper supplier and binder on verso, pp (5-6); dedication 'To VIOLET & VERNON DEAN', verso blank, pp (7-8); fly title, verso blank, pp (9-10); text, including sectional fly titles with versos blank, pp 11-327; blank p (328).

Binding: 8vo, 5 x 7½ins. Olive green cloth; lettered on spine in brick red; publisher's device blind-stamped in centre of back cover; top and fore-edges cut, lower edges rough trimmed; white end papers.

Dust jacket lettered in green and black. Illustrations of pastoral scenes on front cover and spine in black.

Price: 7s.6d. net. Published 3 October 1932.

2,500 copies of the first impression were printed on 9 August 1932; 500 copies of the second impression on 7 November 1932.

Printed in Great Britain in the City of Oxford at the Alden Press. Paper by John Dickinson & Co. Ltd. Bound by A.W. Bain & Co. Ltd.

Notes: *The Blossoming World* (A 110) p 90: 'It would seem that the book was going well and that I hadn't committed another folly; for this is what I wrote to Edward (Garnett): "I feel immensely pleased with it .... I have done roughly 250

pages, which is roughly half way, and I can't hold myself. This is the book I have always wanted to write – the struggle against the soil, the whole exactly a woman struggling to live on the land ..." '

p 91: 'Novels such as *The Fallow Land* ... are not written today [1971]; nor could they be. They are, in a sense, historical novels, portions of a world that has vanished as surely as the world of my boyhood street games has vanished ... However, the completion of *The Fallow Land* was a happy and important event ...'

The author inscribed a copy of *The Fallow Land* to E.E. Kirby thus:

E.E. Kirby,

who Knows my imperfection
as a writer better, —

Condemns them less,

than any other man.

H. E. Bates.

_____

September.   1932.

He wrote of his association with E.E. Kirby at Kettering Grammar School on pp 102–3 in the first volume of his autobiography, *The Vanished World* (A 107). An illustration of E.E. Kirby by John Ward is on p 103.

Reviews: 'The Fallow Land is much the best piece of work which Mr. Bates has done; and that means it is very good indeed. *The Fallow Land* carries Mr. Bates a step forward, and marks him as one of a handful who can write of the country with grace and authority.' *The Spectator*

'*The Fallow Land* is a poem of the English countryside which never loses its lyric intensity, its delicacy and yet its strength, from first to last.' *Times Literary Supplement*

'Beauty and sorrow become one in a single poignant harmony, binding the succession of incidents into a unity which is also a unison. Especially striking is the complete adequacy of detail. Every descriptive phrase, each metaphor, each adjective even is right, and with a natural, a wholly spontaneous rightness. Every character, like each instrument in an orchestra, has his or her appointed place and part, yet is vividly and individually alive; one comes to know them, to understand them, to feel with them.' *The Times*

The first American issue was published in 1933 by R.O. Ballou, New York.

A 18   THE STORY WITHOUT AN END   1932
         and THE COUNTRY DOCTOR

THE STORY | WITHOUT AN END | and | THE COUNTRY DOCTOR | by | H.E. BATES | (publisher's device) | THE WHITE OWL PRESS | LONDON | 1932

Collation: (A-E)^4 (F)^6 (G)^4 60 pp, consisting of blank leaf, pp (1–2); title-page, verso blank, pp (3–4); fly title THE STORY WITHOUT AN END, verso blank, pp (5–6); notice of publication, verso blank, pp (7–8); PART I text, pp (9)–20; PART II, verso blank, pp (21–22); text, pp (23)–36; fly title THE COUNTRY DOCTOR, verso blank, pp (37–38); text, pp (39)–51; blank page, p (52); three blank leaves, pp (53–58); blank leaf pasted down to form back endpaper, pp (59–60).

Binding: 8vo, $5\frac{5}{8}$ x $8\frac{1}{2}$ins. Quarter grey cloth; pastel blue grained boards; lettered along spine in blue; all edges cut; front end papers white.

Yellow dust jacket; lettering on front cover with design of two cog-wheels and publisher's device enclosed within double-rule border, all in black.

Price: 5/- net. Published December 1932. The edition, numbered and signed by the author, limited to 130 copies, of which 125 were for sale. Copies 1–25 were printed on hand-made paper with orange vellum boards and provided with a slipcase. In these copies the certificate of issue with the author's signature appeared at p (1); a woodcut illustration occurred as a frontispiece on the verso of the half-title-page. One sheet of the original manuscript of *The Country Doctor* was inserted.

Notes: An illustration incorporating the lettering PART ONE occurs at the head of p (9).

The manuscript of *The Story Without An End* was sold by the author to Sir Louis Sterling in 1954. University of London Sterling Catalogue: 'The author's holograph manuscript written in ink on one side of thirty-seven sheets of ruled quarto paper, with interlinear and other corrections. Inscribed by the author on the title page: "The Story without an End was written during 1932 at Little Chart, Kent. The MS. is now in the possession of Louis Sterling. H.E. Bates, Jan. 1934." Enclosed with the manuscript of "The House with the Apricot" (v.No.43) in a cloth

case, a label with the titles and author written by him in ink on the spine. A letter
to Sir Louis Sterling offering him the manuscripts inserted. Published with "The
Country Doctor" in 1932.' (v. Part II, No.50).

A 19   THE HOUSE WITH THE APRICOT   1933
            AND TWO OTHER TALES

THE HOUSE WITH | THE APRICOT | AND TWO OTHER | TALES BY |
H.E. BATES | (publisher's device) | Printed and made in Great Britain by the |
GOLDEN COCKEREL PRESS | TEN STAPLE INN, LONDON | 1933

Collation: (a)^4 b-e^8 (viii) + 64 pp, consisting of two blank leaves, pp (i–iv); title-
page, verso blank, pp (v–vi); dedication 'To MALACHI WHITAKER', verso blank,
pp (vii–viii); text, pp 1–(60); printer's and publisher's imprint with certificate of
limitation, verso blank, pp (61–62); blank pp (63–64).

Binding: 8vo, 6$\frac{1}{4}$ x 9$\frac{1}{2}$ins. Quarter green morocco; orange and dark green cloth
sides decorated with a design of stars incorporating the initials HEB and GCP;
lettering on spine in gold; top edges gilt, fore and lower edges uncut; white end
papers.

Price: £1 1s. Published December 1933. The edition limited to 300 copies each
signed by the author.
    This was the seventh book in The Golden Cockerel Series of first editions by
famous authors.
    The format designed by Robert Gibbings.
    The four wood engravings by Agnes Miller Parker occur at pp 1, 20, 43 and
51. Printed and published by Christopher Sandford, Francis J. Newbery and Owen
Rutter at the Golden Cockerel Press, London. Compositors: F. Young and A.H.
Gibbs. Pressman: A. Curran.

Contents: 'The House with the Apricot' (first publication); 'The Man from Ja-
maica' (first publication, see B 56.1); 'The Pink Cart' (first publication, see B 64.1).

Notes: Malachi Whitaker was a friend of Bates, and a fine writer of short stories.
    The manuscript was sold by the author to Sir Louis Sterling in 1954. University
of London Sterling Catalogue: 'The author's holograph manuscript written in ink
on one side only of seventy sheets of ruled quarto paper, with corrections in ink and
pencil. Enclosed in a brown cloth case, a label with the title and author written
by hand on the spine. The author has added the following note on a separate
sheet: "This MS. of The House with the Apricot is the only version in existence
and was written at Little Chart in Kent during the autumn of 1932. It is now in the
possession of Louis Sterling. H.E. Bates. 1934." Published in December 1933 by
the Golden Cockerel Press in an edition limited to 300 copies.' (v. Part III No.182).

A 20   THE WOMAN WHO HAD   1934
IMAGINATION AND OTHER STORIES

The Woman | who had Imagination | and other Stories by | H.E. Bates | (publisher's device) | Jonathan Cape | Thirty Bedford Square London | and at Toronto

Collation: (A)-S⁸ 288 pp, consisting of half-title, By the same author on verso, pp (1–2); title-page, notice of publication, publisher's, printer's, paper-maker's, binder's and cloth-maker's imprint on verso, pp (3–4); Contents, verso blank, pp (5–6); dedication 'To David Garnett', verso blank, pp (7–8); fly title, verso blank, pp (9–10); text, pp11–288 (a list of other books by H.E. Bates loosely inserted).

Binding: 8vo, 5 x 7½ins. Grey cloth; lettered in green on front cover; lettered in green on spine; publisher's device in green on back cover; top and fore-edges cut; lower edges untrimmed; white end papers.
    Dust jacket lettered in green and black. Design on front cover in black and on spine in green.

Price: 7s. 6d. net. Published 26 February 1934. 2,000 copies were printed on 4 January 1934; the type was distributed on 31 August 1934.
    Printed in Great Britain in the City of Oxford at The Alden Press. Paper made by John Dickinson & Co., Ltd. Bound by A.W. Bain & Co., Ltd., in cloth, fast to light and washable, made by Morton Sundour Fabrics Ltd.

Contents: The Lily - The Story Without An End - The Gleaner - The Woman Who Had Imagination - Time - A German Idyll - For the Dead - The Wedding - The Waterfall - Innocence - Millenium Also Ran - Sally Go Round the Moon - The Brothers - Death of Uncle Silas

Reviews: 'The Woman Who Had Imagination is, to my mind, the first volume of Mr. Bates's complete maturity. In his previous books he has worked out all the superficial aspects of literary influence, and in his new volume he shows himself an artist of magnificent originality with a vitality quite unsuspected hitherto. I cannot enough admire the title story. This story and at least one other, *"The Wedding"* seem to me to deserve a place among the finest English short stories.' Graham Greene, *The Spectator*
    The first American edition was published in 1934 by Macmillan Co., New York.

A 21   THIRTY TALES   1934

THIRTY TALES | by | H.E. BATES | (publisher's device) | WITH AN INTRODUCTION BY | DAVID GARNETT | LONDON | JONATHAN CAPE 30 BEDFORD SQUARE

Collation: (A)-H¹⁶: I-I*¹⁸ (iv) + 288 pp, consisting of THE TRAVELLERS' LIBRARY, a star and half-title, publisher's advertisement on verso, pp (i–ii); title-page, notice of first issue in The Travellers' Library 1934 with publisher's, printer's, binder's and paper-maker's imprint on verso, pp (iii–iv); CONTENTS, verso blank, pp (1–2); dedication 'TO E.E. KIRBY', verso blank, pp (3–4); INTRODUCTION, pp 5–8; text, pp 9–288. pp 40, listing books in The Travellers' Library bound in at end.

Binding: 8vo, $4\frac{1}{2}$ x $6\frac{3}{4}$ins. Dark blue cloth; publisher's monogram blind-stamped on back cover; lettering with decorations and publisher's device on spine in gold; all edges cut; white end papers.

Dust jacket in yellow and green; front cover lettered and bordered in black with ornamental design in black and green. Back cover carries publisher's advertisement for The Travellers' Library and The Life and Letters Series in black within single-rule green border. Lettering and publisher's device on spine in black with illustration of a ship in black and green.

Price: 3s.6d. net. Published 9 April 1934. 3,000 copies were printed on 7 February 1934.

Travellers' Library Catalogue No. 198. Printed and bound by The Garden City Press Limited Letchworth Herts & London. Paper made by John Dickinson & Co Limited.

Contents: Introduction - Alexander - The Mother - Death in Spring - The Holiday - Harvest - Charlotte Esmond - A Flower Piece - The Hessian Prisoner - Fishing - The Baker's Wife - The Child - On the Road - Blossoms - The Flame - Fear - A Comic Actor - The Idiot - The Birthday - The Barber - The Fuel-Gatherers - The Spring Song - The Father - Two Candles - A Love Story - The Schoolmistress - The Mower - The Voyage - Lanko's White Mare - A Tinker's Donkey - A Threshing Day for Esther

Notes: H.E. Bates had dedicated his first book, *The Last Bread* (A 2), to Kirby in 1926. Their association began in 1919 when Kirby took up a teaching post at Kettering Grammar School where H.E. Bates was a pupil. Kirby had returned from the war having suffered serious wounds, vividly described by Bates at p 102 in the first volume of his autobiography, *The Vanished World* (A 107). At p 103 he continued to write of Kirby: 'If it is possible to change human vision, or at least to waken it, by the stimulus or shock of a single experience, then this is the perfect example of it. I do not think I am putting it either too highly or fancifully to say that in that one morning in the autumn of 1919 I not only grew up; I grew up in what I was to be. Fanciful as it may sound, I date my literary career from that moment. "Write me," the young ex- infantry officer said to us, "an essay on Shakespeare. I mean from your own point of view. Don't tell me he was born in Stratford-upon-Avon in 1564. I already know that. Don't tell me either that he wrote *Macbeth* or *The Merchant of Venice*. I already know that too.'

Throughout the lifetime of H.E. Bates the two men sustained a very close friendship. Kirby himself contributed to and reviewed many books on country matters. Bates sent him many of his own books as presents and often sought his advice before publication.

'The Travellers' Library' by Graham Greene *(Now and Then,* 1934, and later repeated in *Then and Now* 1935):

'With the publication of *Thirty Tales by H.E. Bates, Green Hell* by Julian Duguid, and *But for the Grace of God* by J.W.N. Sullivan, The Travellers' Library reaches its two hundredth volume and a chance is given to estimate the publisher's achievement.... It is the complete absence of standardization which is the most marked characteristic of the Travellers' Library.

'Take Mr. Bates for example. No writer to-day owes less to his contemporaries. His debt to Tchekoff is obvious, but the influence is a direct one, not by way of Katherine Mansfield, and he has naturalized Tchekoff in a way that Katherine Mansfield, perhaps because of her colonial birth and lack of local root, was unable to do. To my mind Mr. Bates is a more conscious and controlled writer. His stories express mood by means of severe limitation. His own emotions are not allowed to lap over the edge of his stories as Katherine Mansfield's so often did. This first selection of his tales adds distinction to a library which has made less compromise with popularity than any other series at the price .... In the tone of its prose, in the sense of poetic imagination working in a localized area, *Thirty Tales* takes its place beside *Dubliners*. And *Dubliners* contains surely the finest short story written in English since the death of James - I mean "The Dead".'

A 22   THE POACHER   1935

A22a First English edition

THE POACHER | by | H.E. BATES | (publisher's device) | JONATHAN CAPE | THIRTY BEDFORD SQUARE | LONDON

Collation: (A)-T^8. 304 pp, consisting of blank leaf, pp (1-2); half-title, By the same author on verso, pp (3-4); title-page, notice of publication, publisher's, printer's, paper maker's and binder's imprint on verso, pp (5-6); CONTENTS, verso blank, pp 7-(8); dedication 'To SAM', verso blank, pp (9-10); fly title, PART I, verso blank, pp (11-12); text, including fly titles PARTS II, III and IV, pp 13-303; blank p (304).

Binding: 8vo, 5 x 7$\frac{1}{2}$ins. Brown cloth; lettered in green on front cover; lettering with three rules in green on spine; top and fore-edges cut, lower edges untrimmed; white end papers.

Dust jacket: front cover green with white lettering and illustration in black and white. Spine green, lettered in white with illustration in black on white background. Back cover white with reviews of *The Fallow Land* (A 17) in black.

Price: 7s.6d. net. First published 21 January 1935. Printed in Great Britain in the City of Oxford at The Alden Press. Paper made by John Dickinson & Co., Ltd. Bound by A.W. Bain & Co., Ltd. 3,000 copies of the first impression were printed on 5 December 1934; 1,000 copies of the second impression on 12 February 1935. The type was distributed on 7 June 1935.

Contents: PART I Youth - PART II The Murder - PART III The Land - PART IV The New Century

Notes: Bates dedicated *The Poacher* to Sam Smith of Rushden, whose association with him is described in *The Blossoming World* (A 110), pp 37-8.

Reviews: 'The author of *The Poacher* it was affirmed in these columns must be deemed to stand in the front rank of living English writers under thirty. It might have been at once more generous and no less precise to have declared him frankly and without further qualification the occupant of a place of his own among our contemporary novelists and short-story writers of whatever age .... If Mr. Bates should write no more, still something of his would stand as a contribution to current literature unique in its own kind .... He is primarily a lyric writer, and his impulse has so far found its purest expression in his briefer fictions. His total qualities may be as well studied in his maturer novels, and perhaps nowhere so aptly as in his newest and maturest story *The Poacher*, as fresh and in parts as moving as anything he has written.' *Times Literary Supplement,* 24 January 1935

A22b First American edition

(single rule) | THE POACHER | (single rule) | BY | H.E. BATES | (ornament) | New York | THE MACMILLAN COMPANY | 1935

Collation: (A)-(S)^8 (viii) + 280 pp, consisting of half-title, publisher's device on verso, pp (i–ii); title-page, notices of copyright and publication, March 1935 and printer's imprint on verso, pp (iii–iv); dedication 'To SAM', verso blank, pp (v–vi); CONTENTS, verso blank, pp (vii–viii); fly title, PART I, verso blank, pp (1–2); text, including fly titles PARTS II, III and IV, pp 3–273; blank page, p (274); three blank leaves, pp (275–280).

Binding: 8vo, $5\frac{3}{8}$ x $7\frac{3}{4}$ins. Fine green cloth; front cover lettered in gold on black within single rule gilt and ornamental black border; spine lettered in gold on black within black ornamental border; top edges dyed brown; fore and lower edges untrimmed; white end papers.
   Dust jacket: front and spine illustrated with winter snow scene in black, orange, blue and white; lettered in black and orange. Back cover carries advertisement for new Macmillan novels in black.

Price: $2.00. First published March 1935. Set up and printed in the United States of America by The Stratford Press Inc., New York.

A 23   FLOWERS AND FACES   1935

FLOWERS | AND | FACES | BY | H.E. BATES | (short rule) | ENGRAVINGS | BY | JOHN NASH | THE | GOLDEN COCKEREL | PRESS

Collation: (a)^9:b-c^8:d^5 (iv) + 56 pp, consisting of two blank leaves, pp (i–iv); title-page bordered by engravings, Printed and made in Great Britain on verso, pp (1–2); dedication 'To MY LITTLE FLOWERS ANN AND JUDITH', verso blank, pp (3–4); FOREWORD, pp 5–(6): recto blank, full-page engraving on verso, pp (7–8); text, pp 9–18; full-page engraving, verso blank, pp (19–20); text, pp 21–28; full-page engraving, verso blank, pp (29–30); text, pp 31–40; full-page engraving, verso blank, pp (41–42); text, pp 43–(53); Certificate of issue and author's signature, publisher's device engraved, p (54); blank leaf, pp (55–56).

Binding: 4to, 7⅜ x 9¾ins. Quarter green morocco; white cloth sides marbled in red, blue, green and brown; lettering and publisher's device on spine in gold; top edges gilt, fore and lower edges uncut. Bound by Sangorski and Sutcliffe, London.

Price: 2 guineas. Published June 1935.
The edition limited to 325 copies, of which numbers 1–6 were printed on vellum and 7–325 on Batchelor Hand-made paper. Numbers 301–325 were not for sale. The books were signed by the author.
Printed in Golden Cockerel type by Christopher Sandford, Francis J. Newbery, Owen Rutter and Joan Grant at the Golden Cockerel Press and completed on the first day of June, 1935. Compositors: A.H. Gibbs and E.J. Ward. Pressman: H. Barker.

Notes: Dedicated to his children.
The Blossoming World (A 110) p 117: 'Those were the days, the mid thirties, when select Private Presses flourished and there was in the air a certain slight madness about first editions. One result of this was that the Golden Cockerel Press had, in 1935, commissioned me to write a book for them ... it was in June 1935 that Christopher Sandford and his fellow directors at The Golden Cockerel kindly arranged to give the book, *Flowers and Faces*, an afternoon party in Kensington, the party being in the afternoon so that the guests could also see the King and Queen go past on their Jubilee Procession.'
Book-Production Note 'MR. BATES AND HIS GARDEN The Golden Cockerel, like Mr. Bates himself, breaks new ground in this wholly charming book. When the author wished to shift his home from the Midlands to the South, for two years he searched in vain not so much for a house as for a garden in "a modest, solid quiet place in which to work and grow flowers." At length he became the owner of an old Kentish barn, standing in a farmyard run to waste, which had become dumping ground for "an old clutter of stuff; cart-wheels, beams, buckets, rat-eaten sacks, sheets of corrugated iron." The barn was turned into a spacious dwelling-house:

> for the price of a jerry-built semi-detached monstrosity in a suburban
> street we had the very cottage we had been so vainly seeking, a place of
> solid and beautiful workmanship, dry as a granary must be, and planned
> inside and out to suit every one of our fads and fancies.

And the farmyard was transformed into a garden, where it seems to be always spring.
'The book is printed on Batchelor's paper in the Golden Cockerel type. If the strong blacks and delicately engraved white lines of Mr. John Nash's flower-pieces fail by the nature of the medium to suggest the riot of colour which Mr. Bates enjoys in his earthly paradise, that cannot be said of the marbled cloth sides which Messrs. Sangorski and Sutcliffe have used in the casing of the book. In the marbling Mr. Cockerell has applied red, blue, green and brown to the white sides of the cloth.'
London Mercury and Bookman, August, 1935, p 379

A 24   THE DUET   1935

THE GRAYSON BOOKS | Edited by JOHN HACKNEY | (double rule) | THE
DUET | (ornament) | H.E. BATES | (double rule) | GRAYSON & GRAYSON
| LONDON : MDCCCCXXXV

Collation: (A)-E⁴ (40) pp, consisting of blank leaf, pp (1–2); half-title, verso
blank, pp (3–4); certificate of issue and author's signature, verso blank, pp (5–6);
title-page, verso blank, pp (7–8); text, pp (9–31); blank p (32); By the same author,
NOVELS, SHORT STORIES, PLAYS, POEMS, CHILDREN, ANTHOLOGIES, pp
(33–35); blank p (36); note of full-page illustrations in the Grayson Books, verso
blank, pp (37–38); publisher's, printer's and paper-maker's imprint dated A.D.
mdccccxxxv, verso blank, pp (39–40).

Binding: 8vo, $5\frac{5}{8}$ x $8\frac{5}{8}$ ins.   Black cloth; lettering and designs on front cover
in gold; publisher's device on back cover in gold; cream vellum end papers with
designs and publisher's device in green; top edges dyed green; fore and lower edges
untrimmed.
   Dust jacket front cover fully illustrated in green and brown. 285 copies of this
first edition of *The Duet* were printed; 250, numbered and signed by the author,
were for sale.

Price: 10/6.   Printed and made by The Garden City Press Ltd., Letchworth,
Herts.

Notes: *The Duet* was numbered 1 in the series of twelve Grayson Books published
by Grayson & Grayson, 66 Curzon Street, London, W.1.
   The note on p 37 states that the full-page illustrations in The Grayson Books
are by Joy Lloyd. Two other illustrations, not full-page, occur at pp (9) and (31).

A 25   CUT AND COME AGAIN   1935

CUT AND COME AGAIN | FOURTEEN STORIES | by | H.E. BATES |
(Publisher's device) | JONATHAN CAPE | THIRTY BEDFORD SQUARE |
LONDON

Collation: (A)-S⁸ 288 pp, consisting of half-title, By the same author on verso,
pp (1–2); title-page, publisher's, printer's, paper supplier's and binder's imprint on
verso, pp (3–4); contents, verso blank, pp (5–6); dedication 'To Edward J. O'Brien',
verso blank, pp (7–8); fly title, verso blank, pp (9–10); text, pp 11–285; blank p 286;
blank pp (287–288); 8-page catalogue of novels chosen from fiction and published
by Jonathan Cape bound in at end.

Binding: 8vo, 5 x $7\frac{1}{2}$ ins.   White cloth, flecked with blue and brown; lettered
on front cover in blue; lettering and publisher's device on spine in blue; top and
fore-edges cut; lower edges untrimmed. White end papers.
   Dust jacket white with black lettering.   Designs on front cover and spine in
yellow. Review from *The Times* of the author's work in black on back cover.

Price: 7s. 6d. net. Published 28 October 1935.

2,000 copies were printed on 17 September 1935. The type was distributed on 30 April 1936.

Printed in Great Britain in the City of Oxford at The Alden Press. Paper made by John Dickinson & Co., Ltd. Bound by A.W. Bain & Co. Ltd.

Contents: Beauty's Daughters - Cut and Come Again - The Mill - The Revelation - Waiting Room - Little Fish - The Station - The House with the Apricot - The Irishman - The Plough - Jonah and Bruno - The Bath - Harvest Moon - The Pink Cart

Notes: *The Blossoming World* (A 110) p 123: '...one day I accepted with alacrity an invitation from Graham Greene to lunch with him at a restaurant he had just discovered .... Neither of us enjoyed, up to that time, anything more than a *succès d'estime*, to which on my behalf Graham had contributed a generous appraisal of *Cut and Come Again*. In it he had compared me fairly and squarely with Tchehov, saying that he didn't think me the lesser artist. In consequence my literary stock stood pretty high...'

Reviews: *Cut and Come Again* has the hardness and assurance of emotional and technical maturity. The word "greatness" has been cheapened by the Sunday Press and yellow-jacket advertising, in any case it is too vague a word to use in reference to these splendidly objective stories, but if one set Mr. Bates's best tales against the best of Tchehov's I do not believe it would be possible with any conviction to argue that the Russian was a finer artist. Mr. Bates is supreme among English short-story writers; and the work of most authors beside his appears shoddy, trivial or emotional.' Graham Greene, *The Spectator* 22 November 1935

'He stands alone to-day, an artist unaffected by his social environment of change and disorder. He works only with the elementary things of life: love, work, the soil, warmth and cold, silence and noise .... His new collection of stories shows him growing more powerful, more realistic. His style is harder, more austere, but with this gain in force, Mr. Bates has lost none of his lyrical beauty, his singleness of theme.' Richard Church, *John O'London's Weekly*, 9 November 1935

A 26   A HOUSE OF WOMEN   1936

A 26a First English edition

A HOUSE OF WOMEN | by | H.E. BATES | (publisher's device) | JONATHAN CAPE | THIRTY BEDFORD SQUARE | LONDON

Collation: (A)-T^8:U^{10} 324 pp, consisting of half-title, By the same author on verso, pp (1-2); title-page, publisher's, printer's, paper supplier's and binder's imprint on verso, pp (3-4); Contents, verso blank, pp 5-(6); dedication 'to Rupert Hart-Davis', verso blank, pp (7-8); fly title, BOOK ONE, verso blank, pp (9-10); text, pp 11-324, including fly titles of BOOKS TWO, THREE, FOUR and FIVE, pp (89), (127), (181), (229) with versos blank; an 8-page catalogue of novels chosen from fiction published by Jonathan Cape bound in at end.

Binding: 8vo, 5 x 7½ ins. Pale green cloth; lettered on front cover in blue; lettering with publisher's device on spine in blue; top and fore edges cut; lower edges untrimmed; white end papers.

Dust jacket front cover and spine purple, lettered in white; reviews of other books by H.E. Bates on back cover in black.

Price: 7/6d. net. Published 7 May 1936.

First and second impressions of 2,000 copies each were printed on 31 March 1936, all sheets being delivered on 7 April 1936. A third impression of 1,000 copies was printed on 25 May 1936. The type was distributed on 10 September 1936.

Printed in Great Britain in the City of Oxford at The Alden Press. Paper made by John Dickinson & Co., Ltd. Bound by A.W. Bain & Co., Ltd.

Contents: The Angel - The Farm - Frankie - A House of Women - Change and Decay

Notes: Rupert Hart-Davis had been appointed a director of the publishers, Jonathan Cape, in 1933.

Reviews: A House of Women is the best novel that he [Bates] has so far written; it is the first of his novels which I should rank as a finished work of art above the best of his short stories. This means that it is very good indeed: a novel of the very first rank which one will be sure to re-read in ten and again perhaps in twenty years' time .... An intense feeling for natural beauty, for every blade of grass and every sound in the dew-soaked May morning, for the enchanted dreams of childhood, was the feature of Bates's early work ...' David Garnett, *New Statesman and Nation*

A 26b First American edition

A House of Women | BY | H.E. BATES | (publisher's device) | NEW YORK | HENRY HOLT AND COMPANY

Collation: (A)-(U)⁸ (viii) + 312 pp, consisting of: blank leaf, pp (i–ii); title-page, notice of copyright and printing in THE UNITED STATES OF AMERICA on verso, pp (iii–iv); dedication to Rupert Hart-Davis, verso blank, pp (v–vi); CONTENTS, verso blank, pp (vii–viii); text, pp 1–305; blank p (306); blank pp (307–312).

Binding: 8vo, 5 x 7⅜ ins. Green cloth; lettered on front cover and spine in black; top edges dyed green; all edges cut; white end papers.

Dust jacket front cover black with title lettered in white and black, author lettered in green; illustration on front cover in green and black; spine black, lettered in black and white; back cover white with publisher's list of 'Fall Publications - 1936' in black.

Price: $2.00

A 27 THROUGH THE WOODS 1936
The English Woodland
- April to April

A 27a First English edition

THROUGH | the WOODS | (engraving on wood) | The English Woodland - April to April | By | H.E. BATES | With 73 Engravings on Wood | By AGNES MILLER PARKER | VICTOR GOLLANCZ LTD COVENT GARDEN | 1936

Collation: (Aw)-Iw^8 144 pp, consisting of half-title, verso blank, pp (1–2); title-page, dedication, notice of publication and printer's imprint on verso, pp (3–4); Contents, verso blank, pp (5–6); Engravings on Wood, pp (7–9); blank p (10); text, pp 11–(142); blank pp (143–144).

Binding: 4to, $7\frac{3}{4}$ x $10\frac{1}{4}$ ins. Terracotta cloth; lettered on spine in gold; all edges cut; white end papers.
  Dust jacket: an engraving on wood, in brown, of a squirrel on an oak tree occurs on the front cover and is one of the 73 engravings on wood by Agnes Miller Parker (see *Notes*). Lettered on front cover and spine in brown.
  In addition to a dust jacket, the book was paper-banded: 'BERNARD SHAW writes:- "A look through these miraculous engravings is better than a real woodland walk. You can actually feel the fur and smell the leaves."
  This band unfortunately conceals the names of author and artist, who are H.E. BATES and AGNES MILLER PARKER 10/6 NET.'

Price: 10/6 net. Published October 1936. Printed by The Camelot Press Ltd., London and Southampton.

Contents: The Wood in April - The Other Wood - Trees in Flower - Flowers and Foxes - Oaks and Nightingales - The Villain - Woods and Hills - The Height of Summer - Woods and the Sea - Poachers and Mushrooms - The Heart of Autumn - Winter Gale and Winter Spring - Snows of Spring - Primroses and Catkins - The Darling Buds of March - The Circle is Turned.

Notes: The 73 wood-engravings by Agnes Miller Parker: in brown on front cover of dust jacket; title-page p (3); 71 in the text, pp 11–(142) - listed on pp (7)–(9).

'Snows of Spring' was first published in *The Spectator*, London, 1 February 1935 as 'The Snows of Spring' (see C 26.1). Considerable changes to the text were made in *Through The Woods*.
  On 8 October 1936, Bates wrote to Edward Garnett: 'I think my own part in it is as good as I've done, and some of the woodcuts are masterly. Let me know what your impressions are ...'
  Later that month he expressed his thanks to Garnett: 'I'm delighted to hear that you like the book so much ... it warms my heart to hear your praises ...'
  Sam Smith, of Rushden, to whom Bates had previously dedicated *The Poacher* (A 22), received a copy inscribed: 'For Sam, who will understand & love, in this book, a great many things a great many other people have not understood & have hated. Ever, H.E. BATES'

In *The Blossoming World* (A 110), pp 37–8, Bates wrote of Sam Smith: 'Of the half dozen people to whom I could talk literature and companion things two were younger than I; one twenty years older. All came from working-class families. Sam Smith, the older man, unlike Constance Garnett, was virtually self-educated, though later, as a shoehand in his forties, he was offered a scholarship to Cambridge, an opportunity he declined. A small, virile, athletic man, not entirely uninterested in the arts of boxing and ladies, as well as pubs and literature, he had been a soldier in the First World War; rifleman, stretcher-bearer, foot-slogging it out in a very different wasteland. We too found common ground in books, countryside, flowers and even boxing.'

Reviews: 'It is no exaggeration to say that now, at least in the power of evoking the scent, touch, sound and movement of the English scene, Mr. Bates is comparable to W.H. Hudson. He has a like faculty for suggesting the lavish by means of a simple statement, unadorned with adjectives. He has learned to balance his sensuous excitements of eye and ear against an ordered curiosity. He controls his rather dangerous, Keats-like responses to immediate impressions, as it were setting them aside to cool while he finds a place for them in his pattern. The intellectual intervention, paradoxically, only adds to the richness of the material, just as an ecstasy can often be heightened by sceptical examination.' Richard Church, *New Statesman*, 2 January 1937

A 27b First American impression

THROUGH | the | WOODS | (engraving on wood) | The English Woodland - April to April | By | H.E. BATES | With 73 Engravings on Wood | By AGNES MILLER PARKER | NEW YORK | THE MACMILLAN COMPANY | 1936

Notes: Apart from the Macmillan imprint on the title-page and lack of printer's imprint on p (4), the contents and binding are identical to those of the first English edition.

The basic colour of beige for the dust jacket is as the English edition. However, the additional engraving in brown on the front cover of the English jacket is not repeated here and designs in brown of the last engraving in the book, 'Through the Woods', are continuous on the jacket, with lettering on front cover and spine in brown. A blurb is printed in brown on front and back flaps.

'Printed in Great Britain' occurs at the foot of p (4).

A 28   SOMETHING SHORT AND SWEET   1937

SOMETHING | SHORT AND SWEET | Stories | by | H.E. BATES | (publisher's device) | JONATHAN CAPE | THIRTY BEDFORD SQUARE | LONDON

Collation: (A)-S^8 288 pp, consisting of blank leaf, pp (1–2); half-title, By the same author on verso, pp (3–4); title-page, publisher's, printer's, paper supplier's and binder's imprint on verso, pp (5–6); Contents, verso blank, pp (7–8); dedication

'To H.A. Manhood', verso blank, pp (9–10); fly title, verso blank, pp (11–12); text, pp 13–288; an 8-page catalogue of novels chosen from fiction published by Jonathan Cape bound in at end.

Binding: 8vo, 5 x 7½ ins. Blue cloth; lettering, ornament and publisher's device on spine in gold; top and fore-edges cut; lower edges untrimmed; white end papers.
     Dust jacket front cover and spine black with floral designs in black, white, green and brown; lettered in white. Reviews of other books on back cover in black and red.

Price: 7/6d. net. Published 16 July 1937. 2,000 copies of the first impression were printed on 5 June 1937; 1,000 copies of the second impression on 14 August 1937.
     The type was distributed on 14 January 1938; the jacket blocks were scrapped on 17 June 1940.
     Printed in Great Britain in the City of Oxford at The Alden Press. Paper made by John Dickinson & Co., Ltd. Bound by A.W. Bain & Co., Ltd.

Contents: Cloudburst - Purchase's Living Wonders - Something Short and Sweet - The Captain - Italian Haircut - *The Palace - Finger Wet, Finger Dry - The Kimono - Mister Livingstone - The Case of Miss Lomas - The Sow and Silas - The Landlady - No Country - Breeze Anstey - The Man Who Loved Cats - Spring Snow
     *A note in the Jonathan Cape ledger states: "In the event of this book being reprinted at any time after 17/1/47 the story The Palace must be omitted". See also Note to *Country Tales* (A 30).

Notes: H.A. Manhood was a contemporary of H.E. Bates, both authors having many short stories published by Jonathan Cape in the 1930s.

A 29   DOWN THE RIVER   1937

A29a First English edition

DOWN THE RIVER | (engraving on wood) | BY H.E. BATES | With 83 Engravings on Wood | BY AGNES MILLER PARKER | (engraving on wood) | VICTOR GOLLANCZ LTD COVENT GARDEN | LONDON : MCMXXXVII

Collation: (AR)-IR⁸:KR⁴ 152 pp, consisting of half-title, verso blank, pp (1–2); title-page, printer's imprint on verso, pp (3–4); Contents, verso blank, pp (5–6); Engravings on Wood, pp (7–9); blank p (10); text, pp 11–(151); blank p (152).

Binding: 4to, 7¾ x 10¼ ins. Dark blue cloth; lettering on spine in gold; all edges cut; white end papers.
     Dust jacket: an engraving on wood, in blue, of ducks on a mill pond on front cover and included in index of the total of 83 engravings on wood by Agnes Miller Parker. Lettered on front cover and spine in blue.

Price: 10/6 net. Published December 1937. Printed by The Camelot Press Ltd, London and Southampton.

DOWN the RIVER

By H. E. BATES

WITH EIGHTY-THREE WOOD-ENGRAVINGS

By AGNES MILLER PARKER

By THE AUTHOR & ARTIST OF

THROUGH the WOODS

Contents: The Twin Rivers - A Boy's Brook - The First River - Fish and Fish-ermen - The Flood - The Frost - The Second River - Water Flowers and Water Creatures - Flowers of Childhood - The Water-Mill - The Lace-Makers - Otters and Men - The Rivers of England - Down to the Sea
'The Lace Makers' was first published in the *New Statesman and Nation*, 28 April 1934, see (C 20.)

Notes: The 83 engravings on wood by Agnes Miller Parker: one in blue on front cover of dust jacket; two on title-page p (3) 80 in the text, pp 11–(151), listed on pp (7)–(9).

A29b First American impression

DOWN THE RIVER | (engraving on wood) | BY H.E. BATES | With 83 Engravings on Wood | BY AGNES MILLER PARKER | (engraving on wood) | HENRY HOLT AND COMPANY | NEW YORK: 1937

Notes: Apart from the imprint of HENRY HOLT AND COMPANY above and lack of printer's imprint on p (4) the contents and binding are identical to those of the first English edition.
A note, 'Printed in Great Britain', occurs at the foot of p (4).
Dust jacket not seen.

A 30   COUNTRY TALES   1938
Collected Short Stories

COUNTRY | TALES | Collected Short Stories | by | H.E. BATES | LONDON | READERS' UNION LTD. | 1938

Collation: (A)-N^{16} (iv) + 412 pp, consisting of blank leaf pasted down as front end paper, pp (i–ii); blank pp (iii–iv); half-title, notice of special compilation for READERS' UNION on verso, pp (1–2); title-page, POINT, notice of publication and printer's imprint on verso, pp (3–4); CONTENTS, verso blank, pp 5–(6); THE WRITER EXPLAINS, pp 7–10; fly title, verso blank, pp (11–12); text; pp 13–405; blank p (406); two blank leaves, pp (407–410), blank leaf pasted down as back end paper, pp (411–412).

Binding: 8vo, $4\frac{7}{8}$ x $7\frac{5}{16}$ ins. Pale green boards; title with design of cockerel within single-rule border, H.E. BATES · READERS' UNION within single-rule border, all in red on front cover. Lettered on spine in red. Top edges dyed red; all edges cut; white end papers. Cellophane wrapper.
22,000 copies were printed on 24 August 1938 with Readers' Union imprint. The type was distributed on 10 April 1941 (see A 36).
Published September 1938. Printed by The Alden Press, Oxford, for Readers' Union Limited, Chandos Place by Charing Cross, London.

Contents: The Easter Blessing - Never - The Black Boxer - Death in Spring - The Story Without an End - The Gleaner - The Woman Who Had Imagination - Time

- The Waterfall - Innocence - Sally Go Round the Moon - The Brothers - Beauty's Daughters - Cut and Come Again - The Mill - Waiting Room - Little Fish - The Station - The House with the Apricot - The Plough - Jonah and Bruno - The Bath - Harvest Moon - The Pink Cart - Cloudburst - Italian Haircut - The Palace - The Kimono - The Landlady - Breeze Anstey

Notes: The book was specially compiled for Readers' Union by arrangement with the author and Jonathan Cape Ltd. The notice at p (2) stated that an edition for the general public would be issued in the winter of 1939. That edition was published in 1940 with the same title (A 36). There was a change in the contents. The story, 'The Palace', was not then included due to a lawsuit following its publication in *Something Short and Sweet* (A 28).

The POINT at p (4) stated: 'The edition for Readers' Union members only is possible by co-operative reader demand and by sacrifice of ordinary profit margins by all concerned. Such conditions cannot apply under the normal hazards of production and distribution.'

A 31   SPELLA HO   1938

A 31a First English edition

SPELLA HO | A Novel by | H.E. BATES | (publisher's device) | JONATHAN CAPE | THIRTY BEDFORD SQUARE | LONDON

Collation: (A)-Z^8 AA-CC^8 416 pp, consisting of half-title, By the same author on verso, pp (1–2); title-page, notice of publication, printer's, paper-maker's and binder's imprint on verso, pp (3–4); CONTENTS, verso blank, pp 5–(6); dedication 'To FRANK WHITAKER', verso blank, pp (7–8); fly title, BOOK ONE SPELLA HO : 1873, verso blank, pp (9–10); text, including sectional fly titles, pp 11–414; blank pp (415–416).

Binding: 8vo, $5\frac{1}{4}$ x $7\frac{3}{4}$ ins. Turquoise fine weave cloth; lettering with ornament and publisher's device on spine in gold; top edges dyed green; top and fore-edges cut, lower edges rough trimmed; white end papers.

Dust jacket lettered on front cover in white with illustration in black, white orange and yellow; spine lettered in white, orange and yellow; back cover in white with orange border and comment on the author by David Garnett in black.

Price: 8s.6d. net. Published 1 September 1938.

4,000 copies of the first impression were printed on 14 July 1938; 1,000 copies each of the second and third impressions were printed on 10 September 1938; 1,000 copies each of the fourth and fifth impressions were printed on 30 September 1938.

The type was distributed on 22 August 1939. Printed in Great Britain in the City of Oxford at The Alden Press. Paper by Spalding & Hodge Ltd. Bound by A.W. Bain & Co. Ltd.

Notes: Spella Ho was first serialized in the *Atlantic Monthly*, Boston, Mass. clxii, August–November, 1938, pp 260–90; 409–38; 555–84; 703–32.

The dust jacket for the first English edition is a perfect example of the work of Hans Aufseeser in gouache on black paper. He became Hans Tisdall in 1939 and worked almost exclusively for the best part of twenty-five years as a jacket designer for Jonathan Cape. Features of his brilliant designs were his unique method of calligraphy with outstanding colouring.

The Blossoming World (A 110) pp 125–27: 'The theme seemed to me to call for bold and powerful treatment; it was no pastoral sketch. I saw in it not only a personal struggle but a piece of social history, a segment of the late Industrial Revolution that had marked my native landscape with so many soulless, hideous red-brick scars .... I forged ahead with the Chronicle of Bruno with a conscious strength and confidence I had not experienced before .... I had called the novel, which spans the years 1873–1931, *Spella Ho*. I had taken the title from a chance map-reference of the county of Northamptonshire. The reference, Spella Ho clearly indicated Spella House, but there seemed to be something far more arresting and dramatic in the brevity of Spella Ho and so it became.

'I well remember that Ellery Sedgewick, the editor of the *Atlantic Monthly*, who had asked Sylvia Townsend Warner, on a visit to England, who were the young English writers he ought to be most looking out for and had received the reply "H. E. Bates"... The proofs of *Spella Ho* duly arrived in Boston and one spring evening I was astonished to receive a cable from there not only offering me good terms for the book itself but a sum of no less than 5000 dollars for the serialization of the book in the *Atlantic Monthly*. I went about for days in a startling state of crazy disbelief.'

Also pp 133, 136, 141, 147 and 148.

A 31b First American edition

(single rule) | SPELLA HO | BY | H.E. BATES | (publisher's device) | BOSTON | LITTLE, BROWN AND COMPANY | 1938 | (single rule)

Collation: (viii) + 382pp, consisting of half-title, BY THE SAME AUTHOR on verso, pp (i–ii); title-page; notices of copyright and publication, publisher's and printing imprints on verso, pp (iii–iv); dedication 'To FRANK WHITAKER', verso blank, pp (v–vi); CONTENTS; verso blank, pp (vii–viii); fly title, BOOK ONE SPELLA HO : 1873, verso blank, pp (1–2); text, pp (3) - 382.

Binding: 8vo, $5\frac{7}{16}$ x $8\frac{1}{10}$ ins. Pictorial paper wrappers; all edges cut; white end papers.

Cover painting by J. O'H. COSER. Published October 1938. The publisher's imprint states: THE ATLANTIC MONTHLY PRESS BOOKS ARE PUBLISHED BY LITTLE, BROWN AND COMPANY IN ASSOCIATION WITH THE AT-LANTIC MONTHLY COMPANY.

Printed in the United States of America.

A 32   'Carrie and Cleopatra'   April 1939

Unpublished

(four hyphens) | CARRIE | and | CLEOPATRA | A | Play | In | Four | Acts | By | H.E. | BATES

Collation: 4to, 8 x 10 ins; pp (rectos only) (iii) + 27 (Act I), 29 Act II, 25 Act III, 20 Act IV, consisting of : title-page, p (i); CHARACTERS, p (ii); SCENES for the four Acts, The Action and Time, p (iii); ACT I, pp 1–27; ACT II, pp (1)–29; ACT III, pp (1)–23; ACT IV, pp (1)–20.

Binding: Stapled.

Notes: The script was typewritten. A photo-copy is in the possession of the author's son, Richard Bates.
       Despite lengthy negotiations with Jonathan Cape, the play was not published. A dispute had arisen between publisher and author; the argument would appear to have centred on other books having been published by Gollancz and Batsford and the effect this had on options being taken up by Jonathan Cape. The author's relations with Cape worsened and in 1943 their association ended, following further disputes concerning his 'Flying Officer X' material. Laurence Pollinger then became his agent and Michael Joseph his publisher.
       'Carrie and Cleopatra' was performed at the Torch Theatre in London in April 1939 with Louise Hampton taking one of the lead roles. It was not received with much enthusiasm and was taken off after a brief run, never to reach a major theatre.
       The World in Ripeness (A 114) p 119: '...a piece called Carrie and Cleopatra, which was put on, thanks to the tireless interest of that ever-present help in trouble, Violet Dean, at the Torch Theatre, one of London's many little theatres at that time, just before the war. Though giving good acting scope to several of its actors, it wasn't very well received. I was not unnaturally disappointed, though undeterred.'

A 33   I AM NOT MYSELF   1939

I AM NOT | MYSELF | (publisher's device) | H.E. | BATES

Collation: (A-H)⁴ (64) pp, consisting of blank leaf pasted down as front end paper, pp (1–2); four blank leaves, pp (3–10); title-page, verso blank, pp (11–12); text, pp (13–53); blank p (54); certificate of limitation signed by the author and publisher's imprint, verso blank, pp (55–56); three blank leaves, pp (57–62); blank leaf pasted down as back end paper, pp (63–64).

Binding: 4to, 7¾ x 11 ins. Quarter green morocco; fine cream linen sides marbled in brown and green; lettered along spine in gold; top edges gilt, fore and lower edges uncut; white end papers.
       Published in June 1939.
       Thirty-five copies were printed in 18-pt Corvinus Light type on a parchment paper made by Batchelor. Of three copies reserved for the Author and Printer, two

lettered 'A' and 'B' were printed on a green Batchelor hand-made paper and one copy lettered 'C' was printed on a buff Milbourne hand-made paper. All copies were numbered and signed by the author. The book was completed at the Corvinus Press during June 1939. A slip-case was provided.

A 34 THE FLYING GOAT 1939

THE | FLYING GOAT | by | H.E. BATES | (publisher's device) | JONATHAN CAPE | THIRTY BEDFORD SQUARE | LONDON

Collation: A-U^8 320 pp, consisting of blank leaf, pp (1–2); half-title, By the same author on verso, pp (3–4); title-page, notice of publication, printer's, paper maker's and binder's imprint on verso, pp (5–6); CONTENTS, verso blank, pp 7–(8); dedication 'To RICHARD CHURCH', verso blank, pp (9–10); fly title THE FLYING GOAT, verso blank, pp (11–12); text, pp 13–315; blank p (316); two blank leaves, pp (317–320); an 8-page catalogue of novels chosen from fiction published by Jonathan Cape bound in at end.

Binding: 8vo, 5 x 7½ ins. Lime green cloth; lettered in blue on front cover; lettering, ornament and publisher's device on spine in blue; top and fore-edges cut; lower edges untrimmed; white end papers.

Dust jacket designed by Hans Aufseeser. Front cover and spine black; back cover white, lettered in blue, mauve, white and orange. The designs on front cover and spine are of a garlanded goat in the sky surrounded by clouds and stars.

Price: 7s. 6d. net. Published 1 September 1939.

3,000 copies of the first impression were printed on 29 June 1939. The type was distributed on 2 January 1940.

Printed in Great Britain in the City of Oxford at The Alden Press. Paper made by John Dickinson & Co. Ltd. Bound by A.W. Bain & Co. Ltd.

Contents: The White Pony - Every Bullet Has Its Billet - A Funny Thing - Château Bougainvillaea - The Ship - Perhaps We Shall Meet Again... - The Machine - I Am Not Myself - The Flying Goat - The Late Public Figure - The Blind - Shot Actress–Full Story - The Dog and Mr. Morency - The Wreath - Elephant's Nest in a Rhubarb Tree - The Ox.

A 35 MY UNCLE SILAS 1939

MY UNCLE SILAS | (drawing) | Stories by | H.E. BATES | Drawings by | EDWARD ARDIZZONE | JONATHAN CAPE 30 BEDFORD SQUARE LONDON

Collation: (As)-Ms^8 192 pp, consisting of half-title, verso blank, pp (1–2); recto blank, frontispiece, pp (3–4); title-page, notice of publication, printer's, paper-maker's and binder's imprint on verso, pp (5–6); CONTENTS, verso blank, pp

(7–(8); PREFACE, pp 9–12; fly title THE LILY with a drawing, p (13); text, including fly titles each with a drawing, pp 14–190; drawing, verso blank, pp (191–192).

Binding: 4to, $7\frac{1}{4}$ x $9\frac{7}{8}$ ins.   Green cloth; the frontispiece repeated in black on front cover; lettering with an ornament and publisher's device on spine in gold; top edges green; fore-edges cut; lower edges untrimmed; white end papers.

Dust jacket cream, lettered on front cover and spine in black. Drawing on p (43) repeated on front cover with orange as second colour.

Price: 10s. 6d. net. Published 27 October 1939.

2,000 copies of the first impression were printed on 15 September 1939. The type was distributed on 2 February 1940.

Printed in Great Britain by The Camelot Press Ltd., Southampton and London. Paper made by John Dickinson & Co. Ltd. Bound by A.W. Bain & Co. Ltd.

Contents: Preface - The Lily - The Revelation - The Wedding - Finger Wet, Finger Dry - A Funny Thing - The Sow and Silas - The Shooting Party - Silas The Good - A Happy Man - Silas and Goliath - A Silas Idyll - The Race - The Death of Uncle Silas - The Return

Notes: The book contains 27 full-page drawings and 21 smaller illustrations by Edward Ardizzone.

In 1984 when republished by the Oxford University Press in a series of Twentieth Century Classics, V.S. Pritchett, President of the Society of Authors, wrote in his introduction: 'Do not mistake the Uncle Silas stories for old-style bucolic farce. Every detail of Silas's unwashed ugliness and of his domestic habits as the village liar and boozer is truthfully put before us, as if we were sitting in his house with him or had been sent down to the cellar to bring up another dreadful bottle of his home-made wine. And Bates has had the art to make us see the villain through the memory of a small boy who is fascinated by the old man, if also, every now and then, sceptical.

'...Bates had the art that enabled him to write many kinds of story. The poet could be the comedian, saved from slapstick by his resources of style and observation. And he was always at his best in the country landscape of his childhood where the hours seemed fuller and longer.'

Forty-five years earlier, in 1939, the following had appeared in the *Sunday Times*: 'Uncle Silas ... is a wencher, a liar, a poacher, a toper. ... No wonder that he developed in Mr. Bates's mind through several stories, until he has a book to himself. Edward Ardizzone's drawings show just the right quality.'

A 36   COUNTRY TALES   1940

COUNTRY | TALES | Collected Short Stories | by | H.E. BATES | (publisher's device) | JONATHAN CAPE | THIRTY BEDFORD SQUARE | LONDON

Collation: (A)-N^{16} (iv) + 412 pp, consisting of blank leaf pasted down as front end paper, pp (i–ii); blank leaf, pp (iii–iv); half-title, By the Same Author on verso, pp (1–2); title-page, notice of publication, publisher's, printer's, paper supplier's and binder's imprints on verso, pp (3–4); CONTENTS, verso blank, pp 5–(6); THE WRITER EXPLAINS, pp 7–10; fly title, verso blank, pp (11–12); text, pp 13–405; blank p (406); two blank leaves, pp (407–410); blank leaf pasted down as back end paper, pp (411–412).

Binding: 8vo, $4\frac{7}{8}$ x $7\frac{7}{16}$ ins. Beige cloth; lettered on front cover in green; lettering, with an ornament and publisher's device on spine in green; all edges cut; white end papers.
    Dust jacket; front cover and spine black, back cover white. All lettering in white excepting title on front cover in scarlet.

Price: 7s. 6d. net. Published 5 July 1940.
    2,000 copies of the first impression with the Jonathan Cape imprint were printed on 24 August 1938. The type was distributed on 10 April 1941.
    Printed in Great Britain in the City of Oxford at The Alden Press. Paper supplied by Spalding & Hodge. Bound by A.W. Bain & Co. Ltd.

Contents: With one exception the contents and page numbers were identical with those in the 1938 edition of *Country Tales* (Readers' Union imprint) (A 30). Owing to a lawsuit concerning publication of 'The Palace' in *Something Short and Sweet* (A 28). 'The Captain' was substituted.
    See also Note to A 30.

A 37   THE SEASONS & THE GARDENER   1940

THE SEASONS & THE GARDENER | A Book for Children by | H.E. BATES and illustrated | with drawings by C.F. TUNNICLIFFE | (scraperboard vignette) | CAMBRIDGE: AT THE UNIVERSITY PRESS, 1940

Collation: Four leaves; BSG1–BSG9⁴ (viii) + 72 pp, consisting of half-title, publisher's imprint on verso, pp (i–ii); title-page, printer's imprint on verso, pp (iii–iv); DEDICATION (see below), verso blank, pp (v–vi); text, pp 1–(69); blank p (70); blank pp (71–72).

Binding: 4to, $6\frac{5}{8}$ x $8\frac{7}{8}$ ins. Quarter black cloth; green boards with orange fleck; lettering with full decorative scraperboard on front cover in black; lettering along spine in green; all edges cut; white end papers.
    Dust jacket; the full decorative scraperboard on the binding was repeated on front of dust-jacket with orange as a second colour. Lettering on both covers and spine black.

Price: 6s. net. Published 1 November 1940. The publishers have no record of the print quantity. They state: 'It had sold 1,981 copies by 27 February 1941, and did not reprint until 1945, so the first impression was probably greater than 5,000 copies (*if* we can draw conclusions from war-time statistics, when the market was bound to be unpredictable). Sales and stocks of the book had evidently dwindled considerably by 1945, but the reprint had been held up due to the paper shortage; in other words, it is very hard to guess whether more or less than 5,000 were originally printed.'

Printed in Great Britain by W. Lewis, MA, at The Cambridge University Press.

Contents: PART I Introduction, and some explanations. PART II Spring - The Flower Garden - The Rock Garden - The Greenhouse - The Vegetable Garden - Seed Sowing. PART III Summer - Weather Changes - Enemies and Friends - Birds - Full Summer. PART IV Autumn - A Change in the Light - Autumn Colour and Autumn Seed - Saving Seeds - Preparing for Winter - First Frosts. PART V Winter - Winter Flowers - Tools - Catalogues - From Winter to Spring - A Last Word.

Illustrations by C.F. Tunnicliffe. 51 scraperboard vignettes occur in the text: pp 1, 3, 5, 6, 7, 8, 9, 10, 11, 13, 14, 15, 18, 19, 21, 23, 25, 27, 28, 30, 32, 34, 35 (two), 36, 37, 38, 39, 40 (repeated on title-page), 42, 43, 44, 45, 46, 47, 48, 49, 51, 52, 54, 55, 56, 58, 59, 61, 62, 64, 65, 66, 67, (69).

Dedication: Dear Ann, Judith, Richard and Jonathan,

I have often promised you, at least the two eldest of you, that I would write you a book. I think you hoped that this would be a book about fairies or ships or elephants or perhaps some of the strange old ladies with ear-trumpets I sometimes imitate for you. You probably never thought it would be a book about gardens.

But here it is. Of course, I haven't written it specially for you, but I have tried to write it as if I were talking to you. By doing that I hoped that many more children besides yourselves would be able to listen to, and understand, what I was trying to say about flowers and birds and bees and all the rest of the interesting and beautiful things that go to make up a garden. Of course, you are lucky because you know the garden I am writing about, and because you have a small garden of your own in it. That little garden of yours, with its daffodils and turnips and primroses and radishes and forget-me-nots and marrows all mixed up in the same bed, has already given you a lot of pleasure. When you look back on it, and the days you spent there under the pink plum tree, you may perhaps think of it as one of the happiest things in your life. But one day also you will, most probably, want to make a different, larger and better garden for yourselves.

It is then, I hope, that you will look at this book. For that is why I have written it: because I hope that it will not only be easy for children to understand but also full of sensible advice that will help you, and other children, to grow flowers and make gardens successfully. So many people know nothing of the simplest garden rules and flowers because, unlike you, they did not learn when they were young. This book will, I hope, do something to change that. And if it does so for only a handful of people I shall be quite happy.

This, then, is your book. It has come, so to speak, out of our garden. In time I hope gardens of your own will come out of it.

H.E.B.

A 38   THE BEAUTY OF THE DEAD   1940
AND OTHER STORIES

THE | BEAUTY OF THE DEAD | and Other Stories | by | H.E. BATES
| (publisher's device) | JONATHAN CAPE | THIRTY BEDFORD SQUARE |
LONDON

Collation: (A)-Q^8 256 pp, consisting of half-title, By the same author on verso,
pp (1–2); title-page, publisher's, printer's, paper-maker's and binder's imprint on
verso, pp (3–4); CONTENTS, verso blank, pp 5–(6); fly title, verso blank, pp (7–8);
text, pp 9–255; blank p (256).

Binding: 8vo, 5 x 7½ ins. Pale green cloth flecked with white; lettering on front
cover in red; lettering, an ornament and publisher's device on spine in red; top and
fore-edges cut, lower edges untrimmed; white end papers.
    Dust jacket; front cover and spine black, lettered in deep pink and white, back
cover white with list of Books by H.E. Bates and note by David Garnett in deep
pink and black.

Price: 7s. 6d. net. Published 6 December 1940.
    2,500 copies of the first impression printed on 22 October 1940. Printed in Great
Britain in the City of Oxford at The Alden Press. Paper made by John Dickinson
& Co. Ltd. Bound by A.W. Bain & Co. Ltd.

Contents: The Beauty of the Dead - The Bridge - Fuchsia - The Ferry - The
Loved One - Old - The Banjo - A Scandalous Woman - Love is not Love - Quartette
- Mr. Penfold - The Goat and the Stars - The Earth - Time to Kill - The Little
Jeweller

Notes: 'The Beauty of the Dead' and one other short story, 'The Bridge', were
published by the Corvinus Press in May 1941 in a limited edition of 25 copies (A
39).

A 39   THE BEAUTY OF THE DEAD   1941
AND ONE OTIIER SIIORT STORY

THE BEAUTY | OF THE DEAD | AND ONE OTHER | SHORT STORY |
By H.E. BATES

Collation: (66) pp, consisting of two blank leaves, pp (1–4); title-page, verso
blank, pp (5–6); blank leaf, pp (7–8); fly title, THE BEAUTY OF THE DEAD,
verso blank, pp (9–10); text, pp (11–25); blank page, p (26); blank leaf, pp (27–28);
fly title, THE BRIDGE, verso blank, pp (29–30); text, pp (31–59); blank p (60);
certificate of issue, verso blank, pp (61–62); two blank leaves, pp (63–66).

Binding: 4to, 6½ x 9$\frac{9}{10}$ ins. Quarter dark blue buckram backed boards; publisher's devices on front and back covers of blue hair-line paper; lettered in gold
along spine; top edges gilt, others untrimmed. Blue hair-line end papers.

Published May 1941.

20 numbered copies of the book, set in 13 point Times type were printed on a blue hair-line paper made in America. 2 copies, lettered A and B, were printed on Finnish paper made by Terwakoski. 2 copies, lettered C and D, were printed on a streaked paper made by Millbourne. 1 copy, lettered E, was printed on a Dutch paper made about 1790. All copies were signed by the author and completed at The Corvinus Press in May 1941.

A 40   THE MODERN SHORT STORY   1941

THE | MODERN SHORT STORY | A CRITICAL SURVEY | by | H.E. BATES | THOMAS NELSON AND SONS LTD | LONDON EDINBURGH PARIS MELBOURNE | TORONTO AND NEW YORK | 1941

Collation: (1)-14^8 15^4 232 pp, consisting of half-title, By the same author on verso, pp (1–2); title-page, publisher's imprint on verso, pp (3–4); CONTENTS, dedication 'To A.J.J. RATCLIFF' on verso, pp (5–6); PREFACE, pp 7–12; text, pp 13–223, blank page, p (224); INDEX, pp 225–231; printer's imprint, p (232).

Binding: 8vo, 5$\frac{3}{8}$ x 7$\frac{7}{8}$ ins. Half terracotta cloth, beige cloth sides, the two colours divided by a single gilt rule; lettered on spine in gold; all edges cut; top edges dyed terracotta; white end papers.

Dust jacket; beige lettering and publisher's device on front cover, spine and back cover in red.

Price: 7/6 net. Published July 1941.

Printed in Great Britain at the Press of the Publishers.

Contents: Preface - Retrospect - Origins : Gogol and Poe - American Writers After Poe - Tchehov and Maupassant - Tolstoy, Wells and Kipling - Katherine Mansfield and A.E. Coppard - The Irish School - American Renaissance - Lawrence and the Writers of To-Day - Prospect - Index

A second edition, published in 1972 by Michael Joseph, London, contained a new preface.

The first American edition was published in December 1941 by Thomas Nelson & Sons Ltd., New York.

A 41   THE GREATEST PEOPLE IN   1942
THE WORLD AND OTHER STORIES

THE | GREATEST PEOPLE | IN THE WORLD | AND OTHER STORIES | By | FLYING OFFICER "X" | (publisher's device) | JONATHAN CAPE | THIRTY BEDFORD SQUARE, LONDON

Collation: (A)-B^{16} C^8. 80 pp, consisting of half-title, verso blank, pp (1–2); title-page, notice of publication, publisher's imprint, Book Production War Economy Standard emblem and notice, paper-maker's and printer's imprint on verso, pp (3–4); CONTENTS, dedication 'TO HILARY ST. GEORGE SAUNDERS' on verso, pp (5–6); text, pp 7–79; blank p (80).

Binding: 8vo, 4$\frac{1}{2}$ x 7$\frac{1}{4}$ ins. Blue cloth; lettering and design on front cover in silver; top and fore-edges cut; lower edges untrimmed; white end papers.
        Dust jacket; front cover and spine blue, lettered in white; back cover white.

Price: 2s. net. Published September 1942.
        A Directorate of Public Relations (Royal Air Force) Monograph, 'Propaganda and Publicity' (Reference AIR 41/9), filed at the Public Record Office, Kew, records that 16,319 copies were first issued in September 1942.
        Made and printed in Great Britain by Hazell, Watson & Viney, Ltd, London and Aylesbury.
        A cheap edition, priced 6d., was published simultaneously in September 1942 for the British Publishers Guild by Jonathan Cape. This book was No.16 of a series of Guild Books presented by the Guild, a large group of publishers co-operating with the object of issuing and maintaining a comprehensive list of good books in uniform cheap editions.
        The author, inscribing a copy of this 6d. edition to E.E. Kirby, was obviously displeased with the lack of generosity shown by Jonathan Cape.

Contents: It's Never in the Papers - There's No Future In It - The Young Man from Kalgoorlie - It's Just The Way It Is - The Sun Rises Twice - No Trouble At All - A Personal War - K for Kitty - The Greatest People in the World
        These nine stories, together with the six stories in *How Sleep the Brave and Other Stories* (A 47), were published in 1944 in one volume, *Something in the Air* (A 52), not to be confused with the American edition of *There's Something in the Air* (A 45), published in 1943.

Notes: In *The World in Ripeness* (A 114) the author tells of the circumstances which inspired him to write 'The Sun Rises Twice' and 'The Young Man from Kalgoorlie':
        p 18. 'One evening a pilot, an extraordinarily good and tough one, let fall the casual statement that sometimes, not returning from ops over Germany until dawn was breaking, he would see the sun rise twice, once from several thousand feet up and a second time after he had landed. I could scarcely wait to get this down on paper and when I did I called it 'The Sun Rises Twice'.
        pp 18-19. 'The second incident fell from the lips of the young Australian. ...There had been, it seemed, on a remote sheep-farm in Victoria, a couple with an only son. So precious and useful were his hands in the running of the sheep-farm that when war broke out the parents instantly resorted to every kind of trick and subterfuge in order to keep the news from him. Newspapers were cancelled, letters were opened, hidden or burnt, the radio was put out of action. All this, combined with the extreme remoteness of the station, enabled them to keep the stark fact of war from him for an entire year. Then, inevitably, there came a day when he drove a hundred miles to the nearest good-sized town for a few days' holiday, went

into a barber's saloon for a haircut, picked up a newspaper and was stunned by the greatest shock of his young life. He enlisted the very next day and I called his story "The Young Man from Kalgoorlie" '.

p 21. Bates tells of Hilary Saunders, to whom the book was dedicated, having been inspired to invent the pseudonym Flying Officer X. (The stories first appeared in the *News Chronicle* under that *nom de plume.*)

p 29. Hilary Saunders subsequently negotiated with Wren Howard, Jonathan Cape's partner, for the publication of two separate editions in 1942. With promise of an unlimited supply of paper, described by Bates at that time of the war as 'precious as platinum', Hilary Saunders suggested, 'What we have in mind is that our edition should be a sort of Penguin, selling at sixpence, but that you may do your own hard-back edition at, perhaps, half-a-crown.'

p 32-33. Bates describes the break between himself and Jonathan Cape, brought about by having received no financial reward whatsoever from the countless thousands of copies sold by Cape of this book and of *How Sleep the Brave*. The literary agent Laurence Pollinger became his champion and took charge of his affairs. The publisher chosen in place of Cape was Michael Joseph.

A 42   IN THE HEART OF THE COUNTRY   1942

IN THE HEART | OF THE COUNTRY | H.E. BATES | Illustrated by C.F. Tunnicliffe | (vignette) | LONDON : COUNTRY LIFE LIMITED | 2–10 Tavistock Street, Covent Garden, W.C.2

Collation: (A)-I⁸ K⁴. x + 142 pp, consisting of blank leaf, pp (i–ii); half-title, verso blank, pp (iii–iv); title-page, notice of publication and printer's imprint on verso, pp (v–vi); Contents, verso blank, pp vii–(viii); List of Illustrations, verso blank, pp ix–(x); text, pp 11–150; blank pp (151–152).

Binding: 4to, $7\frac{1}{4}$ x $9\frac{3}{4}$ ins. Green cloth; lettered on front cover and spine in gold; top edges cut; fore and lower edges untrimmed; white end papers.

   Dust jacket: pale green, lettered on front and spine in black. The vignetted scraperboard facing p 114 is repeated on front cover in black; another vignetted scraperboard appears on back cover.

Price: 10s. 6d. net.

   Printed in Great Britain by Billing and Sons Ltd., Guildford and Esher.

Contents: Sudden Spring - Fisherman's Luck - Overture to Summer - Fruit Blossom Time - "Clouded August Thorn" - Strange Battlefields - The Great Snow - A Summer Spring - "...Bring Forth May Flowers" - Victorian Garden - Wealden Beauty - The Strangeness of Fish - The Parish Pump - Flowers and Downland

Notes: In 1949 the publication by Michael Joseph Limited, London, of *The Country Heart* (A 62) brought together in considerably revised and amended form *O More Than Happy Countryman* and *In The Heart of the Country*. The notice of publication at p (6) of *The Country Heart* did not include the word 'In' when referring to *In The Heart of the Country*.

The above Contents appeared in Part I of *The Country Heart* as Chapters 1–14, pp (15)–123.

Illustrations by C.F. Tunnicliffe: title-page vignette; 14 full-page vignetted scraperboards facing pp 14, 24, 36, 44, 50, 64, 78, 82, 92, 102, 114, 124, 134, 146. A further 14 vignetted scraperboards within the text at pp 11, 19, 32, 41, 48, 61, 75, 81, 88, 100, 111, 123, 132, 142 are not included in the List of Illustrations at p (ix).

A 43   WAR PICTURES BY BRITISH   1942
ARTISTS No.3 R.A.F.

(three-rule border) | R.A.F. | With | an Introduction by | H.E. BATES | 1942 | OXFORD UNIVERSITY PRESS | LONDON · NEW YORK · TORONTO | (two-rule border)

Collation: (A-D)⁸ 64 pp, consisting of half-title, publisher's note on verso, pp (1–2); title-page, notice of Crown copyright and printer's imprint on verso, pp (3–4); INTRODUCTION by H.E. BATES, pp 5–7; blank p (8); reproductions of drawings and paintings numbered 1–48, pp (9–56); Notes on the Pictures, pp 57–64.

Binding: 8vo, 4¾ x 7½ ins. Plain white card, loosely covered with white paper wrapper, front cover with designs in black, white and blue, lettering in black and white, all within ruled border of black and blue; publisher's note on p (2) repeated on front inside flap; names of artists and titles in the series lettered in black within black ruled border on back cover; lettered along spine in black.

Price: 1s. 3d. net.
Printed in Great Britain by Harrison & Sons, Ltd., Printers to His Majesty the King, 44–47 St. Martin's Lane, London, W.C.2.

Notes: Introduction by H.E. Bates dated December 1941.
The 48 drawings and paintings reproduced in the book were made by artists working under the official direction of the Air Ministry on the recommendation of the Ministry of Information Artists' Advisory Committee. The artists contributing were Robert Austin, ARA, Robin Darwin, T.C.Dugdale, ARA, Richard Eurich, Keith Henderson, Eric Kennington, Dame Laura Knight, RA, J. Mansbridge, Raymond McGrath, Paul Nash, Roy Nockolds, Cuthbert Orde, Sir William Rothenstein, Graham Sutherland.
The Blossoming World (A 110) pp 177–78: 'Soon afterwards came the letter from Cecil Day Lewis. It contained the interesting suggestion that I might care to look at some portraits done by Eric Kennington, Paul Nash, Laura Knight, Sir William Rothenstein, Graham Sutherland, Keith Henderson and others of some of the pilots who had fought in the Battle of Britain. I knew of course of Kennington's work from his vividly admirable portraits of British and Arab leaders alike in T.E. Lawrence's *Seven Pillars of Wisdom*.
'...it was Cecil Day Lewis' idea that I should look at the Kennington and Nash portraits of the Battle of Britain pilots, see what I thought of them and then

annotate them for a small book to be put out by the M.O.I. When the portraits arrived I was instantly struck by several things; first the great variation in the faces of the men themselves, which varied from the glamorised types with their fancy neckerchiefs ... to Sergeant Pilots of calm and unglamorised composure and resolve and sensitive men who might have been poets, Oxford dons, picture restorers or prelates or indeed anything at all. The great variation of those faces was infinitely fascinating. I duly did my annotations and the little book was duly published. I had given it the title of You Have Seen Their Faces. Little though I was aware of it at the time, the title was to a degree prophetic. The faces that had fought the Battle of Britain had been little seen or known until Kennington and other artists drew them. But behind them were many other faces of whose characteristics the greater part of the population of Britain were also entirely ignorant.'

A 44   THE BRIDE COMES TO EVENSFORD   1943

The | BRIDE | Comes To | EVENSFORD | By | H.E. BATES | (publisher's device) | JONATHAN CAPE | THIRTY BEDFORD SQUARE | LONDON

Collation: (A)-D^8 64 pp, consisting of half-title, By the same author on verso, pp (1–2); title-page, notice of publication, publisher's imprint, Book Production War Economy Standard emblem and notice, printer's, paper-maker's and binder's imprint on verso, pp (2–3); dedication 'To Dilys Powell and Leonard Russell', p (5); text, pp 6–60; blank pp (61–62); blank leaf pasted down as back end paper, pp (63–64).

Binding: 8vo, 5 x 7$\frac{5}{8}$ ins. Blue cloth; lettering with design on front cover in silver; top and fore-edges cut; lower edges untrimmed; white end papers.
     Dust jacket designed by Hans Tisdall (formerly Aufseeser). Design on front cover in blue, crimson and white, lettered in crimson and white; back cover white; spine lettered in black.

Price: 3s. 6d. net. Published 1 February 1943.
     3,000 copies of the first impression were printed on 24 November 1942.
     Printed in Great Britain in the City of Oxford at The Alden Press. Paper made by Spalding and Hodge Ltd. Bound by A.W. Bain & Co. Ltd.

Notes: Dilys Powell was a contributor to *The Saturday Book*; Leonard Russell was its editor when the story was first published in *The 1943 Saturday Book* (Hutchinson, London. October 1942, Part 5, pp 147–89 (B 165.1).
     The story was subsequently published in *The Bride Comes to Evensford And Other Tales* (A 63), with the same design on the front cover of the jacket.

A 45   THERE'S SOMETHING IN THE AIR   1943

(illustration of an aeroplane) | THERE'S | SOMETHING IN | THE AIR | BY | FLYING OFFICER X | (H.E. BATES) | (publisher's device) | NEW YORK: ALFRED A KNOPF: 1943

Collation: (A-F)^{16} 3 + 1 + vi + 174 pp, consisting of recto blank, Review of 'East of Farewell' by Howard Hunt on verso, pp (1–2); half-title, verso blank, pp (3–4); title-page, notices of copyright and publication on verso, pp (i–ii); dedication 'TO HILARY ST. GEORGE SAUNDERS', verso blank, pp (iii–iv); CONTENTS, pp (v)–vi; fly title, verso blank, pp (1–2); text, pp 3–170; glossary of RAF slang, pp 171–172; publisher's device, compositor's, printer's and binder's imprint, verso blank, pp (173–174).

Binding: 8vo, 5$\frac{1}{4}$ x 7$\frac{3}{4}$ ins. Blue cloth; top edges dyed light red; fore and lower edges cut; lettering and design in gold on spine.
     Published 17 May 1943.

Contents: It's Never in the Papers - There's No Future In It - The Young Man from Kalgoorlie - It's Just The Way It Is - The Sun Rises Twice - No Trouble At All - A Personal War - K for Kitty - The Greatest People in the World - Macintyre's Magna Charta - The Beginning of Things - Li Tale - The Disinherited - Sorry, No Saccharine - Sergeant Carmichael - O'Callaghan's Girl - Yours is the Earth - Morning Victory - Free Choice, Free World - Here We Go Again - There's Something in the Air - Glossary of R.A.F. Slang

Notes: Set in Electra, a Linotype type face designed by W.A. Dwiggins. This face cannot be classified readily as either 'modern' or 'old-style'. It is not based on any historical model, nor does it echo any particular period or style. It avoids the extreme contrast between 'thick' and 'thin' elements that mark most 'modern' faces, and attempts to give a feeling of fluidity, power and speed. The book was composed, printed and bound by The Plimpton Press, Norwood, Mass.

A 46   COUNTRY LIFE   1943

COUNTRY LIFE | BY | H.E. BATES | (publisher's device) | PENGUIN BOOKS | HARMONDSWORTH MIDDLESEX ENGLAND | 300 FOURTH AVENUE NEW YORK U.S.A.

Collation: (A)-D^{16} E^8 (viii) + 136 pp, consisting of half-title, portrait of the author and biographical note on verso, pp (i–ii); title-page, notice of publication, paper-maker's and printer's imprint on verso, pp (iii–iv); FOREWORD, pp (v–vi); CONTENTS, AUTHOR'S NOTE on verso, pp (vii–viii); text, pp 9–144.

Binding: 8vo, 4$\frac{3}{8}$ x 7$\frac{1}{8}$ ins. Paper covers; front cover and spine in three divisions, centre white with yellow above and below; in the top division PENGUIN BOOKS lettered and bordered in black on white; central division lettered in black and

yellow; publisher's device in bottom division in black and white; lettering and serial
number (401) on spine in black, publisher's device in black and white; commercial
advertisement on back cover in black, yellow and white; inside covers white with
commercial advertisements in black; all edges cut.

Made and printed in Great Britain for Penguin Books Limited, by Richard Clay
and Company Ltd., Bungay, Suffolk.

Contents: (A selection of notes which appeared in *The Spectator* in a column
called 'Country Life') Foreword - The Birds - Country Problems, Country Govern-
ment - The Seasons and the Weather - The Countryside at War - Flowers and Trees
- Eat and Drink - Country Ways, Country Folk - Animals - Landscape - On the
Land - In the Garden - Prunings and Clippings

A 47   HOW SLEEP THE BRAVE   1943
AND OTHER STORIES

First English edition

HOW SLEEP THE | BRAVE | AND OTHER STORIES | By | FLYING OF-
FICER "X" | (publisher's device) | JONATHAN CAPE | THIRTY BEDFORD
SQUARE, LONDON

Collation: (A)-E^8 80 pp, consisting of half-title, By the Same Author on verso,
pp (1–2); title-page, CONTENTS, dedication 'To JOHN PUDNEY', notice of publication, publisher's, paper-maker's and printer's imprint on verso, pp (3–4); text,
pp (5)–80. (Book Production War Economy Standard notice and emblem appears
at the foot of p 80.)

Binding: 8vo, 4⅝ x 7 ins. Blue cloth; lettering with design on front cover in silver;
all edges cut; white end papers.

Dust jacket; front cover and spine blue with lettering in white; back cover bordered with blue at spine, lettered in white.

Price: 2s. 6d. net. Published August 1943.
Made and printed in Great Britain by C. Tinling & Co., Ltd., Liverpool, London
and Prescot.

A Directorate of Public Relations (Royal Air Force) Monograph 'Propaganda
and Publicity' (Ref. AIR 41/9) at the Public Record Office, Kew, records that
10,331 copies were first issued in August 1943. *Contents:* PART I - How Sleep
the Brave. PART II - The Beginnings of Things - The Disinherited - Croix De
Guerre - Yours is the Earth - There's Something in the Air

A 48   O MORE THAN HAPPY   1943
COUNTRYMAN

First English edition

O MORE THAN HAPPY | COUNTRYMAN | by | H.E. BATES | Illustrated by C.F. Tunnicliffe | (design) | LONDON : COUNTRY LIFE LIMITED | 2-10 Tavistock Street, Covent Garden, W.C.2

Collation: (A)-F^8 G^4 104 pp, consisting of half-title, full-page vignetted scraperboard on verso as frontispiece, pp (1-2); title-page, notice of publication, BOOK PRODUCTION WAR ECONOMY STANDARD emblem and notice, printer's imprint on verso, pp (3-4); Contents, list of full-page illustrations on verso, pp (5-6); text, pp 7-104.

Binding: 4to, $7\frac{1}{4}$ x $9\frac{3}{4}$ ins. Dark green cloth; lettered on front cover and along spine in white; all edges cut; cream end papers.
    Dust jacket green, lettered on front cover and spine in black. Illustration from p 65 is repeated on front cover, and from p 52 on back cover.

Price: 8s. 6d. net.
    Printed in Great Britain by Billing and Sons Ltd., Guildford and Esher.

Contents: Et Decorum Est Pro Patria Mori - The Great House - Sea Days, Sea Flowers - Mr. Pimpkins - The Future Garden - The Garden on Leave - The New Country - The Old Tradition - The Green Hedges - O More Than Happy Countryman

Notes: The contents were later published in 1949 by Michael Joseph Limited as Nos. 1-10 in Part Two of *The Country Heart* (A 62), described as a considerably revised and amended edition of *O More Than Happy Countryman* and *The Heart of the Country (In The Heart of the Country* (A 42)).
    Illustrations by C.F. Tunnicliffe: full-page vignetted scraperboards; frontispiece p (2), and pp 9, 17, 23, 33, 49, 55, 65, 75, 85, 101. A further 15 vignetted scraperboards in the text: pp 7, 13, 14, 19, 20, 29, 38, 52, 53, 59, 72, 79, 80, 93, 104. Illustrations on p 65 and p 52 repeated on jacket.

A 49   THERE'S FREEDOM IN THE AIR   1944

(THE OFFICIAL STORY OF THE ALLIED AIR FORCES FROM THE OCCUPIED COUNTRIES)

There's Freedom in the Air | LONDON : HIS MAJESTY'S STATIONERY OFFICE (illustration of Spitfires in flight, continuous with inside of front cover)

Collation: One gathering only, stapled. 36 pp, consisting of title-page, emblems of the Polish, Fighting French, Dutch and Greek allies, Contents and Notice of Crown Copyright on verso, pp (1-2); FOREWORD, Notice of publication, printer's imprint and emblems of the Norwegian, Czechoslovak, Belgian and Yugoslav allies, p (3); Text, including map and photographs, pp (4-36).

Binding: 8vo, 6⅞ x 9 ins. Illustrated paper covers; title in yellow, price in white on front cover; continuous yellow border (⅞ ins. wide) at foot of covers, lettered in black; all edges cut.

Price: 6d. net. Published March 1944.
Prepared for The Air Ministry by The Ministry of Information and printed by The Whitefriars Press Ltd., London and Tonbridge.
A Directorate of Public Relations (Royal Air Force) Monograph, 'Propaganda and Publicity' (Reference AIR 41/9) at the Public Record Office, Kew, records that 399,900 copies were first issued in March 1944.

Notes: A copy is in the Public Record Office, Kew, Richmond, Surrey, filed in AIR 20/4870. It is dated, with corrections and amendments, April and October 1944.
The manuscript, approximately 30,600 words, is typed on eighty-four sheets of foolscap paper and contains thirteen chapters.
The World in Ripeness (A 114): At p 35 the author describes the events leading to his meeting with Air Chief Marshal Portal (later Lord Portal) who chose him to write the pamphlet.
At pp 36 and 37 Bates wrote: '...he proceeded to explain that someone should write the story of the Night Battle of Britain, a perilous affair whose near catastrophic events had already been allowed to slip back into a darkness as Stygian as that in which it had in fact been fought in the winter of 1941 ...the Night Battle had somehow slid away into the limbo of nightmares best forgotten.
It was Portal's idea that this state of affairs should be put right. He proceeded to elaborate by comparing the two battles: the day battle an affair largely waged by one force, one section of the populace so small that its members had already been honoured as the Few; the night battle waged by comparison with scores of varied units drawn from all sections of the community, both service and civilian...
The pamphlet was duly finished but, though approved in high places, was never published. Today it is safely filed away in the Public Records Office, from which it will doubtless never emerge.'

A 50   'The Night Interception Battle 1940-1941' (pamphlet)

A 51   FAIR STOOD THE WIND FOR FRANCE   1944

A 51a First English edition

H.E. BATES | (star ornament) | FAIR | STOOD THE WIND | FOR FRANCE | "Fair stood the wind for France | When we our sails advance, | Nor now to prove our chance | Longer will tarry." | MICHAEL DRAYTON | (1563-1631) | (publisher's device) | MICHAEL JOSEPH LIMITED | 26 Bloomsbury Street, London, W.C.1

Collation: (A)-G¹⁶ 224 pp, consisting of half-title and publisher's note, By the same Author on verso, pp (1-2); title-page; notice of publication, Book Production War Economy Standard emblem and notice, printer's and binder's imprint on verso, pp (3-4); text, pp 5-224.

Binding: 8vo, 5⅛ x 7¼ ins. Brown boards; lettering with two stars and publisher's device on spine in gold; top edges dyed brown; all edges cut; white end papers.

Dust jacket designed by A.E. Barlow. Front cover and spine in shades of deep mauve to purple, lettered in white. Back cover white, listing publisher's 'New Novels for 1944' in black.

Price: 9s. 6d. net. Published November 1944. A total of 87,286 copies were sold.

Set and printed in Great Britain by Tonbridge Printers Ltd., Peach Hall Works, Tonbridge, in Times nine on eleven point. Bound by James Burn.

Notes: *Publisher's Note in the first English edition:* 'This novel contains approximately 110,000 words which, in order to save paper, have been compressed within 224 pages. There are many more words on each page than would be desirable in normal times; margins have been reduced and no space has been wasted between chapters. The length of the average novel is between 70,000 and 90,000 words, which, ordinarily, make a book of between 288 and 352 pages. This novel would ordinarily make a book of about 416 pages.'

The book had first been serialized in America in the *Saturday Evening Post*, 18 March-6 May 1944.

A four-part serialization was televised on BBC 1 in September 1980.

As a play dramatized by Gregory Evans and Michael Napier Brown, its world première was presented at the Royal Theatre, Northampton, 10 April-3 May 1986.

The World in Ripeness (A 114) p 31: 'In periods of leave, at week-ends or whenever I could snatch a spare day I now worked on *Fair Stood the Wind for France*, writing in a frenzy that fitted the mood of the times yet always striving to keep the style of the novel, as in the stories of Flying Officer X, clear and vivid in its pictorial simplicity.'

p 33: 'After twenty years of writing, with its several disasters and constant struggles, *Fair Stood the Wind for France* was my first wide success. The book was translated into many languages, and indeed is still being further translated, and at least one perceptive reviewer saw it, as I had intended it to be, a story epitomising the youth of two countries at a period of great conflict and agony.'

Reviews: 'Ever since he was discovered by that genius-diviner Edward Garnett, I have found Bates' work a source of pleasure. His candour of personality, his honest craftsmanship in the handling of prose, his knowledge of nature, even his occasional touches of spleen; these have been my meat. And above all these, some element of sheer poetry .... Therefore I have never ceased to predict that one day, as the tree ripened, Bates would write a masterpiece. Here is that masterpiece.'

Richard Church, *John O'London's Weekly*

A 51b First American edition

H.E. BATES (within a single rule border surrounded by an ornamental design) |
FAIR STOOD | THE WIND | FOR | FRANCE | AN ATLANTIC MONTHLY
PRESS BOOK | LITTLE, BROWN AND COMPANY · BOSTON | 1944

Collation: (A-G^{16}) (H^{10}) (I^{16}) (iv) + 272 pp, consisting of half-title, verso blank,
pp (i–ii); title-page, notices of copyright and publication, publisher's and printing
imprints on verso, pp (iii–iv); text, pp 3–270; blank pp (271–272).

Binding: 8vo, 5$\frac{1}{8}$ x 7$\frac{1}{2}$ ins. Maroon cloth; title on front cover lettered in gilt on
a black band within single-rule gilt border; title on spine lettered in gilt, author's
and publisher's names in gilt on black bands within single-rule gilt borders above
and below title; all edges cut; cream end papers.
    Dust jacket; coloured drawing on front cover and spine by Nicholas Panesis; front
cover and spine lettered in yellow; back cover white with portrait of the author and
biographical note in black with heading of author's name and title in red.

Price: $2.50. Published May 1944.
    Copyright by The Curtis Publishing Company and H.E. Bates.
    An Atlantic-Little, Brown book published by Little, Brown and Company in
association with The Atlantic Monthly Press and printed in The United States of
America.

A 52   SOMETHING IN THE AIR   1944

First English edition

SOMETHING | IN THE AIR | Comprising | The Greatest People in the World |
and | How Sleep the Brave | Stories by | FLYING OFFICER "X" | (publisher's
device) | JONATHAN CAPE | THIRTY BEDFORD SQUARE LONDON

Collation: (A)-D^{16} E^{10} 148 pp, consisting of half-title, verso blank, pp (1–2);
title-page; notice of publication in two volumes and the collection in this volume,
publisher's imprint, Book Production War Economy Standard emblem and notice,
paper-maker's and printer's imprint on verso, pp (3–4); CONTENTS; notes of original publications and dedications on verso, pp (5–6); text, pp (7)–148.

Binding: 8vo, 4$\frac{5}{8}$ x 7$\frac{1}{8}$ ins. Blue cloth; lettering, with ornament on front cover in
silver; lettering along spine and publisher's device in silver; all edges cut; white end
papers.
    Dust jacket; front cover blue with lettering and design in white; back cover
white, lettering in blue and black; spine blue, lettered with star in white.

Price: 5s. net. Published November 1944.
    Made and printed in Great Britain by C. Tinling & Co., Ltd., Liverpool, London
and Prescot.
    A Directorate of Public Relations (Royal Air Force) Monograph, 'Propaganda
and Publicity' (Reference AIR 41/9) at the Public Record Office, Kew, records that
5,750 copies were first issued in November 1944.

Contents: It's Never in the Papers - There's No Future In It - The Young Man from Kalgoorlie - It's Just The Way It Is - The Sun Rises Twice - No Trouble At All - A Personal War - K for Kitty - The Greatest People in the World - How Sleep the Brave - The Beginning of Things - The Disinherited - Croix De Guerre - Yours is the Earth - There's Something in the Air

Reviews: 'Flying Officer X's identity is now an open secret, and this one-volume edition of the stories of *The Greatest People in the World* and *How Sleep the Brave* can be added to the collections of H.E. Bates's work.

'His material is, of course, magnificent, and he makes very moving use of it. And if at times the emotion of the stories presses too closely upon us, we must blame the time for that, not Mr. Bates. Each reader has a personal, as well as a general, imaginative relationship with these simple, glorious, brave themes, but whatever pain they may bring it would surely be impossible to read them without deriving increase of gratitude and hope and courage.' *The Spectator*

A 53   'The Battle of the Flying-Bomb'   1945

Unpublished

Notes: The pamphlet, on duplicated sheets, is of approximately 30,000 words and is filed in the Public Record Office, Kew, under Reference AIR 20/4140.

Norman Longmate, an eminent historian of the Home Front in World War II, quoted from the pamphlet at pp 62–3, 66, 104, 162, 317, 332, 352–3, 354, 382–3, 394, 400, 402, 424, 449 in his book, *The Doodlebugs: The Story of the Flying-Bombs* (London: Hutchinson, 1981).

At pp 484–7 he explained in detail the circumstances in which H.E. Bates (then a Squadron Leader in the Royal Air Force) wrote the pamphlet and the reasons for it remaining unpublished:

'The flying-bomb offensive had hardly begun when, on 29 June 1944, a wing commander in the PR3 branch of the Air Ministry wrote to the Director of Public Relations suggesting that the same author should be invited to compile a similar account of the RAF's anticipated triumph over the V-1. "It should be possible, if we start preparing it now," he suggested, "to have it on sale within a few weeks of the end of the attack." The project was approved, and when it was learned that Hilary St George Saunders, who had anonymously written *The Battle of Britain*, was not available, the task was entrusted to Squadron Leader Bates, better known as the novelist H.E. Bates, the Air Ministry's "writer in residence". Bates had enterprisingly been recruited earlier in the war to the Public Relations Branch and had already scored a great success with his stories of the bomber crews, published under the pseudonym "Flying Officer X". As usual in large organizations, while one talented man did the work, others with time on their hands created difficulties. The publication, one civil servant warned the Director of Public Relations on 5 September, would take four months to prepare and three more to produce, even if unillustrated. In the meantime a full-scale press conference, complete with maps and photographs, was planned – that held two days later by Duncan Sandys and

already described elsewhere – and "this ... may satiate the public appetite for this
particular subject in these tremendous days". To this the wing commander who
had originally proposed the idea replied effectively on 8 September, after the press
conference had been held. Squadron Leader Bates, he pointed out, had already
gone to France to begin his research on the ground, and – an even more powerful
argument – the RAF would benefit by receiving the chief credit in his booklet for
defeating the flying-bomb. By now the original modest plan for a short, 5000-word
pamphlet, produced by the RAF and selling at threepence, had been lost sight of
as the War Office, the Ministry of Home Security and - most formidable of all, on
this particular battle-field - the Ministry of Information all became involved. At a
meeting of representatives of all the interested parties, except the author himself,
on 11 September, it emerged that a 40,000-word book was now contemplated, to be
published by the Ministry of Information for His Majesty's Stationery Office. Every
department was eager to ensure that its share of the credit was not stolen by a rival.
By 13 October the pamphlet's "founding father" in the Air Ministry was writing
a little despairingly to his director to report that even the Ministry of Health –
presumably because of their responsibility for housing – were demanding a say in
the contents, while two months later poor H.E. Bates, now back from France and
hard at work, was encountering opposition even from within his own department.
"There is", wrote one officer of the Air Intelligence Branch, in response to a very
reasonable request for details of the cost of the battle in Allied aircraft, "strong
security objection against publishing the figure of our losses." By 2 January 1945 -
a week after the Christmas raid on Manchester – Bates caused further consternation
by requesting details of airlaunched V-1s and on 2 March, with the war almost over
and not a line yet set in type, came an official ruling that the text must be treated
as secret until passed by the censor.

'Victory in Europe, so that the last excuse for delay was removed, seems to
have passed almost unnoticed by those happily engaged in the controversy over *The
Battle of the Flying-Bomb*, as the booklet had been provisionally entitled. By now
the argument had developed a momentum of its own and in the files new names and
ever more impressive sets of abbreviations blossomed daily as more and more under-
employed bureaucrats generated a weight of paper far more voluminous than the
work they were discussing. The matter had even reached the War Cabinet which
had, not very helpfully, simply instructed the Ministry of Information to issue a
book about all the Crossbow operations. Wing Commander Barker, who had now
been fighting this particular battle for nearly a year, promptly asked for guidance
from the Ministry of Information. Was Bates's work, he wanted to know, to be used
as the basis? Was he to continue to amass information? Or was all his effort to be
wasted? No clear answer was forthcoming, for reasons which Barker explained to
a superior: "I gather, confidentially", he wrote on 11 May 1945, "that the truth is
the Ministry of Information are extremely loath to produce any book at all if they
are not to be allowed to explain the Mimoyecques installation, as they feel that,
now that the German war is over, to withhold the information would be to deceive
the public."

' "The Mimoyecques installation" consisted of a battery of long-range, high-
powered guns, unconnected with the flying-bomb and never used in action, and
there was therefore every possible ground for ignoring them. They proved, however,
a convenient stick to use against a project about which, presumably because it had

originated elsewhere, the Ministry had never been enthusiastic. The Ministry of Information believed, explained an internal Air Ministry memorandum of 3 October 1945, "that unless a chapter on these structures is included the pamphlet will lose much of its appeal to the public" – although the public had not even known they existed.

'It was all sadly reminiscent of the rivalry between the German Army and the Luftwaffe which had bedevilled the secret weapons project and why the Ministry of Information, if the guns really were still a danger, did not simply omit all reference to them – as Bates himself wished – is something of a mystery. In the event, however, the arguments for doing nothing prevailed. By an interesting twist of fate, it was left to a future Poet Laureate, C. Day Lewis, to make a final effort to save his fellow writer's work. "In a letter from Mr. Day Lewis of the Publications Division of the M. of I.," one officer of the Air Ministry Public Relations Division reported to his superiors on 1 November 1945, "he says he understands that 'the details of the Mimoyecques installations can be described and that all the Chiefs of Staff ask is that there should be formal security review of the actual text'.... It may well be that the War Office can be persuaded to allow us to use some of the details which M. of I. require." The final sentence of the same letter made clear, however, that time was finally running out for 'The Battle of the Flying-Bomb', after a struggle which had lasted sixteen months – far longer than the events it described. "S/Ldr. Bates...," the writer pointed out, "is to be demobilised next week." With his departure into civilian life – followed by that of many of the officers who had fought so valiantly on his behalf in Section PR3, which surely deserves to be remembered among other, more famous formations in the annals of the Royal Air Force – the attempt to tell the story of the V-1s to the British public was finally abandoned. Bates's manuscript, which finally ran to 30,000 words, remains unpublished to this day, although the substantial extracts from it quoted in this book illustrate what a loss its suppression was.'

A 54   THE DAY OF GLORY   1945

H.E. BATES | (ornament) | The Day | of | Glory | (ornament) | A Play in | Three Acts | (publisher's device) | MICHAEL JOSEPH LTD. | 26 Bloomsbury Street, London, W.C.1.

Collation: (A)-E^8 80 pp, consisting of half-title; By the same Author on verso, pp (1–2); title-page; notices of publication and performing rights, printer's and binder's imprint on verso, pp (3–4); CHARACTERS, SCENE and TIME, verso blank, pp (5–6); text, pp 7–(79); blank p (80).

Binding: 8vo, 4$\frac{3}{4}$ x 7$\frac{1}{4}$ ins. Deep blue cloth; lettered along spine in gold; all edges cut; white end papers.

Dust jacket white; front cover lettered in black within blue rectangle surrounded by ornamental design in black and two-rule border in blue and black. Back cover lettered in black and blue. Spine lettered, with two ornaments, in black.

Price: 6s. net. Published August 1945. 3,090 copies of the first edition were sold.

Set and printed in Great Britain by Tonbridge Printers, Ltd., Peach Hall Works, Tonbridge, in Bembo eleven on twelve point, and bound by James Burn.

Notes: *Characters*: Colonel Sanderson, DSO, Millicent Sanderson, Diana Sanderson, Squadron Leader Jack Sanderson, DFC, Pilot Officer L. Radwanski, Julia, Catherine Delacourt, Charles. *Scene*: The Lounge of the Sandersons' house in the South of England. *Time*: The action takes place within twenty-four hours in the summer of 1942.

Publisher's Note: 'The Day of Glory is not so much a play about the RAF as a play about the impact of war on the individual. It is true that some of its characters are pilots of the RAF, but what it really sets out to depict is the clash of war on three generations of a single family. The drama of that impact is compressed into a single day of action as it affects the family of a young and successful fighter pilot. Through the eyes of his uncle, a colonel mentally wrecked by one war; of his young sister, adoring and in her adoration utterly oblivious of the future;...of his pre-war fiancée and her pre-war standards and ideals which she sees being destroyed before her eyes; of his lover, with her clarity and tenderness born out of the knowledge that the lives of pilots are shorter and more tense and more rarified than our own; and lastly of his mother, who with the brilliant and painful vision of motherhood sees the destruction of three generations exemplified by a single tragedy.'

The World In Ripeness (A 114) p 120: 'Not that the idea of the play was dead; on the contrary it continued to be agitated with life and finally became, later in the war, *The Day of Glory*.

'Unhappily it proved impossible to produce it until the war was over*, – a fact that undoubtedly mitigated against any possible commercial success. By that time all fervour for the war had been dissipated and when at last *The Day of Glory* was produced at the Embassy Theatre one could only sense, on the first night, an atmosphere cold and disillusioned. Several parts in the play were also badly miscast, the result being that what I had wanted to say never got put over. The play fared far better on tour, under the auspices of the Arts Council, finding far better acting and far warmer audiences in the provinces than in London, where hard-bitten first night audiences often do as much to kill a play's chances of success as the hostility of critics. *The Day of Glory* is, however, still performed and has even achieved, in Holland, a state of some permanency as an annual event.'

* The play was produced at Salisbury on 31 October 1945 and broadcast by the BBC on 5 November 1945

Reviews: 'In my opinion, for what it is worth, it is the best play dealing with a war subject that I have read. I shall be very surprised if Sq. Ldr Bates does not surpass, as a dramatist, his already established reputation as a novelist and short-story writer.' Val Gielgud, *Radio Times*

A 55   'The Spider Love'   (1946)

Unpublished

(design of three stars) | THE | SPIDER | LOVE | A | Play | In | Three | Acts | By | H.E. | BATES | (design of three stars)

Collation: (iii) + 46 pp (rectos only), (Act I, p 20 numbered as 20.–21.) + 1 + 36 + 1 + 54 (with an addition p 18a), consisting of title-page, p (i); "But oh! self traitor I do bring The Spider Love, which transubstantiates all." - John Donne, p (ii); CHARACTERS, action and TIME, p (iii); ACT I, pp (1.I)–46.I with p 20 numbered 20.–21 I; ACT II, (1.II–36.II; ACT III SCENE I, (1.I.III)–32.1.III (including an additional p 18a.1.III); ACT III SCENE II 33–54.2.III.

Binding: 4to, 8 x 10 ins. Plain brown paper covers, stapled. ACTS I and II and II and III divided by single sheets of plain blue paper.

Notes: The above details taken from a carbon copy in possession of the author's son, Richard Bates, the original having been typewritten by Ethel Christian, 36-38 Southampton Street, Strand, London, W.C.2 and carries the stamp of Margery Vosper Ltd., 32 Shaftesbury Ave., London, W.1 on the title-page.
      The author refers to the play not having been performed at p 120 of *The World in Ripeness* (A 114): 'I followed. . . with a dark, Ibsen-like piece called *The Spider Love* (I culled the title from Donne's great lines *But O, self traitor, I do bring The spider love, which transubstantiates all, And can convert manna to gall*) but its demands on actors are incontestably formidable and it is probably for this reason that it has never been performed.'

A 56   THE CRUISE OF THE BREADWINNER   1946

A 56a First English edition

H.E. Bates | (single rule in brown) | The Cruise of | THE BREADWINNER | (single rule in brown) | MICHAEL JOSEPH LTD. | 26 Bloomsbury Street, London, W.C.1 (the whole within a $\frac{3}{16}$ ins. brown border)

Collation: (A)-D^8 64 pp, consisting of half-title; Also by H.E. BATES (within a brown border), pp (1–2); title-page, notice of publication, printer's and binder's imprint on verso, pp (3–4); text, pp 5–63; blank p (64).

Binding: 8vo, $5\frac{1}{8}$ x $7\frac{4}{5}$ ins. Black cloth; design in silver on front cover; author and publisher lettered along spine in silver; title lettered along spine in black on a silver background; all edges cut; end papers illustrated in brown and white by Broom Lynne.
      Coloured pictorial dust jacket designed by Broom Lynne, the end paper illustrations being repeated; front cover and spine lettered in black and white.

Price: 5s. net. Published July 1946. A total of 20,160 copies were sold.
      Set and printed in Great Britain by Tonbridge Printers, Ltd., Peach Hall Works, Tonbridge, in Bembo twelve on thirteen point, and bound by James Burn.

Notes: The end paper illustrations by Broome Lynne are printed in brown and repeated in colours on the dust jacket. An illustration in brown at the top of p 5 is repeated as a design in silver on front cover.

The Cruise of
THE BREADWINNER

A 56b First American edition

H.E. BATES (within an ornamental border) | The Cruise | of the | Breadwinner | An Atlantic Monthly Press Book | Little, Brown and Company · Boston | 1947

Collation: (A-H)^{16} (x) + 118 pp, consisting of blank leaf pasted down to form front end paper, pp (i–ii); blank leaf, pp (iii–iv); recto blank, By H.E. BATES on verso, pp (v–vi); half-title, verso blank, pp (vii–viii); title-page, notices of copyright, reservation of rights and publication, publisher's and printing imprints on verso, pp (ix–x); fly title, The Cruise of the Breadwinner, verso blank, pp (1–2); text, pp 3–112; two blank leaves, pp (113–116); blank leaf pasted down to form back end paper, pp (117–118).

Binding: 8vo, 4¾ x 7⅛ ins. Maroon cloth; publisher's device blind-stamped on front cover; gilt lettering on spine; top edges cut; fore and lower edges trimmed; white end papers.

Dust jacket designed by Samuel Bryant. Front cover and spine maroon; back cover white. 'The Breadwinner' is pictured in colours on front cover with lettering of the title and author in white with 'Author of FAIR STOOD THE WIND FOR FRANCE' in pink. Lettered on spine in white; back cover carries portrait of the author in black and white, and biographical note in black with author's name in blue.

Price: $1.50. Published March 1947.

Published by Little, Brown and Company in association with The Atlantic Monthly Press and printed in The United States of America.

A 57   THE TINKERS OF ELSTOW   1946

THE TINKERS OF ELSTOW | (vignette) | By H.E. BATES | Illustrations by | RANDOLPH SCHWABE | (single rule) | The story of the Royal Ordnance | Factory managed by J. Lyons | & Company Limited for the | Ministry of Supply during | the World War of 1939–1945.

Collation: (A-C)^8 50 pp, consisting of free end paper counted in pagination, pp (1–2); half-title; the signatures of the author and illustrator, certificate of limitation, printer's and paper-maker's imprint on verso, pp (3–4); title-page, illustration of the Church of Elstow on verso, pp (5–6); Prologue, pp 7–13; blank page, p (14); text, pp 15–47; illustration of "Elstow from the Air", p 48; Epilogue, pp 49–50.

Binding: 8vo, 5$\frac{3}{8}$ x 8$\frac{1}{4}$ ins. Dark blue leather with gold ornamental border on insides of front and back covers to edges of paste-downs; gold lettering on front cover; all edges cut; white end papers.

This first edition was limited to 300 copies, each signed by the author and illustrator; printed on Millbourn hand-made paper by Bemrose & Sons Ltd., London and Derby.

The second edition (1946) was printed by Bemrose & Sons Ltd., London and Derby, on paper made by Edward Collins & Sons, of Kelvindale. Bound in maroon cloth with the title in red on a yellow label on front cover; 'by H.E. Bates' in gold below the label.

Notes: Illustrations by Randolph Schwabe: vignette on title-page, p (5), pp (6), 16, 21, 23 (full page); 30, 34, 41 and 48.

A 58   OTTERS AND MEN   1947

OTTERS AND MEN | By H.E. BATES | (short rule)

Collation: One gathering. 4 pp, consisting of title, quotations from *The Shooting Times, Otters and Otter-hunting* and *The Shooting Times and British Sportsman* followed by commencement of text, p (1); text, pp (2–3); completion of text, note of reprinting from *Down the River* by H.E. Bates (Victor Gollancz Ltd., London, 1937) by special permission of the author and publishers, publisher's imprint and note of OTHER PUBLICATIONS, Publication No. and Price, p (4).

Binding: 8vo, 5 x 8$\frac{1}{4}$ ins. White paper, not stapled.

The pamphlet is numbered 37, published by the National Society for the Abolition of Cruel Sports, 4 Tavistock Square, London, W.C.1.

Price: 1d.

Notes: The text is an abridgement of the author's essay, 'Otters and Men', in
Down the River (A 29).

A 59   THE PURPLE PLAIN   1947

A 59a First English edition

H.E. BATES | (ornament) | The | Purple Plain | (publisher's device) | London
| MICHAEL JOSEPH LTD

Collation: (A)-G^{16} 224 pp, consisting of half-title, Also by H.E. BATES on verso,
pp (1–2); title-page as above, notice of publication, publisher's, paper-maker's and
printer's imprint on verso pp (3–4); text, pp 5–224.

Binding: 8vo, 5$\frac{1}{8}$ x 7$\frac{3}{4}$ ins. Purple boards; lettering, with ornament and publisher's device on spine in silver; all edges cut; white end papers.
   Dust jacket designed by A.E. Barlow. Front cover and spine in shades of purple,
lettered in white; back cover white, lettered in black and purple.

Price: 10s. 6d. net. A total of 60,088 copies were sold.
   Made and printed in Great Britain by Purnell and Sons Ltd., Paulton (Somerset)
and London.

Notes: The manuscript is owned by the Bates family.
   The World in Ripeness (A 114) p 97: 'Readers of *The Purple Plain* will not
need to be told, I think, that the incidents ... are part of the early fabric of that
novel: the drive across the scalding plain, the laughing Burmese children crowding
on the jeep, the little Burmese house, the lime-juice, Dorothy and her sister, the
talk, the precious stones. They will know that in the book the Padre becomes a
doctor, that my fuss-pot tent-sharer becomes Blore, that Dorothy becomes Anna,
that my place is taken by Forrester, a shattered RAF pilot .... The little ideas and
pictures I gathered up that morning, the unconsidered trifles, were the genesis of
the book.'
   In a presentation copy of the book, Bates appended the following note:
   Publication date Nov 27. Literary Guild choice in America – meaning, they tell
me, 500,000 copies.
   In 1954 the book was made into a film by General Film Distributors. Gregory
Peck took the leading role.

A 59b First American edition

(design of two pairs of chevrons) | H.E. BATES | (design of two pairs of chevrons)
| (publisher's device) | An Atlantic Monthly Press Book | Little, Brown and
Company · Boston | 1947

Collation: (A-K)^{16} (viii + 312 pp, consisting of blank leaf, pp (i–ii); recto blank,
BY H.E. BATES on verso, pp (iii–iv); half-title, verso blank, pp (v–vi); title-page,

notices of copyright and publication, publisher's and printing imprints on verso, pp (vii–viii); fly title, verso blank, pp (1–2); text, p 3–308; two blank leaves, pp (309–312).

Binding: 8vo, $5\frac{1}{4}$ x $7\frac{3}{4}$ ins. Buff cloth; publisher's device on front cover in blue; title lettered along spine within a single-rule border, single rules below author's name and above publisher's name with four pairs of chevrons bordering the top and bottom rules of the title border, all in blue.

Dust jacket designed by Charles Lofgren. Pictorial illustration on front cover and spine in buff, blue and black with lettering in black and white. Back cover white with biographical note and portrait of the author, his name in blue, the remainder in black.

Price: $2.75. Published December 1947.

Copyright by the Curtis Publishing Company and H.E. Bates.

Published by Little, Brown and Company in association with The Atlantic Monthly Press.

Printed in The United States of America.

A 60   THIRTY-ONE SELECTED TALES   1947

THIRTY-ONE | SELECTED TALES | by | H.E. BATES | (publisher's device) | JONATHAN CAPE | THIRTY BEDFORD SQUARE | LONDON

Collation: (A)-I⁸; K-U⁸; X-Z⁸; AA-CC⁸ 416 pp consisting of half-title, By the same author on verso, pp (1–2); title-page, note on selection of the Tales, notice of publication, printer's and binder's imprints on verso, pp (3–4); CONTENTS, verso blank, pp 5–(6); fly title, verso blank, pp (7–8); text, pp 9–414; blank leaf, pp (415–416).

Binding: 8vo, $4\frac{7}{8}$ x $7\frac{1}{2}$ ins. Turquoise cloth; lettering, with an ornament and publisher's device on spine in gold; top and fore-edges cut, lower edges untrimmed; white end papers.

Dust jacket; design of grapevine on front cover and spine in black, yellow ochre and mauve with black lettering; plain back cover.

Price: 10s. 6d. net. Published 9 June 1947.

Printed in Great Britain in the City of Oxford at The Alden Press. Bound by A.W. Bain & Co. Ltd., London.

3,900 copies of the first impression were printed on 24 February 1947 and the delivery of 4,000 was completed on 21 April 1947. 1,000 copies of the second impression were printed on 20 May 1949. 2,000 copies of the third impression were printed on 26 April 1951 and published in the Evensford Edition on 29 October 1951.

Notes: The Tales were selected from *The Woman Who Had Imagination and Other Stories* (A 20); *Cut and Come Again* (A 25); *Something Short and Sweet* (A 28); *The Flying Goat* (A 34); *The Beauty of the Dead and Other Stories* (A 38).

Contents: The Ox - Château Bougainvillaea - A German Idyll - For The Dead
- Every Bullet Has Its Billet - The Irishman - Spring Snow - Millenium Also Ran
- The Blind - Elephant's Nest in a Rhubarb Tree - The Dog and Mr. Morency -
The Banjo - Fuchsia - The Man Who Loved Cats - Mister Livingstone - Something
Short and Sweet - I Am Not Myself - The Wreath - The Machine - The Ship - The
Beauty of the Dead - Mr. Penfold - The Bridge - The Ferry - The Loved One -
Time to Kill - The Little Jeweller - Love is not Love - The Earth - The White Pony
- No Country

A 61   THE JACARANDA TREE   1949

A 61a First English edition

H.E. BATES | (ornamental rule) | The | Jacaranda Tree | MICHAEL JOSEPH
LTD. | & | THE BOOK SOCIETY LTD.

Collation: (A)-G^{16} 224 pp, consisting of half-title, Also by H.E. BATES on verso,
pp (1–2); title-page, notice of publication, paper-maker's and printer's imprint on
verso, pp (3–4); text, pp 5–223; blank p (224).

Binding: 8vo, $5\frac{1}{8}$ x $7\frac{3}{4}$ ins. Blue boards; lettering, with a star ornament and
publisher's device on spine in silver; top edges dyed blue; fore and lower edges cut;
white end papers.
    Dust jacket designed by A.E. Barlow; front cover and spine black and white
shading, lettered in white with floral designs in mauve and green; back cover white,
lettered in black and green.

Price: 9s. 6d. net. Published January 1949.
    A total of 74,423 copies were sold. A Book Society choice issued on first publi-
cation by The Book Society Ltd., in association with Michael Joseph Ltd.
    Made and printed in Great Britain by Purnell and Sons Ltd., Paulton, Somerset
and London.

Notes: *The World in Ripeness* (A 114) p 110: 'When the book finally appeared it
achieved an even greater sale than *The Purple Plain*, again enlarging my readership.
But again there were dissentient voices from friends whose critical judgement I had
learned to respect. Yet again it was useless to point out the compulsion of all
the circumstances that lay behind the book – the East's unforgettable vividness
of scene, the catastrophic nature of the retreat itself, the fatalism, the relentless
heat,...'
    p 111: 'The effect of my visit to India and Burma, brief though it may have
been, had been almost to give me a disease. Its toxins had somehow to be got out
of my system or paralyse me for ever, and writing about it all was, as I saw it, the
only cure.'
    In November 1948 *The Jacaranda Tree* was the first serial to be published in the
magazine *John Bull.*

A 61b First American edition

(ornamental border) | H.E. BATES | The | Jacaranda Tree | (publisher's device) | An Atlantic Monthly Press Book | Little, Brown and Company · Boston | 1949

Collation: (A-I)^{16} (K)^8 (iv) + 300 pp, consisting of half-title, ornamental border and BY H.E. BATES on verso, pp (i–ii); title-page; notices of copyright and publication, publisher's and printer's imprints on verso, pp (iii–iv); fly title, verso blank, pp (1–2), text, pp 3–299; blank p (300).

Binding: 8vo, $5\frac{1}{4}$ x $7\frac{3}{4}$ ins. Grey cloth; author and publisher lettered top and bottom of spine in blue; title lettered along spine within ornamental borders, all in blue; all edges cut; white end papers.

Dust jacket designed by Charles Lofgren. Illustration on front cover and spine in black and pink against grey and white; front cover lettered in pink and white; back cover white with portrait of author and biographical note; author's name in pink, text in black.

Price: $2.75. Published January 1949.

Copyright 1949 by H.E. Bates. Published by Little, Brown and Company in association with the Atlantic Monthly Press and printed in The United States of America.

A 62   THE COUNTRY HEART   1949

The Country Heart | by | H.E. Bates | Drawings by John Minton | Michael Joseph | London (the lettering incorporated in a full-page design; all in green)

Collation: (A)-P^8 240 pp, consisting of half-title, with drawing in green, Also by H.E. Bates on verso, pp (1–2); recto blank, frontispiece, pp (3–4); title-page, note of revised edition of O! MORE THAN HAPPY COUNTRYMAN and THE HEART OF THE COUNTRY, notice of publication, printer's, paper-maker's and binder's imprint on verso, pp (5–6); Contents, p (7); Contents continued with a drawing, p 8; Introduction: Yesterday, pp (9)–12; Part One, the lettering incorporated in a full-page drawing, verso blank, pp (13–14); text, pp (15)–123; blank page, p (124); Part Two, the lettering incorporated in full-page drawing, verso blank, pp (125–126); text, pp (127)–239; blank p (240).

Binding: 8vo, $5\frac{1}{4}$ x $7\frac{7}{8}$ ins. Beige cloth; title-page lettering and design repeated on front cover in green; lettering, with ornament and publisher's device on spine in green; top edges dyed green; fore and lower edges cut; white end papers.

Pictorial dust jacket designed by John Minton; lettered on front cover in green and black; lettered on spine in yellow and black; additional drawing in blue occurs above blurb on front flap.

Price: 12s. 6d. net. 9,921 copies were sold.

Set and printed in Great Britain by Unwin Brothers Ltd, at the Gresham Press, Woking, in Plantin type, ten point, leaded, on paper made by John Dickinson and bound by James Burn.

Contents: *INTRODUCTION*: Yesterday *PART ONE:* Sudden Spring - Fisherman's Luck - Overture to Summer - Fruit Blossom Time - 'Clouded August Thorn' - Strange Battlefields - The Great Snow - A Summer Spring - '...Bring Forth May Flowers' - Victorian Garden - Wealden Beauty - The Strangeness of Fish - The Parish Pump - Flowers and Downland

     PART TWO: Et Decorum Est Pro Patria Mori - The Great House - Sea Days, Sea Flowers - Mr. Pimpkins - The Future Garden - The Garden on Leave - The New Country - The Old Tradition - The Green Hedges - O More Than Happy Countryman - Epilogue: Tomorrow

Notes: This book brought together in considerably revised form two books of country life, *O More Than Happy Countryman* (A 48) and *In The Heart of the Country* (A 42)*.

     *On p (6) in the note which stated that *The Country Heart* was a revised and amended edition of these books, both titles were incorrectly printed. An exclamation mark was added following O in *O More Than Happy Countryman* and the word 'In' was omitted from *In the Heart of the Country*. These mistakes are frequent in later years where books 'Also by H.E. Bates' are listed.

     Bates said that the two books, *O More Than Happy Countryman* and *In The Heart of the Country*, were like two windows from which he looked out, with feelings of tension and insecurity, on the wartime country world. The disintegration of country life carried one stage further by war, the last shattering blow to great houses and their traditions, the closer alliance between town and country: these are some, but not all of the themes with which he deals.

     Illustrations by John Minton: on the half-title page, p (1), frontispiece, p (4), title-page, p (5), pp 8 and (9), full-page, p (13), (15), (21), (31), (37), (38), 43, (44), (53), 63, (64), 68, (69), 74, (75), 83, (84), 92, (93), (102), 108, (109), 116, (117), 123, (125–full-page), (127), 133, (134), (139), (148), (157), (173), 178, (179), (193), (201), 215, (216), 228, (229), 239. In addition the title-page design is repeated on the front cover and the dust jacket designed as described above.

A 63   THE BRIDE COMES TO   1949
EVENSFORD AND OTHER TALES

THE | BRIDE COMES TO | EVENSFORD | And Other Tales | by H.E. BATES | (publisher's device) | JONATHAN CAPE | THIRTY BEDFORD SQUARE | LONDON

Collation: (A)-O⁸ 224 pp, consisting of blank leaf, pp (1–2); half-title, By the same author on verso, pp (3–4); title-page, note of previous publications, printer's and binder's imprint on verso, pp (5–6); CONTENTS, dedication 'TO DILYS POWELL and LEONARD RUSSELL' on verso, pp (7–8); fly title, verso blank, pp (9–10); text, pp 11–221; blank p (222); blank (223–224).

Binding: 8vo, 5 x 7⅝ ins. Fawn cloth; lettered on front cover in blue; also on spine with ornament and publisher's device in blue; top and fore-edges cut; lower edges untrimmed; white end papers.

Dust jacket designed by Hans Tisdall. Design on front cover in blue, crimson and white, lettered in crimson and white; back cover plain white; spine crimson with black lettering.

Price: 9s. net. Published 14 November 1949. 3,000 copies of the first impression were printed on 16 August 1949. The type was distributed on 2 January 1951.

Printed in Great Britain in the City of Oxford at The Alden Press. Bound by A.W. Bain & Co. Ltd., London.

Contents: The Bride Comes to Evensford - The Black Boxer - On the Road - A Love Story - Charlotte Esmond - A Flower Piece - The Mower - The Hessian Prisoner - Death in Spring - Sheep - The Russian Dancer - A Threshing Day for Esther

A 64   DEAR LIFE   1949

A 64a First American edition

H.E. BATES | Dear Life | (publisher's device) | An Atlantic Monthly Press Book | Little, Brown and Company · Boston | 1949 (the whole within ornamental and ruled border with three compartments)

Collation: (A-K)^8 viii + 152 pp, consisting of blank leaf, pp (i–ii); recto blank, By H.E. Bates on verso, pp (iii–iv); half-title, verso blank, pp (v–vi); title-page, notices of copyright and publication, publisher's and printer's imprints on verso, pp (vii–viii); fly title, verso blank, pp (1–2); text, pp 3–149; blank p (150); blank pp (151–152).

Binding: 8vo, $4\frac{3}{4}$ x $7\frac{1}{8}$ ins. Lime-green cloth; publisher's device on front cover in blue; lettered on spine in blue; top edges cut; fore and lower edges rough-trimmed; white end papers.

Dust jacket designed by Charles Lofgren. Front cover and spine in shades of green, lettered in black and white. Back cover white with portrait of the author and biographical note in black.

Price: $2.00. Published November 1949.

Copyright 1949, by H.E. Bates. Published by Little, Brown and Company in association with The Atlantic Monthly Press and printed in The United States of America.

A 64b First English edition

H.E. BATES | (ornament of a single star) | Dear | Life | (an illustration in red by Ronald Searle) | London | MICHAEL JOSEPH

Collation: (A)-H^8 128 pp, consisting of half-title and drawings by Ronald Searle, Also by H.E. BATES on verso, pp (1–2); title-page, notice of publication, printer's and binder's imprint on verso, pp (3–4); text, pp 5–(128).

Binding: 8vo, 5⅛ x 7⅞ ins. Beige cloth; lettering and illustration in red on front cover; lettering with ornament and publisher's device on spine in red; all edges cut; end papers vertically lined in grey and white with illustrations in red.

Dust jacket scarlet, lettered in black; front cover illustration repeated on front and back covers of jacket in black; title-page illustration repeated in reduced form in red above blurb on front flap.

Price: 7s. 6d. net. Published February 1950. 14,342 copies were sold.

Set and printed in Great Britain by Tonbridge Printers Ltd., Peach Hall Works, Tonbridge, in Garamond eleven on thirteen point, and bound by James Burn.

Notes: The drawings by Ronald Searle in A 64b occur in red on the title-page p (3), repeated on front flap of dust jacket; both end papers; front cover of book and repeated in black on both covers of dust jacket.

The manuscript (235 pp, quarto) was presented by the author to the King's School, Canterbury for the Hugh Walpole Collection.

A 65   EDWARD GARNETT   1950

H.E. BATES | EDWARD GARNETT | with eight plates in photogravure | three illustrations in line | MAX PARRISH LONDON | 1950 (all within an ornamental border)

Collation: (A-E)⁸ (F)⁴ 88 pp, consisting of half-title with names of editors of PERSONAL PORTRAITS, verso blank, pp (1–2); title-page, publisher's and printer's imprint on verso, pp (3–4); AUTHOR'S NOTE, INDEX OF ILLUSTRA-TIONS IN LINE on verso, pp (5–6); INDEX OF PLATES IN PHOTOGRAVURE, illustration of Edward Garnett's bookplate on verso, pp (7–8); text, pp 9–87; blank p (88).

Binding: 8vo, 4¼ x 7⅛ ins. Brown cloth; design on front cover in gold; lettered along spine in gold; all edges cut; white end papers.

Dust jacket; deep cream with two white bands on front and back covers; the plate facing p 32 of Edward Garnett repeated on front cover; lettering on front cover and along spine in red.

Price: 6s. net. Published December 1950.

Published by Max Parrish & Co. Ltd., Adprint House, Rathbone Place, London W.1 in association with Chanticleer Press Inc., 41 East 50th Street, New York 22, NY. Adprint Limited London.

The text set in Monotype Garamond 11 on 12 pt and printed in Great Britain by Clarke & Sherwell Ltd., Northampton.

Notes: This volume was one of a series of 'Personal Portraits', edited by Patric Dickinson and Sheila Shannon.

When H.E. Bates first met Edward Garnett in 1926 he was an unknown young man of twenty and Garnett a formidable literary figure who had already discovered, nurtured and helped to bring fame to such men as Conrad, Galsworthy, Hudson and D.H. Lawrence. Garnett was a man of penetrative and withering judgment, of sage experience, of eccentricity and ironic humour, and above all of inexhaustible enthusiasm for literature and those who made it. In this book, beginning with his first meeting with that 'enormous and grizzly' figure and continuing until Garnett's death twelve years later, Bates has not only painted a portrait of one of the most remarkable and influential literary characters of the last fifty years but has provided a picture himself which he described as '–the first note in autobiography'.

Illustrations in line (p 6): p 8 Edward Garnett's bookplate by Ford Madox Brown. This was used as a device on the title-page of *A Beggar* by Grace Black, the only book Garnett published under his own imprint.

p 27: Inscription on the fly-leaf of the Polish translation of Joseph Conrad's *Almayer's Folly.*

p 55: The letter from Edward Garnett to Bates on the subject of 'The Voyagers' *Plates in Photogravure* p (7): Edward Garnett as a young man; Edward Garnett in the uniform of the British Ambulance Unit for Italy, 1915; Edward Garnett. Pastel drawing by Simon Bussy, c. 1905; Edward Garnett; H.E. Bates, aged about twenty, at the beginning of his literary career; Detail from the MS. of *Catherine Foster,* an early work by H.E. Bates; Edward Garnett in 1930; Constance Garnett.

The first American edition was published in 1950 by Folcroft Library Editions, Folcroft, Pa.

A 66   FLOWER GARDENING   1950
A Reader's Guide

FLOWER GARDENING | (short rule) | A Reader's Guide by | H.E. BATES | (wood-engraving by Joan Hassall) | 1950 | PUBLISHED FOR | THE NATIONAL BOOK LEAGUE | BY THE CAMBRIDGE UNIVERSITY PRESS (the whole within an ornamental border enclosed by a double-line rule frame)

Collation: One gathering only, stapled.   24 pp, consisting of title-page, notes on the National Book League and wood-engraving by Joan Hassall with notice of publication on verso, pp (1–2); text, pp 3–part 9; bibliographical note, part p 9; SOME BOOKS TO READ, pp 10–23; notes on THE NATIONAL BOOK LEAGUE, printers' imprint, p (24).

Binding: 8vo, $5\frac{1}{2}$ x $8\frac{1}{2}$ ins. Pink and white paper covers; NBL lettered in pink with other lettering in black within an ornamental border on front cover, below which is an engraving by Joan Hassall followed by the price in black; a list of The Reader's Guides in black on back cover within ornamental border.

Price: One Shilling net. Published 19 May 1950. The Cambridge University Press edition was 1,500 copies.

Text printed in Great Britain by Unwin Brothers Ltd., Woking and London. Cover printed in Great Britain by A.P. Taylor & Co., Ltd., London.

The National Book League had the book printed and supplied stock to the Cambridge University Press for publication, keeping some copies (number not known) back for its own members.

Notes: Wood-engravings by Joan Hassall on title-page and front cover.

A 67   THE SCARLET SWORD   1950

A 67a First English edition

H.E. BATES | (ornamental rule) | The | Scarlet Sword | (publisher's device) | London MICHAEL JOSEPH

Collation: (A)-H^{16} (iv) + 252 pp, consisting of blank leaf pasted down as front end paper, pp (i–ii); blank leaf, pp (iii–iv); half-title, Also by H.E. BATES on verso, pp (1–2); title-page, notice of publication, publisher's, paper-maker's and printer's imprints on verso, pp (3–4); text, pp 5–248; two blank leaves pasted down as back end paper, pp (249–252).

Binding: 8vo, $5\frac{1}{8}$ x $7\frac{3}{4}$ ins. Scarlet boards; lettering, with star and publisher's device on spine in silver; all edges cut; white end papers.

Dust jacket designed by Broom Lynne. Front cover and spine black and grey, lettered in scarlet and white; design of a sword on front cover in scarlet; portrait of the author with facsimile of his signature in black on white back cover.

Price: 10s. 6d. net. 37,223 copies were sold.

Made and printed in Great Britain by Purnell and Sons Ltd. Paulton (Somerset) and London.

A 67b First American edition 1951

H.E. BATES | (design) | THE | Scarlet Sword | (design) | (publisher's device) | An Atlantic Monthly Press Book | Little, Brown and Company · Boston | 1951

Collation: (A-I)^{16} (vi) + 282 pp, consisting of recto blank, BY H.E. BATES on verso, pp (i–ii); half-title, verso blank, pp (iii–iv); title-page, notices of copyright and publication, publisher's and printing imprints on verso, pp (v–vi); fly title, verso blank, pp (1–2); text, pp 3–282.

Binding: 8vo, $5\frac{1}{4}$ x $7\frac{3}{4}$ ins. Pale grey cloth; lettering with design on spine in red; all edges cut; white end papers.

Pictorial dust jacket; painting on the front cover by Denver L. Gillen. Lettered on front and spine in white and black. Portrait of the author by G. Scott Bushe on back cover.

Price: $3.00

Published by Little, Brown and Company in association with The Atlantic Monthly Press and printed in The United States of America.

A 68   COLONEL JULIAN and other stories   1951

A 68a First English edition

H.E. BATES | (short ornamental rule) | Colonel Julian | and other stories | (publisher's device) | London | MICHAEL JOSEPH

Collation: (A)-H^{16} 256 pp, consisting of half-title, ALSO BY H.E. BATES on verso, pp (1–2); title-page, notice of publication, publisher's, printer's, paper-maker's and binder's imprints on verso, pp (3–4); Contents, verso blank, pp (5–6); dedication 'To M.J. [Michael Joseph] with affection and gratitude', verso blank, pp (7–8); text, pp 9–255; blank p (256).

Binding: 8vo, $4\frac{3}{4}$ x $7\frac{1}{4}$ ins. Royal-blue boards; title lettered on spine within an ornamental border with other lettering and publisher's device all in gold; all edges cut; white end papers.

Dust jacket designed by Freda Nichols; front cover, spine and part of back cover printed in bands of deep and light blue; author's name and title on front cover in white, designer's name in black; remainder of back cover white with list of Bates's novels in black and blue.

Price: 10s. 6d. net. Published June 1951. 10,028 copies were sold.

Set and printed in Great Britain by Tonbridge Printers Ltd., Peach Hall Works, Tonbridge, in Baskerville eleven on twelve point, on paper made by John Dickinson at Croxley and bound by James Burn at Esher.

Contents: The Little Farm - Colonel Julian - Time Expired - The Lighthouse - Joe Johnson - The Park - Sugar for the Horse - The Flag - No More the Nightingales - The Bedfordshire Clanger - A Girl Called Peter - The Major of Hussars - Mrs. Vincent - A Christmas Song - The Frontier

A 68b First American edition (1952)

Colonel Julian | AND OTHER STORIES | (ornamental division) | by | H.E. BATES | (publisher's device) | An Atlantic Monthly Press Book | Little, Brown and Company · Boston (the whole within a single rule border)

Collation: (A-H)^{16} (xii) + 244 pp, consisting of blank leaf, pp (i–ii); recto blank, BOOKS BY H.E. BATES on verso, pp (iii–iv); half-title, verso blank, pp (v–vi);

title-page, notice of copyright and reservation of rights, Library of Congress Catalog No. 52-5505, notice of First Edition, publisher's and printing imprints on verso, pp (vii–viii); dedication, verso blank, pp (ix–x); Contents, verso blank, pp (xi–xii); fly title, verso blank, pp (1–2); text, pp (3)–240; two blank leaves, pp (241–244).

Binding: 8vo, 4⅞ x 7⅜ ins. Pale grey boards; lettered on spine in red; all edges cut; white end papers.
    Dust jacket designed by Thomas S. Ruzicka. Design on front cover and spine in blue and red; lettered on front cover in white and on spine in red and white. Back cover white with portrait of the author by G. Scott Bushe and notes of other books by H.E. Bates in black.

Price: $3.00
    Published by Little, Brown and Company in association with The Atlantic Monthly Press and printed in The United States of America.

A 69   THE CRUISE OF THE   1951
          BREADWINNER & DEAR LIFE

THE CRUISE OF | THE BREADWINNER | & | DEAR LIFE | by | H.E. BATES | (publisher's device incorporating the author's monogram) | London | MICHAEL JOSEPH

Collation: (A)-F¹⁶ G⁸ 208 pp, consisting of half-title, Books by H.E. BATES on verso, pp (1–2); title-page, notices of first publication of *The Cruise of the Breadwinner* and *Dear Life* and of this one volume in The Evensford Edition, printer's, paper-maker's and binder's imprint on verso, pp (3–4); fly title *The Cruise of the Breadwinner* with an illustration, verso blank, pp (5–6); text, pp 7–77; blank page, p (78); fly title *Dear Life* with an illustration, p (79); blank page, p (80); text, pp 81–(204); blank leaf, pp (205–206); blank leaf pasted down as back end paper, pp (207–208).

Binding: 8vo, 4⅞ x 7¼ ins. Lime-green boards; publisher's device incorporating the author's monogram in red at bottom right-hand corner of front cover; lettering with ornament and publisher's device on spine in red; all edges cut; white end papers.
    Evensford Edition dust jacket designed by Freda Nichols; front cover blue with design of oak tree in white, black and brown; title, author's and jacket designer's names in black. The Evensford Edition in brown; lettering and publisher's device on spine in black with design of oak leaves in black and brown; back cover white with blue borders, a note on H.E. Bates by David Garnett in black.

Price: 9s. 6d. net. 1,990 copies were sold.
    Set and printed in Great Britain by Tonbridge Printers Ltd., Peach Hall Works, Tonbridge, in Garamond eleven on thirteen point, on paper made by John Dickinson at Croxley, and bound by James Burn at Esher.

Notes: The illustrations in black and white below the fly titles at pp (5) and (79) are repeated from the one in brown at the top of p 5 of *The Cruise of the Breadwinner* (first English edition A 56a), the one in red on the title-page, p (3) of *Dear Life* (first English edition A 64b).

The *Cruise of the Breadwinner* was first published as a book in the UK in July 1946 and in America in March 1947 (A 56), *Dear Life* as a book in America in November 1949 and in the UK in February 1950 (A 64).

A 70   SELECTED SHORT STORIES   1951
          OF H.E. BATES

SELECTED | SHORT STORIES | of | H.E. BATES | chosen and introduced | by the author | POCKET BOOKS (G.B.) LTD. LONDON | by arrangement with | JONATHAN CAPE LTD.

Collation: (A-I)^{16} (vi) + 282 pp, consisting of title-page, notices of publication and copyright, publisher's device, publisher's, paper-maker's, and printer's imprints on verso, pp (i–ii); Preface, pp (iii–iv); Contents, Acknowledgements on verso, pp (v–vi); text, pp 1–281; page of publisher's devices, p (282).

Binding: 8vo, 4 x 6$\frac{3}{8}$ ins. Paper covers; front cover pictorially illustrated by Peter Hale, lettered in white and orange with publisher's device in black and white; back cover yellow and white with lettering in blue and black, publisher's device in black and white against circle of red; the title along spine in black against blue background; inside covers red, illustrated with publisher's devices (trademarks) and description of the trademark lettered in black on white within single-rule black border. All edges cut and dyed red.

Price: 2s.
      Made and printed in Great Britain By Jarrold and Sons, Ltd., Norwich, for Pocket Books (G.B.) Ltd., 37–39 Essex Street, London, WC2.

Contents: PREFACE - The Mill - Waiting-Room - The Station - Beauty's Daughters - A Flower Piece - The Mower - A Threshing Day for Esther - Death in Spring - The Beauty of the Dead - The Bridge - The Earth - The Loved One - Château Bougainvillaea - The Ox - I Am Not Myself - Mr. Penfold - The Sow and Silas

Notes: This book was numbered B 21 in a series of titles chosen from the lists of leading publishers.

A 71   TWENTY TALES   1951

TWENTY | TALES | by | H.E. BATES | (publisher's device incorporating the author's monogram) | JONATHAN CAPE | THIRTY BEDFORD SQUARE | LONDON

Collation: (A)-Q⁸ 256 pp, consisting of half-title, By the same author on verso, pp (1–2); title-page as above, selection of the *Tales*, notice of publication, printer's and binder's imprints on verso, pp (3–4); CONTENTS, verso blank, pp (5–6); fly title, verso blank, pp (7–8); text, pp 9–253; blank p (254); blank pp (255–256).

Binding: 8vo, 4⅞ x 7½ ins. Lime-green boards; publisher's device incorporating the author's monogram in red at bottom right-hand corner of front cover; lettering with ornament and publisher's device on spine in red; top and fore-edges cut; lower edges trimmed; white end papers.

Evensford Edition dust jacket designed by Freda Nichols; front cover blue with a design of oak tree in white, black and brown; the title, '20 Tales', author's and jacket designer's names in black, The Evensford Edition in brown; lettering and publisher's device on spine in black with design of oak leaves in black and brown; back cover white with blue borders, note on H.E. Bates by David Garnett in black.

Price: 10s. 6d. net. Published 3 September 1951. First impression, 3,000 copies printed on 5 June 1951; Second impression, 2,000 copies printed on 21 February 1952; Third impression, 1,500 copies printed on 3 January 1961.

Printed in Great Britain in the City of Oxford at The Alden Press. Bound by A.W. Bain & Co. Ltd., London.

Contents: Perhaps We Shall Meet Again ...- The Flying Goat - The Late Public Figure - Shot Actress–Full Story - Purchase's Living Wonders - The Case of Miss Lomas - Cloudburst - The Captain - Italian Haircut - The Kimono - The Landlady - Breeze Anstey - Old - A Scandalous Woman - Quartette - The Goat and the Stars - Alexander - Lanko's White Mare - A Tinker's Donkey - The Barber

Notes: *Selection of Tales* p (4) 'These Tales are selected from the following volumes: *Thirty Tales* (A 21); *The Flying Goat* (A 34); *The Beauty of the Dead and Other Stories* (A 38); *Something Short and Sweet* (A 28) (the date of first publication is wrongly stated as 1940).

A 72   THE GRASS GOD   1951

THE | CORNHILL | (publisher's device) | SUPPLEMENT No.1 | (short rule) | THE GRASS GOD | By H.E. Bates | EPISODE AT GASTEIN | by William Sansom | (short rule) | JOHN MURRAY, 50 ALBEMARLE STREET, LONDON, W1

Collation: (A)-E⁸ FF*¹⁰ (iv) + 96 pp, consisting of advertisements, pp (i–iv); title-page, publisher's and editorial notes, printer's and publisher's imprint on verso, pp (1–2); fly title, The Grass God BY H.E. BATES, verso blank, pp (3–4); text, pp 5–55; blank page, p (56); fly title, Episode at Gastein BY WILLIAM SANSOM, verso blank, pp (57–58); text, pp 59–96.

Binding: 8vo, 5½ x 8½ ins. Paper covers; front cover red with publisher's device in red and white within ornamental border of black, red and white, lettered in black and white; white spine, lettered in red; back cover pale blue-grey with red border,

list of books written by William Sansom and published by The Hogarth Press in black; all edges cut.
The Cornhill Supplement No.1 No.989

Price: 2s. 6d. net.
Made and printed in Great Britain by Butler & Tanner Ltd., Frome and London and published by John Murray (Publishers) Ltd.

A 73   FAWLEY ACHIEVEMENT   1951

FAWLEY | ACHIEVEMENT | by | H.E. BATES | Illustrated by Roy Coombs | LONDON | ESSO PETROLEUM COMPANY, LIMITED | SEPTEMBER 1951

Collation: One gathering only, stapled. 40 pp, consisting of half-title, verso blank, pp (1–2); title-page, printer's imprint on verso, pp (3)–4; commemorative note, illustration on verso, pp 5–(6); text, pp 7–40.

Binding: 4to, 8 x $9\frac{7}{8}$ ins. Magenta card covers (insides white); lettering with design on front cover in yellow; publisher's device on back cover in yellow; all edges cut; no end papers.
Published September 1951.
Printed in Great Britain at the Anvil Press Limited.

Notes: The book commemorated the official opening on 14 September 1951 of the new Esso Refinery, at Fawley, Hampshire, and was intended as a tribute to the vision, skill and energy of all those who helped to plan and build it.
Full-page illustrations by Roy Coombs in black and yellow ochre occur on pp (6), (11), (15), (17), (25), (31), (33) and (37). The centre pages, pp (20–21), are occupied by a plan of the Refinery, with a key to its eight main parts (in black and yellow ochre). Other illustrations, in black and yellow ochre, occur at pp 9, 13, 27 and 40.

A 74   THE COUNTRY OF WHITE CLOVER   1952

H.E. BATES | The Country | of White Clover | Drawings by | BROOM LYNNE | (drawing) | London | MICHAEL JOSEPH

Collation: (A)-M⁸ 192 pp, consisting of half-title with a drawing, Also by H.E. Bates on verso, pp (1–2); title-page, notice of publication, printer's paper-maker's and binder's imprint on verso, pp (3–4); dedication 'To R.L.', verso blank, pp (5–6); Contents with a drawing, verso blank, pp (7–8); text, pp (9)–190; blank pp (191–192).

Binding: 8vo, $5\frac{1}{8}$ x $7\frac{7}{8}$ ins. Beige cloth; drawing on half-title repeated on front cover within ornamental design, all in deep red; facsimile of author's signature stamped in gold in bottom right-hand corner of front cover; lettering on spine in gold, the title within an ornamental border of deep red; top edges dyed deep red, fore and lower edges cut; white end papers decorated with drawings in brown.

Pictorial dust jacket designed by Broom Lynne. Lettering on front cover and spine in white. Drawings in blue on flaps.

Price: 12s. 6d. net. Published 26 May 1952. 7,765 copies were sold.

Set and printed in Great Britain by Unwin Brothers Ltd., at the Gresham Press, Woking, in Bembo type, thirteen point, leaded, on paper made by John Dickinson and bound by James Burn.

A limited edition of 100 [1] copies, numbered and signed by the author was produced simultaneously. They were printed by Unwin Brothers Ltd., on handmade paper and bound by James Burn. The case chosen was green buckram with a facsimile of author's signature stamped on front cover in gold. Gilt top edges and marker, fore and lower edges uncut. Price: 63/-.

Contents: Journey to Spring - The Country of White Clover - A Piece of England - Trees and Men - Union Rustic - The Face of Summer - Railway Flowers - The Show - All Summer in a Day - The New Hodge - Sea and September - The Turn of the Year

Notes: 'R.L.', Sir Robert Lusty, was appointed editorial and production manager at Michael Joseph Ltd., in 1936, when the company was formed. He left as Deputy Chairman in 1956.

The drawings by Broom Lynne occur on pp (1), (3), (7), (9), (20), 32, (33), 56, (57), 66, (67), 83, (84), 114, (115), 125, (126), 146, (147), 158, (159), 167, (168), 183, (184), 190.

The drawing at the foot of the half-title p (1) is repeated on the front cover in deep red and on front inside flap of dust jacket in blue. The drawing on p (7) (Contents) is repeated on p 83. The drawing on p 147 is repeated and enlarged on front end papers in brown. An additional drawing in blue appears on back inside flap of dust jacket.

A 75   THE FACE OF ENGLAND   1952

THE | FACE OF ENGLAND | By | H.E. Bates | With 40 Photographs | in Colour | by | A.F. Kersting | London | B.T. BATSFORD LTD (the whole within a single-rule border)

Collation: (A-M)[8] 128 pp, consisting of half-title, verso blank, pp (1-2); recto blank, frontispiece, pp (3-4); title-page, notice of publication, and printer's imprint on verso, pp (5-6); CONTENTS, PUBLISHER'S NOTE on verso, pp 7-8; full-page illustration, verso blank, pp 9-(10); LIST OF ILLUSTRATIONS, pp 11-12; text, including illustrations, pp 13-(126); PHOTOGRAPHIC DATA, pp 127-128.

---

[1] When this edition was delivered to the publishers, copy No.44 was missing

Binding: 4to, 7⅜ x 9¾ ins. Deep red cloth; lettering with dividing rules on spine in gold; top edges dyed deep red; fore and lower edges cut; white end papers.

Fawn dust jacket, colour photograph No.24 of the Abbey Church at Dorchester, Oxfordshire, slightly reduced, pasted to front cover within single-rule green borders; lettered on spine in green.

Price: 21s. net.

The manuscript (99pp quarto) was presented by the author to the King's School, Canterbury, for the Hugh Walpole Collection.

Made and printed in Great Britain by William Clowes and Sons, Limited, for the publishers B.T. Batsford Ltd., 4 Fitzhardinge Street, Portman Square, London W1.

A 76   LOVE FOR LYDIA   1952

A 76a First English edition

H.E. BATES | (ornamental rule) | Love | for | Lydia | (publisher's device) | London | MICHAEL JOSEPH

Collation: (A)-E (F)-K¹⁶ 320 pp, consisting of half-title, Also by H.E. Bates on verso, pp (1–2); title-page, notice of publication, printer's, paper-maker's and binder's imprint on verso, pp (3–4); dedication 'To LAURENCE' (Laurence Pollinger), verso blank, pp (5–6); note of fictitious characters, verso blank, pp (7–8); Contents, verso blank, pp (9–10); fly title, Part One, verso blank, pp (11–12); text, including fly titles for Parts Two, Three and Four, pp 13–319; blank p (320).

Binding: 8vo, 4⅞ x 7¼ ins. Red cloth; lettering, with ornament and publisher's device on spine in gold; top edges dyed red; fore and lower edges cut; white end papers.

Dust jacket designed by Broom Lynne; front cover and spine blue, back cover white; on front cover author's name in white outlined in red and yellow, decoration in yellow and red; on spine title in yellow, author's name in white outlined in red, publisher's name and device in red; portrait of author on back cover in black with facsimile of his signature and other lettering in black.

Price: 12s. 6d. net. 61,261 copies were sold.

Set and printed in Great Britain by Tonbridge Printers Ltd., Peach Hall Works, Tonbridge, in Times ten on eleven point, on paper made by John Dickinson at Croxley, and bound by James Burn at Esher.

Notes: Laurence Pollinger was the author's literary agent.

The Vanished World (A 107) pp 136–8: Bates tells of an assignment given to him as a newspaper reporter to go to Rushden Hall and there interview the occupants, Mr and Mrs Sartoris. Having described the Hall he continued: 'All that I bore away with me into the freezing blackness of the winter night was, in fact, in no sense real; it was in some sense both haunting and prophetic. In fact it was not to become real for another thirty years, when that same room became the setting for the first chapters of a novel of mine. But since one room, like one idea doesn't necessarily make a novel, it was opportune that somewhere about the same time I had another experience, even briefer but just as singular in its importance. One morning as I went to catch my morning train, a smart pony-drawn gig drew up at the station and out of it got a tallish, dark, proud, aloof young girl in a black cloak lined with scarlet. I had never seen her before and never saw her again. Such a vision was not, in fact, ever to be seen in that town and I surmised, rightly or wrongly, that she came from the Hall.

'In the writing of novels there must necessarily be a fusion of negative and positive. In this case the cold, dismal, wintry Hall was the negative; the girl in the scarlet-lined cloak, seen for two minutes, was the positive. In fusion, thirty years later, they became *Love for Lydia*.'

In 1976, due to the efforts of H.E. Bates' son Richard, the book was serialized and shown by London Weekend Television; the producer was Tony Wharmby.

A 76b First American edition

H.E. BATES | LOVE for | LYDIA | (publisher's device) | An Atlantic Monthly Press Book | LITTLE, BROWN AND COMPANY · Boston

Collation: (A-L)^{16} (viii) + 344 pp, consisting of recto blank, BY H.E. BATES on verso, pp (i–ii); half-title, verso blank, pp (iii–iv); title-page, notices of copyright and publication, publisher's and printing imprints on verso, pp (v–vi); dedication, statement of fictitious characterizations on verso, pp (vii–viii); fly title PART ONE, verso blank, pp (1–2); text, including fly titles for PARTS TWO, THREE and FOUR, pp 3–344.

Binding: 8vo, 5⅜ x 8 ins. Pale-blue cloth; lettering on spine in deep blue; all edges cut; white end papers.

Pictorial dust jacket designed by Paul Galdone. Portrait of the author on back cover from photograph by O. Scott Bushe. Front cover lettered in black; spine lettered in black with author's name in white.

Price: $3.50. Published in 1953.

Library of Congress Catalog Card No. 52-9066.

Published by Little, Brown and Company in association with The Atlantic Monthly Press and printed in The United States of America.

A 77   THE STORIES OF FLYING   1952
OFFICER 'X'

THE STORIES OF | FLYING OFFICER 'X' | by | H.E. BATES | (publisher's device incorporating the author's monogram) | JONATHAN CAPE | THIRTY BEDFORD SQUARE | LONDON

Collation: (A)-M^8 192 pp, consisting of half-title, By the Same Author on verso, pp (1–2); title-page, notice of publication, printer's and binder's imprint on verso, pp (3–4); CONTENTS, verso blank, pp (5–6); AUTHOR'S NOTE, verso blank, pp (7–8); text, pp 9–190; blank pp (191–192).

Binding: 8vo, $4\frac{7}{8}$ x $7\frac{3}{8}$ ins. Lime-green boards; lettering and publisher's device on spine in red; all edges cut; white end papers.
Standard Evensford Edition dust jacket designed by Freda Nichols (see A 68).

Price: 10s. 6d. net. Published 20 June 1952.
Printed in Great Britain by John Dickens and Co. Ltd., Northampton. Bound by A.W. Bain and Co. Ltd., London.
1st impression, 5,000 printed 2 April 1952; 2nd impression, 2,000, 1 August 1957; 3rd impression 1,000, 2 March 1962; 4th impression, 1,500, 21 October 1964; 5th impression, 2,000, 20 June 1967.

Contents: It's Never in the Papers - There's No Future In It - The Young Man from Kalgoorlie - It's Just The Way It Is - The Sun Rises Twice - No Trouble At All - A Personal War - K For Kitty - The Greatest People in the World - How Sleep The Brave - The Beginning of Things - The Disinherited - Croix De Guerre - Yours is the Earth - There's Something in the Air - The Bell - Free Choice : Free World - Sergeant Carmichael

Author's Note: p (7) 'The original volumes of the Flying Officer 'X' stories, *The Greatest People in the World* and *How Sleep the Brave* (A 41, A 47) were dedicated to the late Hilary St George Saunders, from whose enthusiasm and vision the entire project of writing them derived so much; and to John Pudney whose friendly watchfulness and greater experience in practical Air Force matters saved both them and myself from various pitfalls. Although three new stories have been added to the present collection time has shown no reason why the names of these two friends should not remain coupled on the dedication page. Indeed the untimely death of Hilary St George Saunders only provides another opportunity of paying homage to a man who was so much concerned, both in enthusiasm and affection, with these stories and their genesis.'

A 78   PASTORAL ON PAPER   1953

PASTORAL ON PAPER | by | H.E. BATES | Photographs by | JOHN GAY | Map and Drawings by | LESLIE S. HAYWOOD | THE MEDWAY CORRUGATED PAPER COMPANY LIMITED | MEDWAY (within a single-rule border)

Collation: (M.P.P.-1)^8 M.P.P.-2 - (M.P.P.-9)^4 (M.P.P.-10)^6 pp 92, consisting of blank leaf, pp (1–2); half-title, verso blank, pp (3–4); title-page, verso blank, pp (5–6); CONTENTS, verso blank, pp (7–8); index of PHOTOGRAPHS, pp (9–10); text, pp (11–23); photographs, numbered and described, pp (24–89); blank page, p (90); publisher's, designer's and printer's imprints, verso blank, pp (91–92).

Binding: Double cr. 8vo, $7\frac{1}{4}$ x $9\frac{1}{2}$ ins. Fine ribbed pale green cloth; lettering, with a facsimile of the author's signature on front cover in gold; lettered along spine in gold; pale green and yellow head-band; top edges dyed green; fore and lower edges cut; end papers printed with a map of Kent in colour.

Dust jacket with half-tone plates from photographs by John Gay. Photograph 1 repeated on front cover and on back cover from a different angle; front cover lettered in yellow; spine black, lettered in yellow.

Published by The Medway Corrugated Paper Co. Ltd., New Hythe, Maidstone, Kent (a Division of the Reed Paper Group).

Designed by Godbolds Limited and printed in England by Hazell, Watson and Viney Ltd.

Notes: Drawings by Lesley S. Haywood: a map of Kent in colour on end papers; in black and white, as headpieces to Parts 1–5 pp (11, 14, 16, 19, 22).

Photographs: Nos. 1–4, 6–25, 27–33 by John Gay; No.5 by Peter Holdstock; No.26 by Sweatman Hedgeland.

On Wednesday, 27 May 1953, a party was given at the Savoy Hotel, London, by the Medway Corrugated Paper Co. Ltd., to mark publication. The author was guest of honour. It was later reported in the Company's magazine that the book had been widely circulated to Medway's many connections and had everywhere been received with interest and approval.

In a magazine, *Pottery and Glass*, dated July 1953, the book was reviewed. It was described as being beautifully produced and illustrated although one criticism had come from a citizen of Beckenham who failed to understand why the largest town in Kent had been left out of the map which formed the attractive end papers.

The British Museum Library Catalogue of Printed Books and The New Cambridge Bibliography of English Literature each record the year of publication as 1956.

A 79   THE NATURE OF LOVE   1953

A 79a First English edition

H.E. BATES | The | NATURE | of | LOVE | THREE SHORT NOVELS | (publisher's device) | London | MICHAEL JOSEPH (the title printed on a grey-brown square with double rules above and below)

Collation: (A)-F^{16} G^8 H^{16} 240 pp, consisting of half-title, Also by H.E. BATES on verso, pp (1–2); title-page, notice of publication, printer's, paper-maker's and binder's imprint on verso, pp (3–4); dedication 'To W. SOMERSET MAUGHAM', verso blank, pp (5–6); (Contents), verso blank, pp (7–8); fly title 'Dulcima', verso blank, pp (9–10); text, including fly titles 'The Grass God' and 'The Delicate Nature' (pp 93 and 179), pp 11–240.

Binding: 8vo, $4\frac{7}{8}$ x $7\frac{1}{4}$ ins. Deep blue cloth; lettering, with ornament and publisher's device on spine in blue.

Dust jacket designed by Ruth Levy. Front cover and spine blue, back cover white. Lettering in white with the titles of the three novels in black within design on front cover in black, green and white. 'Daily Mail Book of the Month' within a design on spine in black. Portrait of the author on back cover. (Terracotta paper band, Daily Mail BOOK OF THE MONTH, in black.)

Price: 10s. 6d. net. 16,460 copies were sold.

Set and printed in Great Britain by Tonbridge Printers Ltd., Peach Hall Works, Tonbridge, in Bembo twelve on fourteen point, on paper made by John Dickinson at Croxley, and bound by James Burn at Esher.

Contents: Dulcima - The Grass God - The Delicate Nature

Notes: *The World in Ripeness* (A 114) p 113: '... "The novella", a critic wrote recently, "is a form of notorious difficulty. It must combine the shock or finality of the short story with the psychological complication and density of medium available to the novel." This is well said; but what is highly astonishing is not how few but how many writers of recent times have been eager to accept the challenge, to the singular enrichment of modern literature. Pushkin, Poe, Tchehov, Maupassant, Kipling, Maugham, Mann, Bunin, Crane, Wells, James, Sherwood Anderson, Knut Hamsen, Hemingway, Conrad, Thornton Wilder, Katherine Ann Porter, Graham Greene, D.H. Lawrence, Oscar Wilde, Joyce – the list of brilliant exponents in the form is as rich as it is seemingly endless.

'I now resolved, therefore, to try to add to it myself. The challenge having been taken up I presently produced a volume of four [2] novellas called *The Nature of Love*, only to be warned by my publishers that "of course it won't sell. You must resign yourself to that." In fact it did sell and indeed so well that I have ever since been more attracted to the form, so that now I have written some twenty novellas ...'

A 79b First American edition

THE NATURE | OF LOVE | by | H.E. BATES | (publisher's device) | An Atlantic Monthly Press Book | Little, Brown and Company · Boston (all within a single-rule border)

Collation: (A-O^8) (vi) + 218 pp, consisting of half-title, BY H.E. BATES on verso, pp (i–ii); title-page, Notices of copyright, reservation of rights, Library of Congress Catalog Card No. 54-6866 and of First American Edition, publisher's and printing imprints on verso, pp (iii–iv); Contents, dedication on verso, pp (v–vi); fly title Dulcima, verso blank, pp (1–2); text, including fly titles The Grass God and The Delicate Nature, pp (3)–217; blank p (218)

Binding: 8vo, $5\frac{1}{8}$ x $7\frac{1}{2}$ ins. Deep-blue boards; publisher's device blind-stamped on front cover; lettered on spine in silver; top and lower edges cut, fore edges rough trimmed; white end papers.

Dust jacket designed by Ruth Levy. Front cover identical with jacket of A 79a. Spine lettered in white with portrait of author by G. Scott Bushe on white back cover, with 'Books by H.E. BATES' in black.

Price: $3.50.

Published by Little, Brown and Company in association with The Atlantic Monthly Press and printed in The United States of America.

---

[2] It was of three novellas.

A 80   THE FEAST OF JULY   1954

A 80a First English edition

H.E. BATES | (star) | The Feast | of July | (publisher's device) | London |
MICHAEL JOSEPH

Collation: (A)-O⁸ 224 pp, consisting of half-title, Also by H.E. BATES on verso,
pp (1–2); title-page, notice of publication, printer's imprint on verso, pp (3–4); text,
with a design at the bottom of p (223), pp 5–(223); blank p (224).

Binding: 8vo, $5\frac{1}{8}$ x $7\frac{3}{4}$ ins. Green cloth flecked with white; lettering with ornament and publisher's device on spine in gold; top and fore edges cut, lower edges
uncut; white end papers.
     Dust jacket front cover and spine green, back cover white; author's name on
front cover in black on white background with title in white, shadowed in black;
lettering on spine in black against white background; back cover shows portrait of
the author in black and white, facsimile signature in black.

Price: 10s. 6d. net. A total of 30,057 copies were sold.
     Made and printed in Great Britain by Purnell & Sons, Paulton (Somerset) and
London, and set in Bembo type, 12 point, 1 point leaded.

Notes: The scene of the novel is set in a river valley of the English Midlands at
the end of the nineteenth century. The title derives from the July Sunday of Fifty
Feast that is still celebrated all over the Midlands. These Feasts, once religious in
character, like the pardons of France, are now celebrated as pleasure fairs, but up
to the end of the nineteenth century they were a more robust and colourful part of
English life than they are today.
     Recommended by The Book Society.

A 80a First American edition 1954

The Feast of July | (single ornamental border) | H.E. BATES | (publisher's
device) | An Atlantic Monthly Press Book | Little, Brown and Company · Boston

Collation: (A-Q)⁸ (viii) + 248 pp, consisting of blank leaf, pp (i–ii); recto blank,
BY H.E. BATES on verso, pp (iii–iv); half-title, verso blank, pp (v–vi); title-page,
notices of copyright, reservation of rights, Library of Congress Catalog Card No. 54-
8288 and of First Edition, publishing and printing imprints on verso, pp (vii–viii);
fly title, verso blank, pp (1–2); text, pp 3–246; blank pp (247–248).

Binding: 8vo, $5\frac{3}{8}$ x 8 ins. Yellow ochre cloth; publisher's device on front cover in
brown; lettering with design on spine in brown; all edges cut; white end papers.
     Dust jacket designed by Miriam Woods. Front cover and spine in yellow, blue,
brown and black with brown lettering on front cover; title lettered on spine in black,
author's name in white, publisher in brown; back cover white with lettering and
ornaments in brown.

Price: $3.50
     Published by Little, Brown and Company in association with The Atlantic
Monthly Press and printed in The United States of America.

A 81   THE DAFFODIL SKY   1955

A 81a First English edition

H.E. BATES | (two ornamental rules divided by a star) | The Daffodil Sky | (publisher's device) : London : MICHAEL JOSEPH

Collation: (A)-H^{16} 256 pp, consisting of half-title, ALSO BY H.E. BATES on verso, pp (1–2); title-page, notice of publication, printer's, paper-maker's and binder's imprint on verso, pp (3–4); dedication 'To SIR LOUIS STERLING', verso blank, pp (5–6); CONTENTS, verso blank, pp (7–8); text, pp 9–256.

Binding: 8vo, 4$\frac{7}{8}$ x 7$\frac{1}{4}$ ins. Black boards; lettered on spine with ornamental rules and publisher's device in gold; all edges cut; white end papers.
   Pictorial dust jacket designed by WILDSMITH, coloured black, green and yellow; lettering on front cover in white, and on spine in black and white; back cover white with list of books by H.E. BATES in black within black and green ornamental borders above and below, the lower border divided by publisher's device in black.

Price: 12s. 6d. net. 10,821 copies were sold.
   Set and printed in Great Britain by Tonbridge Printers Ltd., Peach Hall Works, Tonbridge, in Baskerville eleven on twelve point, on paper made by Henry Bruce at Currie, Scotland, and bound by James Burn at Esher.

Contents: (English and American) The Good Corn - The Daffodil Sky - Country Society - Across the Bay - Elaine - The Maker of Coffins - The Treasure Game - Chaff in the Wind - The Small Portion - The Common Denominator - A Place in the Heart - The Evolution of Saxby - Roman Figures - Go, Lovely Rose - Third View on the Reichenbach

A 81b First American impression 1956

H.E. BATES | (two ornamental rules divided by a star) | The Daffodil Sky | An Atlantic Monthly Press Book | Little, Brown and Company · Boston

Collation: (A-H)^{16} As 81a.

Binding: 8vo, 5$\frac{1}{4}$ x 7 ins. Cream cloth; publisher's device on front cover in green; lettering with design on spine in green; all edges cut; cream end papers.
   Pictorial dust jacket in colour designed by Samuel H. Bryant. Front cover and spine black; illustration of daffodil on front cover in yellow and green with lettering in white and yellow; illustration of daffodil on spine in black, white and blue; back cover white with reviews of *The Sleepless Moon* in black.

Price: $3.50
   Published by Little, Brown and Company in association with The Atlantic Monthly Press.
   Set and printed in Great Britain by Tonbridge Printers Ltd., Peach Hall Works, Tonbridge, in Baskerville eleven on twelve point.

A 82   THE SLEEPLESS MOON   1956

A 82a First English edition

H.E. BATES | (short rule) | The Sleepless Moon | (publisher's device) | London | MICHAEL JOSEPH

Collation: (A)-M^{16} 384 pp, consisting of half-title, ALSO BY H.E. BATES on verso, pp (1–2); title-page, notice of publication, printer's, paper-maker's and binder's imprint on verso, pp (3–4); dedication 'To DAVID LEAN', verso blank, pp (5–6); fly title, PART ONE, verso blank, pp (7–8); text, including fly titles for PARTS TWO and THREE, pp 9–(384).

Binding: 8vo, 5 x 7¾ ins. Black cloth; a church scene in gold in lower right-hand corner of front cover; lettering, with ornament and publisher's device on spine in gold; all edges cut; white end papers.
     Dust jacket designed by WILDSMITH. Front cover and spine blue. On front cover the author's name in white and red, the title in green, white and red with church scene in centre in blue, black and white; lettering on spine in white with publisher and device in black, sprays of leaves in green. On back cover list of books also by H.E. Bates in black bordered ornamentally above and below in green with devices in black.

Price: 15s. net. A total of 25,345 copies were sold.
     Set and printed in Great Britain by Tonbridge Printers Ltd., Peach Hall Works, Tonbridge, Kent, in Bembo twelve on thirteen point, on paper made by Henry Bruce of Currie, Scotland, and bound by James Burn at Esher.

Notes: *The Vanished World* (A 107) p 83: The author here refers to the setting of the novel in Higham Ferrers, Northamptonshire:
     'It was my grandfather's practice to buy up, every summer, a small orchard or two, and occasionally even a solitary tree of plums or pears from some private garden whose owner had neither the time or inclination to pick the fruit for himself. Of the solitary trees I most vividly remember a tall conical-shaped tree of honey pears, ripening in August, that grew in an old stone-walled garden side by side with Chichele's charming grammar school, now used for sacred purposes rather than the secular ones for which it was intended six hundred years ago. The tree not only appeared to me very tall and the pears of a singular juicy sweetness, but the whole garden must have made on my young mind an impression at once permanent and endearing, for it is from this garden and its adjoining stone house that the tragic heroine of *The Sleepless Moon*, a novel of mine written more than forty years later, walks to her wedding in the neighbouring church and subsequently to a marriage unconsummated.'

A 82b First American edition 1956

H.E. Bates | THE | SLEEPLESS | MOON | (publisher's device) | An Atlantic Monthly Press Book | Little, Brown and Company | BOSTON TORONTO (enclosed within a ruled border with four cross rules boxing)

Collation: (A-M)^{16} (viii) + 376 pp, consisting of recto blank, By H.E. Bates on verso, pp (i–ii); half-title, verso blank, pp (iii–iv); notices of copyright, reservation of rights, Library of Congress Catalog Card No. 56-5927, publisher's and printing imprints on verso, pp (v–vi); dedication, verso blank, pp (vii–viii); fly title, Part One, verso blank, pp (1–2); text, including fly titles for Parts Two and Three, pp 3–(375); blank p (376).

Binding: 8vo, $5\frac{5}{16}$ x 8 ins. Tan cloth; publisher's device on front cover and lettering on spine in blue; all edges cut; white end papers.
 Pictorial dust jacket designed by Lester Peterson. Comment on recent books (*The Nature of Love, Love for Lydia, The Feast of July, Colonel Julian and Other Stories*) by H.E. Bates on back cover.

Price: $4.00
 Published by Little, Brown and Company in association with The Atlantic Monthly Press and printed in The United States of America.

A 83   DEATH OF A HUNTSMAN   1957
four short novels

A 83a First English edition

DEATH | of a | HUNTSMAN | four short novels | by | H.E. BATES | (publisher's device) | London | MICHAEL JOSEPH

Collation: (A)-G^{16} 224 pp, consisting of half-title, ALSO BY H.E. BATES on verso, pp (1–2); title-page, notice of publication, printer's, paper-maker's and binder's imprint on verso, pp (3–4); (Contents), verso blank, pp (5–6); fly title, Death of a Huntsman, verso blank, pp (7–8); text, p 9–222 (including fly titles, Night Run to the West p (75), Summer in Salander p (121), The Queen of Spain Fritillary p (181); blank pp (223–224).

Binding: 8vo, $5\frac{1}{4}$ x $7\frac{3}{4}$ ins. Deep-blue cloth; lettering, with ornament and publisher's device on spine in gold; all edges cut; white end papers.
 Dust jacket designed by William Belcher. Front cover and spine decoration in mauve, black and scarlet with all lettering in white, back cover white with list of books by H.E. Bates in black with ornamental designs above and below in scarlet and black.

Price: 12s. 6d. net. A total of 11,634 copies were sold.
 Set and printed in Great Britain by Tonbridge Printers Ltd., Peach Hall Works, Tonbridge, Kent, in Bembo twelve on fourteen point, on paper made by Henry Bruce at Currie, Midlothian, and bound by James Burn at Esher, Surrey.

Contents: Death of a Huntsman - Night Run to the West - Summer in Salander - The Queen of Spain Fritillary
 Recommended by The Book Society

A 83   SUMMER IN SALANDER   1957

A 83b First American edition of Death of a Huntsman

H.E. BATES | (ornamental rule) | Summer | in Salander | (publisher's device) |
An Atlantic Monthly Press Book | Little, Brown and Company · Boston · Toronto

Collation: (A-H^{16}) (x) + 246 pp, consisting of blank leaf pasted down to form
front end paper, pp (i–ii); blank leaf, pp (iii–iv); half title, By H.E. Bates on verso,
pp (v–vi); title-page, notices of copyright, reservation of rights, Library of Congress
Catalog Card No. 57-11155, publisher's and printing imprints on verso, pp (vii–
viii); Contents, verso blank, pp (ix–x); fly title Death of a Huntsman, verso blank,
pp (1–2); text, including fly titles Night Run to the West, Summer in Salander and
The Queen of Spain Fritillary, pp (3)–241; blank p (242); blank pp (243–244); blank
leaf pasted down to form back end paper, pp (245–246).

Binding: 8vo, 5 x 7$\frac{3}{8}$ ins. Yellow cloth; publisher's device on front cover in black;
lettered on spine in black; all edges cut; white end papers.
    Pictorial dust jacket designed by Samuel Bryant; lettered on front cover in white,
black and yellow and on spine in white and black; back cover white with a portrait
of the author by Brian Weed and reviews of *The Daffodil Sky* in black.

Price: $3.50
    Published by Little, Brown and Company in association with The Atlantic
Monthly Press and printed in The United States of America.

A 84   SELECTED STORIES   1957

H.E. BATES | Selected Stories | (star) | PENGUIN BOOKS

Collation: (A)-I^{16} 288 pp, consisting of Penguin Books 1243, half-title and publisher's device, By the same author on verso, pp (1–2); title-page, publisher's imprint, note of first publication of the selected stories, notice of publication, printer's
imprint on verso, pp (3–4); CONTENTS, verso blank, pp (5–6); PREFACE, pp
7–(8); text, pp 9–(283); blank p (284); other Penguin fiction, pp (285–288).

Binding: 8vo, 4 x 6$\frac{7}{8}$ ins. Paper covers in cream with orange borders; on front
cover the title, illustration by John Diebel, author's name and publisher's device in
black within continuous single rules in black; publisher and price in orange above
and below the rules; lettering along spine with serial number in black, publisher's
device in orange and cream within the rules; portrait of the author by Mark Gerson,
biographical note and publisher's device, all in black within the rules on back cover
with publisher above and below in orange. On inside of front cover a note on the
selection of the stories with a review from *The Times*; inside back cover reviews of
four other books by the author. All edges cut.

Price: 3/6. Published by Penguin Books Ltd., Harmondsworth, Middlesex.
    Made and printed in Great Britain by Wyman & Sons Ltd., London, Fakenham
and Reading.

Contents: Preface - The Mill - Château Bougainvillaea - The Ox - Cut and Come Again - The Station - Harvest Moon - The Bridge - The Kimono - The Beauty of the Dead - The Loved One - I Am Not Myself - The Earth - Love is not Love - A German Idyll - Mr Penfold - Breeze Anstey

The details of first publications, p (4), are not strictly accurate as they refer generally to publication in collections of short stories. For precise information about first publication as separate stories see Section B.

A 85   SUGAR FOR THE HORSE   1957

SUGAR FOR THE HORSE | by H.E. BATES | (illustration) | ILLUSTRATED BY | Edward Ardizzone | LONDON | MICHAEL JOSEPH

Collation: (A)-G^8 H^4 120 pp, consisting of half-title, verso blank, pp (1–2); title-page, notice of publication, printer's, paper-maker's and binder's imprint on verso, pp (3–4); Contents, verso blank, pp (5–6); text, including illustrations, pp 7–(120).

Binding: 8vo, 5$\frac{1}{4}$ x 8 ins. Blue cloth; lettering of title and author's name on spine in gold against maroon background, bordered above and below with designs in gold; publisher's name and device at foot of spine in gold; all edges cut; white end papers.

Deep pink dust jacket with illustrations on front and back covers by Edward Ardizzone (illustration on front cover also occurs at p 91; illustration on back cover at p 31). All lettering on front cover and spine in black.

Price: 12s. 6d. net. A total of 9,905 copies were sold.

Set and printed in Great Britain by Unwin Brothers Ltd., at the Gresham Press, Woking, in Imprint type, 11 point, leaded, on paper made by Henry Bruce at Currie, Midlothian, and bound by James Burn at Esher, Surrey.

Contents: Sugar for the Horse - The Bedfordshire Clanger - Queenie White - The Blue Feather - The Foxes - The Double Thumb - Aunt Tibby - The Little Fishes - The Widder - The Eating Match - The Singing Pig - The Fire Eaters

The black and white drawings by Edward Ardizzone: on title-page, pp (3); 7, 11, 16, 21, 24, 31*, 36, 43, 50, 55, 60, 65, 68, 75, 77, 83, 86, 91*, 95, 99, 103, 107, 111, 117, (120) (repeated from title-page)

*also on dust jacket

A 86   THE DARLING BUDS OF MAY   1958

A 86a First English edition

H.E. BATES | (short rule) | The Darling Buds | of May | (publisher's device) | London | MICHAEL JOSEPH

Collation: (A)-E^{16} 160 pp, consisting of half-title, ALSO BY H.E. BATES on verso, pp (1–2); title-page, notices of publication and copyright, printer's, papermaker's and binder's imprint on verso, pp (3–4); text, pp 5–(158); blank pp (159–160).

Binding: 8vo, 5 x 7$\frac{3}{4}$ ins. Red cloth; lettering, ornament and publisher's device on spine in gold; all edges cut; white end papers.
    Pictorial dust jacket designed by Broom Lynne. Lettering on front cover and spine in white.

Price: 12s. 6d. net. A total of 65,591 copies were sold.
    Set and printed in Great Britain by Tonbridge Printers Ltd, Peach Hall Works, Tonbridge, Kent, in Bembo twelve on thirteen point, on paper made by Henry Bruce at Currie, Midlothian, and bound by James Burn at Esher, Surrey.

Notes: Recommended by the Book Society. *The Darling Buds of May* was the first of the four Larkins books. Others followed: *A Breath of French Air* (A 87); *When the Green Woods Laugh* (A 90) (*Hark, Hark, the Lark!* in America); *Oh! To Be in England* (A 97)
    The book was filmed under the title The Mating Game, an American production with Paul Douglas and Debbie Reynolds. As a result of the changed title and story Bates was moved to write scathing comments in an article for *Films and Filming*, May 1959. He called his piece, 'When the Cinemagoer complains that - "It Isn't Like The Book" - Who's To Blame?' (C 170). He wrote:
    '...My objections to the curious metamorphosis suffered by *The Darling Buds of May* is based on the fact that what is ordinarily a matter of technical expediency in translating a story from one medium to another has here become a mere pointless display of movie-world lunacy. Those readers already familiar with the book will know that it deals with the joyous doings of the Larkins, a family of strawberry-picking, junk-dealing country spivs of engaging freedom of character to whom morals, income tax and the normal benefits of clergy are mere words.
    'Whatever virtues the story of these extraordinarily happy, uninhibited people may or may not possess one thing is quite certain: the book is as English as pubs, steak-and-kidney pudding and *The Canterbury Tales* of Chaucer. When you add to this the fact that it is also an ironic commentary on the great social revolution this country has suffered through the National Health Service (known to the Larkins as the National Elf Lark) television and other forms of drug addiction generally, you may begin to see what angers me about the transition of the scene from Kent to Maryland, USA, together with the complete Americanisation of all the characters and the changing of the title to The Mating Game.'
    It was subsequently staged as a play at the Saville Theatre, London, starring Elspeth March and Peter Jones, and at Northampton Repertory Theatre.
    The manuscript of the book is owned by the Bates family.

A 86b First American edition 1958

(To right of title page) The | Darling | Buds | of | May (To left of title page) by | H.E. | BATES | (publisher's device) | An Atlantic Monthly Press Book | Little, Brown and Company | BOSTON (flower) TORONTO

Collation: (A-0)^8 iv + 220 pp, consisting of half-title, by H.E. BATES on verso, pp (i–ii); title-page, notices of copyright, reservation of rights, Library of Congress Catalog Card No. 58-7868, notice of First Edition, publisher's imprint, note of printing in The United States of America, pp (iii–iv); fly title, verso blank, pp (1–2); text, pp 3–219; blank page, p 220.

Binding: 8vo, 5$\frac{1}{4}$ x 7$\frac{1}{2}$ ins. Yellow cloth; green tree in flower on front cover; lettering and small flower below title on spine in green; all edges cut; cream end papers.

Dust jacket designed by Barbara Carrigan. Front cover and spine blue-grey; first capital letters of title words green, embellished with blue and brown floral designs, other letters in green with author's name in white; two floral designs on front cover, one repeated on spine lettered in yellow and green; back cover white with portrait of the author by Roest, Amsterdam, and Recent Books by H.E. Bates in black.

Price: TDBOM $3.75.

Published by Little, Brown and Company in assocation with The Atlantic Monthly Press and printed in The United States of America.

A 87   A BREATH OF FRENCH AIR   1959

A 87a First English edition

H.E. BATES | (short rule) | A Breath | of French Air | (publisher's device) | London | MICHAEL JOSEPH

Collation: (A)-E^{16} 160 pp, consisting of half-title and publisher's note, ALSO BY H.E. BATES on verso, pp (1–2); title-page, notices of publication and copyright, printer's, paper-maker's and binder's imprint on verso, pp (3–4); text, pp 5–(159); blank p (160).

Binding: 8vo, 5 x 7$\frac{3}{4}$ ins. Royal-blue cloth; lettering, with ornament and publisher's device on spine in gold; all edges cut; white end papers.

Pictorial dust jacket designed by Broom Lynne, lettered on front cover and spine in white.

Price: 12s. 6d. net. A total of 50,746 copies were sold.

Set and printed in Great Britain by Tonbridge Printers Ltd., Peach Hall Works, Tonbridge, Kent, in Bembo twelve on thirteen point, on paper made by Henry Bruce at Currie, Midlothian, and bound by James Burn at Esher, Surrey.

Notes: The manuscript is owned by the Bates family.

A 87b First American edition 1959

A | BREATH | OF | FRENCH AIR | H.E. BATES | (publisher's device) | An Atlantic Monthly Press Book | LITTLE, BROWN and COMPANY | Boston · Toronto

Collation: (A-O)^8 (x) + 214 pp, consisting of blank leaf pasted down to form
front end paper, pp (i–ii); blank leaf, pp (iii–iv); recto blank, by H.E. Bates on
verso, pp (v–vi); half-title, verso blank, pp (vii–viii); title-page, notices of copyright
and reservation of rights, Library of Congress Catalog Card No. 59-11879, note of
First Edition, publisher's and printing imprints on verso, pp (ix–x); fly title, verso
blank, pp (1–2); text, pp 3–209; blank page, p (210); blank leaf, pp (211–212); blank
leaf pasted down to form back end paper, pp (213–214).

Binding: 8vo, 5 x 7$\frac{1}{4}$ ins. Blue boards; publisher's device blind-stamped on front
cover; author and publisher lettered on spine in pink with title in yellow; all edges
cut; white end papers.

   Pictorial dust jacket designed by Broom Lynne, the design identical with that
of the English jacket, slightly reduced in size and printed on glossy paper. Copy on
flaps, describing the book and providing biographical note of the author, differs.

Price: $3.75
   Published by Little, Brown and Company in association with The Atlantic
Monthly Press and printed in The United States of America.

A 88   THE WATERCRESS GIRL   1959
            and other stories

A 88a First English edition

THE WATERCRESS GIRL | and other stories | by | H.E. BATES | (drawing
| DRAWINGS BY HAZEL POPE | London | MICHAEL JOSEPH

Collation: (A)-G^{16} 224 pp, consisting of half-title and publisher's note, ALSO BY
H.E. BATES on verso, pp (1–2); title-page, notices of publication and copyright,
printer's, paper-maker's and binder's imprint on verso, pp (3–4); CONTENTS,
verso blank, pp (5–6); text, pp 7–222; blank pp (223–224).

Binding: 8vo, 5$\frac{1}{8}$ x 7$\frac{3}{4}$ ins. Blue boards; lettering and publisher's device on spine
in gold; all edges cut; cream end papers.

   Dust jacket designed by Hazel and Ashley Pope. Front cover and spine a grey
weave pattern with lettering and publisher's device in blue; title-page drawing by
Hazel Pope repeated on front cover, enlarged and in brown.

   Back cover white with reviews of *The Darling Buds of May* in brown and black,
bordered above and below with ornamental designs in blue, publisher's device in
brown in centre of lower border.

Price: 13s. 6d. net. A total of 10,148 copies were sold.
   Set and printed in Great Britain by Tonbridge Printers Ltd., Peach Hall Works,
Tonbridge, Kent, in Baskerville eleven on thirteen point, on paper made by Henry
Bruce at Currie, Midlothian, and bound by James Burn at Esher, Surrey.

Contents: (English and American first editions) The Cowslip Field - The Watercress Girl - Let's Play Soldiers - The Far Distant Journey - The Pemberton Thrush

- Death and the Cherry Tree - A Great Day for Bonzo - The Butterfly - Love in a Wych Elm - The House with the Grape Vine - Great Uncle Crow - Source of the World - The Poison Ladies

Notes: Drawings in black and white by Hazel Pope on title-page (repeated on front cover of dust jacket, enlarged and in brown), and on pp 7, 17, 37, 53, 63, 79, 89, 155, 165, 181, 191, 201, 213.

The publisher's note on the half-title page of the English edition does not appear in the American edition but is reprinted on the front inside flap of the dust jacket for that volume:

'Many of the earliest of H.E. Bates's short stories were lyrical sketches, almost prose poems, in which the world and its complexities were seen with crystalline purity through the eyes of children. Now once again, in *The Watercress Girl*, he shows us the child's world with all its strange enlargements and compressions of vision, together with its joyous and painful clarity, its fears, its hopes, its make-believe, its adventurous excursions, and its trust and mistrust of the adult world.

'But though these stories are all about children they are not for children; and though they show us, physically, the world of childhood, what they really reveal, in essence, is the world of grown-ups; a world where we adults still play soldiers, make excursions into the unknown, are afraid of the dark and so often make believe that we are something else than what we really are.'

A 88b First American edition 1960

The Watercress Girl | AND OTHER STORIES | H.E. Bates | (drawing) | DRAWINGS BY HAZEL POPE | An Atlantic Monthly Press Book | LITTLE, BROWN AND COMPANY | Boston · Toronto

Collation: (A-O⁸) (ii) + 222 pp, consisting of half-title, By H.E. Bates on verso, pp (i–ii); title-page, notices of copyright and reservation of rights, Library of Congress Catalog No. 60-5368, note of First American Edition, publisher's and printing imprints on verso, pp (1-2) CONTENTS, verso blank, pp (3-4); fly title, verso blank, pp (5-6); text, pp 7-222.

Binding: 8vo, 5⅜ x 8 ins. Beige cloth; publisher's imprint blind-stamped on front cover; lettered on spine in dark brown; all edges cut; white end papers.

Dust jacket designed by Hazel and Ashley Pope. Design of front cover and spine identical with the English edition, lettering in blue and title-page drawing enlarged on front cover in brown; back cover white with reviews of *The Daffodil Sky* and *The Darling Buds of May* with ornamental borders above and below in blue; the titles in brown, the remainder in black.

Price: $3.75

Published by Little, Brown and Company in association with The Atlantic Monthly Press and printed in The United States of America.

A 89   AN ASPIDISTRA IN BABYLON   1960
            four novellas   .

A 89a First English edition

AN ASPIDISTRA IN BABYLON | four novellas | by | H.E. BATES | (publisher's device) | London | MICHAEL JOSEPH

Collation: (A)-F^{16} G^8 H^{16} 240 pp, consisting of half-title and publisher's note, ALSO BY H.E. BATES on verso, pp (1–2); title-page, notices of publication and copyright, printer's, paper-maker's and binder's imprint on verso, pp (3–4); (Contents), verso blank, pp (5–6); fly title, An Aspidistra in Babylon, verso blank, pp (7–8); text, pp 9–239, including fly titles A Month by the Lake p (61), A Prospect of Orchards p (135), The Grapes of Paradise p (175), with versos blank; blank p (240).

Binding: 8vo, 5 x 7$\frac{3}{4}$ ins. Magenta boards; lettering, with ornament and publisher's device on spine in gold; all edges cut; cream end papers.

    Dust jacket designed by Freda Nichols. Front cover and spine: design in grey and white, lettering in brown and terracotta; back cover white with reviews of *Death of a Huntsman* in black, the title, ornament and publisher's device in terracotta.

Price: 13s. 6d. net. A total of 11,131 copies were sold.

    Set and printed in Great Britain by Tonbridge Printers Ltd, Peach Hall works, Tonbridge, Kent, in Bembo twelve on fourteen point, on paper made by Henry Bruce at Currie, Midlothian, and bound by James Burn at Esher, Surrey.

Notes: 'The Grapes of Paradise' was first serialised in *John Bull,* 10 and 17 March 1956.

A 89b   THE GRAPES OF PARADISE   1960
            First American edition of An Aspidistra in Babylon

The Grapes of Paradise | FOUR SHORT NOVELS | BY | H.E. Bates | (publisher's device) | An Atlantic Monthly Press Book | LITTLE, BROWN AND COMPANY | Boston · Toronto

Collation: (A-O)^8 (P)^{12} ii + 246 pp, consisting of recto blank, By H.E. Bates on verso, pp (i–ii); half-title, verso blank, pp (1–2); title-page, notice of copyright and reservation of rights, Library of Congress Catalog Card No. 60-12206, notice of First American Edition and of publication in England under the title of *An Aspidistra in Babylon,* publisher's and printing imprints on verso, pp (3–4); (Contents), verso blank, pp (5–6); fly title, An Aspidistra in Babylon, verso blank, pp (7–8); text, pp 9–239, including fly titles A Month by the Lake, p (61), A Prospect of Orchards, p (135), The Grapes of Paradise, p (175), with versos blank; blank p (240); three blank leaves, pp (241–246).

Binding: 8vo, 5$\frac{1}{8}$ x 8 ins. Green cloth; lettered on spine in blue; all edges cut; white end papers.

    Dust jacket designed by Edith Allard. Front cover and spine lettered in purple, blue and green. Back cover white with reviews of *The Darling Buds of May* and *The Watercress Girl* in blue.

Price: $3.75
Published by Little, Brown and Company in association with The Atlantic
Monthly Press and printed in The United States of America.

A 90   WHEN THE GREEN WOODS LAUGH   1960

A 90a First English edition

H.E. BATES | (short rule) | When the | Green Woods Laugh | (publisher's
device) | London | MICHAEL JOSEPH

Collation: (A)-E^{16} 160 pp, consisting of half-title and publisher's note, ALSO BY
H.E. BATES on verso, pp (1–2); title-page, notices of publication and copyright,
printer's, paper-maker's and binder's imprint on verso, pp (3–4); stanza from Blake's
Songs of Innocence, verso blank, pp (5–6); text, pp 7–(158); blank leaf, pp (159–
160).

Binding: 8vo, 5$\frac{1}{8}$ x 7$\frac{3}{4}$ ins. Lime-green cloth; lettering, with ornament and publisher's device on spine in gold; all edges cut; white end papers.
Pictorial dust jacket designed by Broom Lynne; lettering on front cover and
spine in white.

Price: 12s. 6d. net. A total of 40,550 copies were sold.
Set and printed in Great Britain by Tonbridge Printers Ltd, Peach Hall Works,
Tonbridge, Kent, in Bembo twelve on thirteen point, on paper made by Henry Bruce
at Currie, Midlothian, and bound by James Burn at Esher, Surrey.

Notes: *Publisher's Note* p (1): 'This novel completes the trilogy of the Larkin
family begun by *The Darling Buds of May* (A 86) and continued in *A Breath of
French Air* (A 87). The scene is the rich fertile heart of the Kentish countryside
already so pungently and lyrically described in *The Darling Buds of May* and the
time is the long, unforgettable summer of 1939. Two new characters, a would-be
stockbroker farmer and his wife - what Pop calls a Piccadilly farmer – descend upon
the Larkins' world, provoking characteristically pungent and mischievous reactions
in Pop and at the same time providing the author with fresh opportunities for gently
satirising those who labour under the illusion that the countryside is exclusively
populated by sows, sheep and simpletons.'
The stanza on p (5) is taken from William Blake's 'Laughing Song'.
The manuscript is owned by the Bates family.

A 90b   HARK, HARK, THE LARK!   1961
First American edition of When the Green Woods Laugh

Hark, Hark, the Lark! | H.E. Bates | (publisher's device) | An Atlantic Monthly
Press Book | LITTLE BROWN AND COMPANY | Boston · Toronto

Collation: (A-K)^8 (ii) + 158 pp, consisting of half-title, By H.E. Bates on verso,
pp (i–ii); title-page, notice of copyright, Library of Congress Catalog No. 61-5310,

Note of First American Edition and that this book was published in England under
the title *When the Green Woods Laugh,* publisher's imprint with note of printing in
The United States of America, pp (1–2); Stanza from Blake's *Songs of Innocence,*
verso blank, pp (3–4); fly title, verso blank, pp (5–6); text, pp 7–(158).

Binding: 8vo, $4\frac{7}{8}$ x $7\frac{3}{8}$ ins. Scarlet cloth; publisher's device blind-stamped on
front cover; lettered on spine in gold; all edges cut; white end papers.
      Dust jacket designed by John Alcorn: yellow ochre, lettered in black. The whole
jacket illustrated with a man and woman caricatured in a bathroom scene.

Price: $3.75
      Published by Little, Brown and Company in association with The Atlantic
Monthly Press and printed in The United States of America.

A 91   NOW SLEEPS THE CRIMSON   1961
**   PETAL and other stories**

A 91a First English edition

H.E. BATES | Now Sleeps the Crimson Petal | AND OTHER STORIES |
(ornament) | (publisher's device) | London | MICHAEL JOSEPH

Collation: (A)-E^{16} F^8 G^{16} 208 pp, consisting of half-title, ALSO BY H.E. BATES
on verso, pp (1–2); title-page, notices of publication and copyright, printer's, paper-
maker's and binder's imprint on verso, pp (3–4); CONTENTS, verso blank, pp
(5–6); text, pp 7–206; blank pp (207–208).

Binding: 8vo, $5\frac{1}{8}$ x $7\frac{3}{4}$ ins. Scarlet cloth; lettering and publisher's device on spine
in gold; all edges cut; cream end papers.
      Dust jacket designed by Charles Gorham. Front cover and spine deep purple
with floral design on front in crimson and green. Lettering on front cover and spine
white and black, crimson on white back cover.

Price: 15s. net. Published April 1961. A total of 12,130 copies were sold.
      Set and printed in Great Britain by Tonbridge Printers Ltd, Peach Hall Works,
Tonbridge, Kent, in Baskerville eleven on thirteen point, on paper made by Henry
Bruce at Currie, Midlothian, and bound by James Burn at Esher, Surrey.

Contents: The Enchantress - Lost Ball - Now Sleeps the Crimson Petal - The
Place where Shady Lay - The Yellow Crab - Daughters of the Village - Where the
Cloud Breaks - Mrs Eglantine - Thelma - The Snow Line - The Spring Hat - An
Island Princess

Notes: The title-page ornament is repeated below the title of each story in the
text.

A 91b   THE ENCHANTRESS and OTHER STORIES   1961
First American edition of Now Sleeps the
Crimson Petal

The Enchantress | AND OTHER STORIES | H.E. Bates | (publisher's device) | An Atlantic Monthly Press Book | LITTLE, BROWN AND COMPANY | BOSTON · TORONTO

Collation: (A-N^8) 208 pp, consisting of half-title, By H.E. Bates on verso, pp (1–2); title-page, notice of copyright, Library of Congress Catalog No. 61-13897, note of First American Edition and publication in England as *Now Sleeps the Crimson Petal*, publisher's imprint and note of printing in The United States of America, pp (3–4); CONTENTS, verso blank, pp (5–6); text, pp 7–206; blank pp (207–208).

Binding: 8vo, 5$\frac{1}{4}$ x 8 ins. Deep-purple cloth; publisher's device blind-stamped on front cover; lettering on spine in silver; all edges cut; white end papers.
Dust jacket designed by Emil Antonucci. White, with designs and lettering on front cover and spine in pink and black; portrait of the author by Hans Roest, Amsterdam, on back cover with notes of recent books by H.E. Bates in black.

Price: $4.00
Published by Little, Brown and Company in association with The Atlantic Monthly Press and printed in The United States of America.

A 92   THE DAY OF THE TORTOISE   1961

(head-piece in scarlet) | THE DAY OF THE TORTOISE | by H.E. BATES | ILLUSTRATED BY PETER FARMER | LONDON | MICHAEL JOSEPH

Collation: (AB)-E^8 F^9 98 pp, consisting of half-title, verso blank, pp (1–2); title-page, notices of publication and copyright, printer's, paper-maker's and binder's imprint on verso, pp (3–4); text, commencing with an ornamental initial 'T' in scarlet, pp 5–(94); acknowledgements for use of words from songs, pp (95–96); blank pp (97–98).

Binding: 8vo, 4$\frac{7}{8}$ x 7$\frac{1}{4}$ ins. Dark-green boards; lettering on front cover and along spine, with two stars, in gold; all edges cut; white end papers.
Dust jacket, pale green, head-piece in scarlet on title-page repeated on front and back; lettering on front, back and spine in scarlet and black.

Price: 7s. 6d. net. Published November 1961. A total of 14,979 copies were sold.
Set and printed in Great Britain by Tonbridge Printers Ltd, Peach Hall Works, Tonbridge, Kent, in Janson eleven on fourteen point, on paper made by Henry Bruce at Currie, Midlothian, and bound by James Burn at Esher, Surrey.

Notes: Illustrations by Peter Farmer:
Head-piece in scarlet on title-page, p (3) and in black p (21); repeated on front and back covers of dust jacket.
In black and white: full page, pp (7), (11), (15), (17), (21), (24), (39), (47), (54), (63), (68), (75), (84); others pp 9, 29, 33, 43, 51, 59, 67, 80, 82, 90.

A 93   ACHILLES THE DONKEY   1962

A 93a First English edition

ACHILLES | THE | DONKEY | by | H.E. BATES | & | CAROL BARKER |
DENNIS DOBSON · LONDON (a small part of the coloured frontispiece continued
on title-page)

Collation: (A)-C⁸ pp (48), consisting of first leaf with full-page coloured illustration pasted down to form front end paper, pp (1–2); continuation of full page
illustration, verso blank, pp (3–4); half-title with coloured illustration, frontispiece
full-page illustration, pp (5–6); title-page, notices of first publication, copyright
of text, and illustrations and reservation of rights, printer's and binder's imprints
on verso, pp (7–8); text, including coloured illustrations, pp (9–46); last leaf with
full-page illustration pasted down to form back end paper, pp (47–48).

Binding: 4to, $8\frac{3}{4}$ x $11\frac{1}{8}$ ins. White boards illustrated in colour with lettering on
front cover and along spine in black; all edges cut; no end papers.
  Dust jacket identical with covers illustrated in colour and lettered in black by
Carol Barker.

Price: 15s. net. Published October 1962.
  Published by Dobson Books Ltd., 80 Kensington Church Street, London W8.
Printed in Great Britain by Taylowe Ltd., Maidenhead. Bound in Great Britain by
Dorstel Press Ltd., Harlow.

Notes: Carol Barker painted the pictures for this book, the first in the 'Achilles'
trilogy, after a visit to Greece. They were shown to H.E. Bates who liked them so
much that he agreed immediately to contribute a text.
  The illustrations occur on the covers of the book (repeated on the dust jacket),
and on pp (2–3 double-page), (5), (6), (7), (9), (10), (11), (12), (13), (14–15 double-
page), (16–17), (18), (19 full-page), (20–21 double-page), (22–23), (24), (25), (26),
(27), (28–29 double-page), (30–31), (33), (34–35), (36–37), (38), (39), (40–41), (42),
(43), (44), (45), (46–47 double-page, identical with (2–3)).

A 93b American issue 1963

  An issue was prepared for America in 1963, uniform with the first English edi-
tion. It bore the imprint, 'FRANKLIN-WATTS INC. NEW YORK', the notice of
publication stating: 'First published in the United States in 1963 by Franklin Watts
Inc., 575 Lexington Avenue, New York 22, N.Y.'
  Dust jacket identical with first English edition.
Price: $3.95
  Library of Congress Catalog Card No. 63-7341.

A 94 THE GOLDEN ORIOLE: five novellas 1962

A 94a First English Edition

THE GOLDEN ORIOLE | five novellas by | H.E. BATES | (publisher's device) | London | MICHAEL JOSEPH

Collation: (A)-E^{16} F^8 G^{16} 208 pp, consisting of half-title and publisher's note, ALSO BY H.E. BATES on verso, pp (1–2); title-page, notices of publication and copyright, printer's, paper-maker's and binder's imprint on verso, pp (3–4); (Contents), verso blank, pp (5–6); fly title, 'The Ring of Truth', verso blank, pp (7–8); text, pp 9–51; blank page, p (52); fly title, 'The Quiet Girl', verso blank, pp (53–54); fly title, 'The Golden Oriole', verso blank, pp (95–96); text, pp 97–125; blank page, p (126); fly title, 'Mr Featherstone Takes a Ride', verso blank, pp (127–128); text, pp 129–169; blank page, p (170); fly title, 'The World is Too Much With Us', verso blank, pp (171–172); text, pp 173–204; two blank leaves, pp (205–208).

Binding: 8vo, 5$\frac{1}{4}$ x 7$\frac{3}{4}$ ins. Terracotta boards; lettering and publisher's device on spine in gold; all edges cut; white end papers.

Dust jacket designed by Charles Gorham. Front cover and spine in black and shades of blue with golden oriole in flight on front cover in black and gold. Lettering on front cover and spine in white with the word 'Golden' in that colour.

Upper part of back cover carries portrait of the author, the lower third white with author's name in blue below which is advertisement for his new full-length novel, *A Crown of Wild Myrtle*, in black.

Price: 16s. net. A total of 11,100 copies were sold.

Set and printed in Great Britain by Tonbridge Printers Ltd., Peach Hall Works, Tonbridge, Kent, in Bembo twelve on fourteen point, on paper made by Henry Bruce at Currie, Midlothian and bound by James Burn at Esher, Surrey.

Contents: (First English and American editions) The Ring of Truth - The Quiet Girl - The Golden Oriole - Mr Featherstone Takes a Ride - The World is Too Much With Us

A 94b First American edition 1962

THE GOLDEN ORIOLE | five novellas by | H.E. BATES | (publisher's device) | An Atlantic Monthly Press Book | LITTLE, BROWN AND COMPANY | BOSTON · TORONTO

Collation: (A-N)^8 (ii) + 206 pp, consisting of blank leaf, pp (i–ii); half-title, by H.E. Bates on verso, pp (1–2); title-page, notices of copyright, reservation of rights, Library of Congress Catalog Card No. 62-18365, notice of First Edition, publisher's and printing imprints, pp (3–4); (Contents), verso blank, pp (5–6); fly title, 'The Ring of Truth', verso blank, pp (7–8); text, pp 9–51; blank page, p (52); fly title, 'The Quiet Girl', verso blank, pp (53–54); text, pp 55–94; fly title, 'The Golden Oriole', verso blank, pp (95–96); text, pp 97–125; blank page, p (126); fly title 'Mr Featherstone Takes a Ride', verso blank, pp (127–128); text, pp 129–169; blank page, p (170); fly title, 'The World is Too Much With Us', verso blank, pp (171–172); text, pp 173–204; blank leaf, pp (205–206).

Binding: 8vo, $5\frac{3}{8}$ x 8 ins. Pale-blue boards; publisher's device blind-stamped on front cover; lettered on spine in yellow; all edges cut; white end papers.

Dust jacket designed by Charles Gorham. Front cover and spine carries same design, slightly enlarged, as for A 94a. Back cover has different portrait of the author (by Hans Roest, Amsterdam), followed by bibliographical note, lettered in black on white.

Price: TGO $4.00

Published by Little, Brown and Company in association with The Atlantic Monthly Press and printed in The United States of America.

A 95   A CROWN OF WILD MYRTLE   1962

A 95a First English edition

H.E. Bates | A CROWN OF | WILD | MYRTLE | (publisher's device) | London | MICHAEL JOSEPH

Collation: (A)-F^{16} 192 pp, consisting of half-title and publisher's note, ALSO BY H.E. BATES on verso, pp (1–2); title-page, notices of publication and copyright, printer's, paper-maker's and binder's imprint on verso, pp (3–4); text, pp 5–(191); blank p (192).

Binding: 8vo, $5\frac{1}{4}$ x $7\frac{3}{4}$ ins. Dark-green boards; lettering with decorations of leaves above and below the title on spine in gold; all edges cut; cream end papers.

White dust jacket designed by John Andrew. On front cover the author's name in dark green, title in orange incorporating design of leaves in dark green; on spine title in white on dark green design; portrait of the author by Mark Gerson appears on back cover with reviews of *The Golden Oriole* in dark green and black.

Price: 15s. net. A total of 16,999 copies were sold.

Set and printed in Great Britain by Tonbridge Printers Ltd., Peach Hall Works, Tonbridge, Kent, in Baskerville twelve on fourteen point, on paper made by Henry Bruce at Currie, Midlothian, and bound by James Burn at Esher, Surrey.

A 95b First American edition 1963

A | Crown | of | Wild Myrtle | (ornament) | By H.E. BATES | FARRAR, STRAUS AND COMPANY | New York

Collation: (A-F^{16}) 192 pp, consisting of half-title, ALSO BY H.E. BATES on verso, pp (1–2); title-page, notice of copyright, Library of Congress Catalog Card No. 63-9923, notes of first printing 1963 and of manufacture in The United States of America on verso, pp (3–4); text, pp 5–(191); blank p (192).

Binding: 8vo, 5⅜ x 8 ins. Quarter green cloth; cerise cloth sides; author's and publisher's names on spine in black, title along spine in gold; all edges cut; white end papers.

Dust jacket designed by Shirley Smith. Front cover white, lettered in black with floral illustration in pink, green and black; spine pink, lettered in black; portrait of the author by Howard Coster on back cover.

Price: $3.95

A 96   ACHILLES AND DIANA   1963

A 96a First English edition

ACHILLES | AND | DIANA | by | H.E. BATES | & | CAROL BARKER | DENNIS DOBSON · LONDON (a small part of the coloured frontispiece continued on title-page)

Collation: (A-C)⁸ (48) pp, consisting of first leaf with full-page coloured illustration pasted down to form front end paper, pp (1–2); continuation of full page illustration, verso blank, pp (3–4); half-title with coloured illustration, frontispiece full page illustration, pp (5–6); title-page, notices of first publication, copyright of text and illustrations and reservations of rights, printer's and binder's imprints on verso, pp (7–8); text, including coloured illustrations, pp (9–46); last leaf with full page illustrations pasted down to form back end paper, pp (47–48).

Binding: 4to, 8¾ x 11¼ ins. White boards with coloured illustration, lettering on front cover and along spine in black; all edges cut; no end papers.

Dust jacket illustrated in colour and lettered in black by Carol Barker, identical with covers.

Price: 15s. net.

Published by Dobson Books Ltd., 80 Kensington Church Street, London W8. Printed in Great Britain by Taylowe Ltd., Maidenhead. Bound in Great Britain by Dorstel Press Ltd., Harlow.

Notes: For this, the second book in the 'Achilles' trilogy, the collaboration between author and illustrator was described by the publisher as being more orthodox. On this occasion H.E. Bates wrote the story which Carol Barker then illustrated.

Illustrations in colour: On cover/dust jacket and on pp (2–3 double page); (5), (6), (7), (9), (10), (11), (12), (13), (15), (16–17 double page), (19 full page); (20), (21), (22), (23), (24–25 double page), (26), (27), (28), (29), (31), (32–33 double page), (34), (35), (36), (37 full page), (38–39 double page), (41), (42), (43), (45), (46–47 double page, identical with pp (2–3)).

A 96b American issue 1964

Notes: An issue was prepared for America in 1964, uniform with first English
edition. It bore the imprint, 'FRANKLIN-WATTS INC. NEW YORK', and stated
'First published in The United States in 1964 by Franklin Watts Inc., 575 Lexington
Avenue, New York 22, N.Y.' Dust jacket as English edition.

Price: $3.95

A 97   OH! TO BE IN ENGLAND   1963

A 97a First English edition

H.E. BATES | (short rule) | Oh! To Be in England | (publisher's device) |
London | MICHAEL JOSEPH

Collation: (A)-D^{16} E^4 F^{16} 168 pp, consisting of half-title and publisher's note,
ALSO BY H.E. BATES on verso, pp (1–2); title-page, notices of publication and
copyright, printer's, paper-maker's and binder's imprint on verso, pp (3–4); dedication 'to STEPHEN JEREMY ANDREW BEVERLEY and EMMA', verso blank,
pp (5–6); text, pp 7–(167); blank p (168).

Binding: 8vo, 5$\frac{1}{8}$ x 7$\frac{3}{4}$ ins. Blue cloth; lettering, with ornament and publisher's
device on spine in gold; all edges cut; cream end papers.
      Dust jacket designed by John Alcorn. Front cover and spine white with coloured
design on front cover. Lettering on front cover and on spine in scarlet and black
with publisher's device in scarlet.
      Back cover has portrait of the author in black and white.

Price: 15s. net. A total of 22,958 copies were sold.
      Set and printed in Great Britain by Tonbridge Printers Ltd., Peach Hall Works,
Tonbridge, Kent, in Bembo twelve on fourteen point, on paper made by Henry
Bruce at Currie, Midlothian, and bound by James Burn at Esher, Surrey.

Notes: The book is dedicated to the author's grand-children.
      The manuscript is owned by the Bates family.

A 97b First American issue

H.E. Bates | Oh! | To Be in England | NEW YORK | FARRAR, STRAUS
AND COMPANY

Collation: (A-D)^{16} (E)^4 (F)^{16} 168 pp, consisting of half-title, ALSO BY H.E.
BATES on verso, pp (1–2); title-page, notice of copyright, Library of Congress
Catalog Card No. 64-11452, notices of First Printing 1964 and of manufacture in
the USA, pp (3–4); dedication, verso blank, pp (5–6); text, pp 7–(167); blank p
(168).

Binding: 8vo, 5⅜ x 8 ins. Blue cloth; author and publisher lettered on spine in green; title lettered along spine in gold; top edges dyed black; fore and lower edges cut; brown end papers.

Dust jacket designed by John Alcorn, as A 97a.

Price: $4.50

A 98   SEVEN BY FIVE   1963

A 98a First English edition

SEVEN by FIVE | Stories by H.E. Bates | 1926–1961 | With a Preface by | HENRY MILLER | (publisher's device) | London | MIICHAEL JOSEPH

Collation: (A)^{16} B^2 B*^{18} C-N^{16} 0^4 P^{16} (viii) + 456 pp, consisting of half-title, ALSO BY H.E. BATES on verso, pp (i–ii); title-page, notices of publication and copyright, printer's, paper-maker's and binder's imprint on verso, pp (iii–iv); AU-THOR'S NOTE, verso blank, pp (v–vi); PREFACE BY HENRY MILLER, pp (vii–viii)(1–2); CONTENTS, pp (3–4) as A98b; fly title, verso blank, pp (5–6); text, pp 7–454; blank pp (455–456).

Binding: 8vo, 5⅜ x 8½ ins. Dark-green cloth; 7 x 5 blind-stamped in centre of front cover; lettering on spine in gold with 7 x 5 blind-stamped below title; all edges cut; cream end papers.

Dust jacket designed by Donald Green. Green, with lettering on front cover and spine in white and scarlet. 7 x 5 on front cover and spine in blue.

Price: 25s. net. A total of 9,625 copies were sold.

Set and printed in Great Britain by Tonbridge Printers, Ltd., Peach Hall Works, Tonbridge, Kent in Period O.S. eleven on twelve point, on paper made by Henry Bruce at Currie, Midlothian, and bound by James Burn at Esher, Surrey.

A 98b   THE BEST OF H.E. BATES [1]   1963
First American edition of Seven by Five

The Best of H.E. Bates | by | H.E. BATES | With a Preface by | HENRY MILLER | (publisher's device) | An Atlantic Monthly Press Book | LITTLE, BROWN AND COMPANY | BOSTON · TORONTO

Collation: (A)^{16} (B)^2 (B*)^{18} (C-N)^{16} (0)^4 (P)^{16} (viii + ′456 pp, consisting of half-title, BY H.E. BATES on verso, pp (i–ii); title-page, notices of copyright, Library of Congress Catalog Card No. 62-10532, and of FIRST EDITION; Note of publication in England under the title *Seven by Five*, publisher's imprint and note of printing in THE UNITED STATES OF AMERICA on verso, pp (iii–iv); AUTHOR's NOTE, verso blank, pp (v–vi); PREFACE BY HENRY MILLER, pp (vii–viii) (1–2); CONTENTS, pp (3–4); fly title, verso blank, pp (5–6); text, pp 7–454; blank pp (455–456).

---

[1] The title should not be confused with *The Best of H.E. Bates: A Selection of Novels and Short Stories* (A 122)

Binding: 8vo, $5\frac{3}{8}$ x $8\frac{1}{4}$ ins. Turquoise cloth; publisher's device blind-stamped on front cover; lettering and a design on spine in blue; all edges cut; white end papers.
     Dust jacket designed by John Alcorn. White; lettered on front cover in black with nine illustrations in colour within single rule borders; spine lettered in black; portrait of the author by Hans Roest, Amsterdam, on back cover with biographical note in black.

Price: $5.75
     Published by Little, Brown and Company in association with The Atlantic Monthly Press and printed in The United States of America.

Contents: The Flame - A Flower Piece - The Mower - Time - The Mill - The Station - The Kimono - Breeze Anstey - The Ox - Colonel Julian - The Lighthouse - The Flag - The Frontier - A Christmas Song - The Major of Hussars - Elaine - The Daffodil Sky - The Good Corn - Country Society - Across the Bay - Chaff in the Wind - The Evolution of Saxby - Go Lovely Rose - The Maker of Coffins - Love in a Wych Elm - Let's Play Soldiers - The Watercress Girl - The Cowslip Field - Great Uncle Crow - The Enchantress - Now Sleeps the Crimson Petal - Where the Cloud Breaks - Lost Ball - Thelma - Mrs Eglantine

Author's Note: 'The earliest of these stories, The Flame, was first published in 1926, having been written a year earlier, when I was twenty; the latest appeared in 1961. The intervening thirty-five years, together with the thirty-five stories I have chosen from that period, therefore give this collection its title, *Seven by Five.** My aim has been to make the book as widely representative of my work as a short-story writer as possible, but I have nevertheless refrained from including any of the war-time stories I wrote under the pseudonym 'Flying Officer X', any of the stories of Uncle Silas and any novellas, since these all belong, in my view, to quite separate categories.'
     *Noted in the American edition as the English title.

A 99   THE FABULOUS MRS V   1964

H.E. BATES | The Fabulous Mrs V | (publisher's device) | London | MICHAEL JOSEPH

Collation: (A)-F^{16} 192 pp, consisting of half-title and publisher's note, ALSO BY H.E. BATES on verso, pp (1–2); title-page, notices of publication and copyright, printer's and binder's imprint on verso, pp (3–4); CONTENTS, verso blank, pp (5–6); text, pp (7)–192.

Binding: 8vo, $5\frac{1}{4}$ x $7\frac{3}{4}$ ins. Deep mauve boards; lettering and publisher's device on spine in gold, single gilt rule dividing the title and author's name; all edges cut; cream end papers.
     Dust jacket designed by Kenneth Farnhill. Design on front cover and spine in pink and white, lettered in green and black; back cover white with reviews of *Seven by Five* in black with title of that book and publisher's device in green.

Price: 16s. net. A total of 9,557 copies were sold.

Set and printed in Great Britain by Unwin Brothers Limited at the Gresham Press, Woking in Spectrum type, ten point leaded, and bound by James Burn at Esher, Surrey.

Contents: And No Birds Sing - The Fabulous Mrs. V - A Couple of Fools - The Ginger-Lily Girl - Afternoon at the Château - A Party for the Girls - The Cat who Sang - The Trespasser - The Diamond Hair-Pin - A Dream of Fair Women - A Nice Friendly Atmosphere - The Lotus Land

A 100 A MOMENT IN TIME 1964

A 100a First English edition

H.E. BATES | A Moment in Time | (publisher's device) | London | MICHAEL JOSEPH

Collation: (A)-F^{16} G^{12} H^{16} 248 pp, consisting of half-title and publisher's note, ALSO BY H.E. BATES on verso pp (1–2); title-page, notices of publication and copyright, printer's, paper-maker's and binder's imprint on verso, pp (3–4); (poem) 'Give them their Life ...', verso blank, pp (5–6); text, pp 7–(248).

Binding: 8vo, 5¼ x 7¾ ins. Deep-blue boards; lettering and publisher's device on spine in gold; all edges cut; white end papers.

Pictorial dust jacket designed by Richard Barton. Author and title lettered on front cover and spine in white; publisher's name on spine in black.

Price: 21s. net. A total of 24,430 copies were sold.

Set and printed in Great Britain by Tonbridge Printers Ltd., Peach Hall Works, Tonbridge, Kent, in Times eleven on thirteen point, on paper made by Henry Bruce at Currie, Midlothian, and bound by James Burn at Esher, Surrey.

Notes: *Publisher's Note* p (1) 'The setting of *A Moment in Time* is Southern England in the summer of 1940, the year of the Battle of Britain ...'

Poem 'Give them their Life', p (5) The poem was written by H.E. Bates when a Squadron Leader in the Royal Air Force and first published in *Air Force Poetry*, edited by John Pudney and Henry Treece (John Lane, The Bodley Head, 1944).

See D 16.

A 100b First American impression 1964

H.E. BATES | A MOMENT | IN TIME | Farrar, Straus and Company New York

Collation: (A-H)^{16} (ii) + 254 pp, consisting of half-title, verso blank, pp (i–ii); ALSO BY H.E. BATES, verso blank, pp (1–2); title-page, Notice of copyright, Library of Congress Catalog Card No. 64-19516, notes of First Printing 1964 and of manufacture in the USA on verso, pp (3–4); (poem), 'Give them their Life ...', verso blank, pp (5–6); text, pp 7–(248); three blank leaves, pp (249–254).

Binding: 8vo, $5\frac{1}{4}$ x 8 ins. Quarter white cloth; deep blue boards; top edges dyed dark red, fore and lower edges cut; blue hair-line end papers.

    Dust jacket designed by Catherine Smolich. Front cover in red, white and blue, lettered in white and black with designs in eight rectangles; spine blue with white lettering; portrait on back cover (by Howard Coster) in black and white with author's name and title in black.

Price: $4.50
    Published by Farrar, Straus and Company, 19 Union Square West, New York 10003, and manufactured in the USA.

A 101   ACHILLES AND THE TWINS   1964

A 101a First English edition

ACHILLES | AND THE | TWINS | by | H.E. BATES | & | CAROL BARKER | DENNIS DOBSON · LONDON (a small part of the coloured frontispiece continued on title-page)

Collation: (AT1)-AT3^8 (48) pp, consisting of first leaf with full page coloured illustration pasted down to form front end paper, pp (1–2); continuation of full page illustration, verso blank, pp (3–4); half-title with coloured illustration, frontispiece full page illustration, pp (5–6); title-page, notices of first publication, copyright of text and illustrations, reservation of rights, printer's and binder's imprints on verso, pp (7–8); text, including coloured illustrations, pp (9–46); last leaf with full-page illustration pasted down to form back end paper, pp (47–48).

Binding: 4to, $8\frac{3}{4}$ x $11\frac{1}{8}$ ins. White boards illustrated in colour with lettering on front cover and along spine in black; all edges cut; no end papers.

    Dust jacket illustrated in colour and lettered in black by Carol Barker and identical with covers.

Price: 15s. net.
    Published by Dobson Books Ltd., 80 Kensington Church Street, London W8. Printed in Great Britain by Taylowe Ltd., Maidenhead. Bound in Great Britain by Dorstel Press Ltd., Harlow.

Notes: This completes the trilogy which began with *Achilles the Donkey* (A 93) and *Achilles and Diana* (A 96).

    Illustrations by Carol Barker: on the covers of the book (repeated on dust jacket), and on pp (2–3 double page), (5), (6), (7), (9), (10–11), (12 full page), (14–15), (17), (18–19 double page), (26), (27), (28–29 double page), (31), (32), (33), (35), (36–37 double page), (38–39), (41 full page), (42), (43), (44–45), (46–47 double page, identical with (2–3)).

A 101b American issue 1965

An issue was prepared for America in 1965, uniform with A 101a. It bore the imprint, 'FRANKLIN-WATTS INC. NEW YORK', the notice of publication stating 'First published in The United States in 1965 by Franklin Watts Inc., 575 Lexington Avenue, New York 22, N.Y.'

Dust jacket identical with first English edition (A 101a).

Price: $3.95

Library of Congress Catalog Card No. 65-10088

A 102   THE WEDDING PARTY   1965

THE | WEDDING PARTY | H.E. BATES | (publisher's device) | London | MICHAEL JOSEPH

Collation: (A)-F^{16} 192 pp, consisting of half-title and publisher's note, ALSO BY H.E. BATES on verso, pp (1–2); title-page, notices of publication and copyright, printer's, paper-maker's and binder's imprint on verso, pp (3–4); CONTENTS, verso blank, pp (5–6); text, pp 7–(192).

Binding: 8vo, $5\frac{1}{8}$ x $7\frac{3}{4}$ ins. Brown boards; lettered on spine in gold with single gilt rule dividing author's name and title, publisher's device in gold; all edges cut; white end papers.

Dust jacket designed by Michael Harvey. Front cover and spine coloured in green and grey-blue; author's name on front cover and spine in yellow, title in white; publisher's name on spine in black; back cover white with reviews of *The Fabulous Mrs V* and *Seven by Five*; author's name and titles in brown, reviews in black.

Price: 21s. net. 8,520 copies were sold.

Set and printed in Great Britain by Tonbridge Printers Ltd, Peach Hall Works, Tonbridge, Kent, in Bembo twelve on fourteen point, on paper made by Henry Bruce at Currie, Midlothian, and bound by James Burn at Esher, Surrey.

Contents: The Winter Sound - The Wedding Party - Early One Morning - Squiff - The Primrose Place - Shandy Lil - The Sun of December - The Courtship - A Teetotal Tale - The Picnic - The Old Eternal - Captain Poop-Deck's Paradise - Coconut Radio

A 103   THE DISTANT HORNS OF SUMMER   1967

H.E. BATES | The | Distant Horns | of Summer | (publisher's device) | London | MICHAEL JOSEPH

Collation: (A)-H^{16} I^2 I*^{10} 280 pp, consisting of half-title, ALSO BY H.E. BATES on verso, pp (1–2); title-page, notices of publication and copyright, printer's and binder's imprint, on verso, pp (3–4); text, pp 5–(277); blank p (278); blank (279–280).

Binding: 8vo, $5\frac{1}{8}$ x $7\frac{3}{4}$ ins. Blue boards; lettering and publisher's device on spine in silver; all edges cut; cream end papers.

Pictorial dust jacket designed by Broom. Lynne, front and back depicting a pastoral scene in colours. Lettered on front cover and on spine in white, with single rule in white dividing the author's name and title.

Price: 25s. net. A total of 14,624 copies were sold.

Set and printed in Great Britain by Tonbridge Printers Ltd., Peach Hall Works, Tonbridge, Kent, in Bembo eleven on twelve point, and bound by James Burn at Esher, Surrey.

A 104   THE FOUR BEAUTIES   1968

H.E. BATES | The Four Beauties | (publisher's device) | London | MICHAEL JOSEPH

Collation: (A)-F^{16} 192 pp, consisting of half-title, ALSO BY H.E. BATES on verso, pp (1–2); title-page, notices of publication and copyright, printer's and binder's imprint on verso, pp (3–4); CONTENTS, verso blank, pp (5–6); text, pp 7–(192).

Binding: 8vo, $5\frac{1}{8}$ x $7\frac{1}{4}$ ins. Magenta boards; lettering, with a star and publisher's device on spine in gold; all edges cut; white end papers.

Dust jacket designed by Michael Harvey. Front cover and spine purple, lettered in white and light blue. Back cover plain white.

Price: 25s. net. Published March 1968. A total of 9,287 copies were sold.

Set and printed in Great Britain by Tonbridge Printers Ltd., Peach Hall Works, Tonbridge, Kent, in Bembo twelve on fourteen point, and bound by James Burn at Esher, Surrey.

Contents: The Simple Life - The Four Beauties - The Chords of Youth - The White Wind

Notes: 'ALSO BY H.E. BATES' p (2). Errors, each repeated in future books by H.E. Bates: 'Short Stories': the title of 'The Flying Goat' was printed as 'The Flying Coat'.

'Essays': the title of 'In The Heart Of The Country' was printed as 'The Heart Of The Country'. This error had been made in previous volumes.

For the title of 'O More Than Happy Countryman', an exclamation mark had been included to read 'O! More Than Happy Countryman'. This error had also been made in previous volumes.

A 105   THE WHITE ADMIRAL   1968

THE | WHITE | ADMIRAL | by | H.E. BATES | illustrated by | PEGGY
CHAPMAN | London | DENNIS DOBSON

Collation: (A-D)⁸ 64 pp, consisting of half-title, full-page colour illustration as
frontispiece, pp (1–2); title-page, notices of copyright in the text and illustrations,
reservation of rights, publisher's, printer's and filmsetter's imprints with SBN 234
779543 on verso, pp (3–4); Dedicated To RICHARD and JONATHAN who got
stung, colour illustration and part list of THE CHARACTERS on verso, pp (5–6);
continuation of THE CHARACTERS, colour illustration, verso blank, pp (7–8);
fly title, full-page colour illustration on verso, pp (9–10); text, including colour
illustrations, pp 11–64.

Binding: 8vo, 6½ x 8¾ ins. Pictorial boards with central panel in deep blue;
front and back covers divided by single white ruled borders to make three panels;
coloured illustrations of butterflies in top and bottom panels; centre panel lettered
in white with illustration of single butterfly in white and blue; lettering on spine
in three sections within blue and white single-rule borders; names of the author,
illustrator and publisher in black against white background; title in white against
central blue background.
      Dust jacket identical with covers.

Price: 18s. net.
      First published in Great Britain in 1968 by Dobson Books Ltd., of 80 Kensington
Church Street, London W8. Published in the Dominion of Canada by General
Publishing Co. Ltd., Don Mills, Ontario. Printed in Great Britain by Taylowe Ltd,
Maidenhead. Filmset by The European Printing Corporation Limited, Dublin,
Ireland.

Notes: Illustrations in colour by Peggy Chapman on covers and dust jacket and
on pp (2, full-page frontispiece), (6), (7), (10, full-page), (15, full-page), (23 full-
page), 26, 27, (30), (39, full-page), 42, 43, (46–47 double-page), 50, 51, (54–55,
double-page), (59, full-page), (63, full-page).
      The dedication is to the author's two sons.

A 106   THE WILD CHERRY TREE   1968

H.E. BATES | The Wild Cherry Tree | (publisher's device) | London | MICHAEL
JOSEPH

Collation: (A)-G¹⁶ 224 pp, consisting of half-title, ALSO BY H.E. BATES on
verso, pp (1–2); title-page, notices of publication and copyright, ISBN 7181 0604
0, printer's and binder's imprint on verso, pp (3–4); CONTENTS, verso blank, pp
(5–6); text, pp 7–(219); blank p (220); two blank leaves, pp (221–224).

Binding: 8vo, $5\frac{1}{8}$ x $7\frac{3}{4}$ ins. Light-blue boards; lettering, with star and publisher's device on spine, in gold; all edges cut; white end papers.

Dust jacket designed by Michael Harvey. Pale blue overall, mottled with white; author's name on back of covers and along spine in dark blue; publisher's name on spine in dark blue; title on front and back of cover and along spine in sage green.

Price: 25s. net. A total of 7,163 copies were sold.

Set and printed in Great Britain by Tonbridge Printers Ltd., Peach Hall Works, Tonbridge, Kent in Bembo twelve on fourteen point, and bound by James Burn at Esher, Surrey.

Contents: Halibut Jones - The Wild Cherry Tree - Some Other Spring - The World Upside-Down - How Vainly Men Themselves Amaze - The First Day of Christmas - The Black Magnolia - Love Me Little, Love Me Long - Same Time, Same Place - The Middle of Nowhere

A 107   THE VANISHED WORLD   1969
An Autobiography
Volume One

A 107a First English edition

H.E. BATES | THE | VANISHED | WORLD | An Autobiography | VOLUME ONE | Illustrated by John Ward | (publisher's device) | LONDON | MICHAEL JOSEPH

Collation: (A)-M⁸ 192 pp, consisting of half-title, ALSO BY H.E. BATES on verso, pp (1-2); title-page, notice of publication, notice of copyright and reservation of rights, ISBN 7181 0430 7, printer's and binder's imprint on verso, pp (3-4); text, including illustrations, pp 5-(189); blank p (190); blank pp (191-192).

Binding: 8vo, $5\frac{7}{8}$ x 9 ins. Blue cloth; author's name and title lettered along spine and divided by star, all in gold; publisher's name lettered at foot of spine in gold; top edges dyed pink; fore and lower edges cut; yellow ochre end papers illustrated in black.

Dust jacket designed by John Ward; pictorial illustration in colour overall; lettered on front cover and spine in red.

Price: 50s. net. £2.50

Set and printed in Great Britain by Tonbridge Printers Ltd., Peach Hall Works, Tonbridge, Kent, in Baskerville eleven on thirteen point, and bound by James Burn at Esher, Surrey.

Notes: Illustrations by John Ward: in colour on dust jacket and in black on front and back end papers; also on pp 6, 7, 9, 10, 11, 13, 14, 16, 18, 20, (23, full-page), 24, 27, (31, full-page), (35, full-page) 37, 40, 41, 43, 44, 46, 49, 52, (55, full-page), 56, 57, (59, full-page), 61, 63, 65, 66, 69, 72, 75, 80, 84, (89, full-page), 97, 99, 103,

(110, full-page), 120 continued (121, full-page), 123, 132, 138, 140, 142, 153, 155, 157, 161, (169, full-page), (173, full-page), 174, (181, full-page), 182, 186, (189).
The author was paid an outright fee of £5,000 for volume and serial rights.
The manuscript is owned by the Bates family.

A 107b First American edition 1969

THE | VANISHED | WORLD | An Autobiography | VOLUME ONE | H.E. BATES | Illustrated by John Ward | UNIVERSITY OF MISSOURI PRESS | COLUMBIA

Collation: (A-F)^{16} (ii) + 190 pp, consisting of half-title, verso blank, pp (i–ii); title-page, notices of first publication in Great Britain and copyright, American publisher's imprint, SBN 8262-0096-6 and Library of Congress Catalog Card No. 77-130667, note of manufacturer in The United States of America, pp (1–2); FORE-WORD TO THE AMERICAN EDITION (WILLIAM PEDEN), pp (3–4); text, pp 5–189; blank p (190).

Binding: 8vo, $5\frac{7}{8}$ x $8\frac{7}{8}$ ins. Dark-blue cloth; lettered along spine in gold; all edges cut; brown end papers.
Pictorial dust jacket in colour designed by John Ward. Yellow ochre, illustrations and lettering in black.

Price: $6.50
Manufactured in The United States of America. *Foreword to the first American edition by Dr William Peden:*
'THE VANISHED WORLD, the first volume of Bates's autobiography, is a recreation of the most memorable events of the author's first twenty years; his childhood as the sensitive son of parents who had gone to work for a few shillings a week before they were twelve; his earliest working-class schooling ("they make me sit next to a boy who stinks"); his falling in and out of calf-love at the age of fifteen; the real beginnings of his creative life, encouraged by a sympathetic schoolmaster and subsequently nourished by his discovery of Chekhov and Conrad and D.H. Lawrence and Stephen Crane; his unsuccessful ventures into the world of business; his meeting the girl who was later to become his wife; his rejection of the religious orthodoxy of his parents; and finally, after many heart-testing literary disappointments and failures, the acceptance of his novel THE TWO SISTERS. THE VANISHED WORLD is a small gem, a book to be cherished, masterly of its kind. In it H.E. Bates has isolated a moment in time and place, and captured it for ever.'

A 108   A LITTLE OF WHAT YOU FANCY   1970

H.E. BATES | (short swelled rule) | A Little of | What You Fancy | (publisher's device) | LONDON | MICHAEL JOSEPH

Collation: (A)-G^{16} (iv) + 220 pp, consisting of two blank leaves, pp (i–iv); half-title, Also by H.E. Bates on verso, pp (1–2); title-page, notices of publication, copyright and reservation of rights, (ISBN) 7181 0764 0, printer's, paper supplier's and binder's imprints on verso, pp (3–4); text, pp 5–(216); two blank leaves, pp (217–220).

Binding: 8vo, $5\frac{1}{8}$ x $7\frac{3}{4}$ ins. Moss-green boards; lettering, with design and publisher's device on spine in gold; all edges cut; white end papers.
      Coloured pictorial dust jacket designed by Oliver Elms. Lettered on front cover in white and black.

Price: 25s. net. £1.25. 15,052 copies were sold.
      Printed in Great Britain by Tonbridge Printers Ltd., Peach Hall Works, Tonbridge, Kent, in twelve on thirteen point Bembo, on paper supplied by P.F. Bingham Ltd., and bound by James Burn, Royal Mills, Esher, Surrey.

A 109   THE TRIPLE ECHO   1970

(drawing in mauve) | THE TRIPLE ECHO | by H.E. BATES | DRAWINGS BY RON CLARKE | Michael Joseph : London

Collation: (A)-E⁸ 80 pp, consisting of recto blank, ALSO BY H.E. BATES on verso, pp (1–2); half-title, verso blank, pp (3–4); title-page, notices of publication, copyright and reservation of rights, ISBN 7181 0814 0, printer's, paper supplier's and binder's imprint on verso, pp (5–6); text, including illustrations, pp 7–(80).

Binding: 8vo, $5\frac{1}{4}$ x $7\frac{3}{4}$ ins. Cream and grey designed boards; the author, title and publisher lettered along spine and divided by two stars, all in gold on a brown background; all edges cut; mauve end papers.
      Mauve dust jacket; lettered on front cover in black and red with enlarged drawing in black from p 15; lettered on spine in black and red; back cover advertises *The Blossoming World* (title in red), with reviews of *The Vanished World*, all in black.

Price: 16s. net. £0.80. A total of 8,710 copies were sold.
      Printed in Great Britain by Tonbridge Printers Limited, Peach Hall Works, Tonbridge, Kent, in twelve on thirteen point Bembo, on paper supplied by P.F. Bingham Ltd., and bound by James Burn, Royal Mills, Esher, Surrey.

Notes: Illustrations by Ron Clarke: On the title-page, p (5), in mauve, and in black and white on pp 7, 15, 21, 23, 27, 31, 34, 39, 51, 53, 57, 61, 72, (80).
      The drawing on p 15 is repeated and enlarged on front of dust jacket.
      The novella was first published in *The Daily Telegraph Magazine* as a three-part serial on 5, 12 and 19 December 1969.
      The World in Ripeness (A 114) pp 113–14:
      '...I have now written some twenty novellas, the most recent being *The Triple Echo*, itself a supreme example of the form's "notorious difficulty".
      '*The Triple Echo* in fact took precisely twenty-five years to write, its genesis having begun in the darker days of the war, in 1943, its completion coming in 1968 - shades of "the path of art endlessly difficult" of which Edward Garnett had warned me long ago in his preface to *The Two Sisters* (A 3). I will not of course

mislead the reader by pretending that every day of that twenty-five years was spent in wrestling with that one particular story; it is enough to say that the challenge, the problem and the complexity were always there, constantly kicking away at the womb of the mind, the story apparently unwilling to be born but ever restless in its tireless determination finally to come to life.

'Any writer of fiction will tell you that inevitably, from time to time, he finds it necessary to invent a new character to do the work of unravelling his narrative for him. In the case of *The Triple Echo* the exact reverse was true. What had so long inhibited the birth of my story was not the lack of a character but the fact that, as I belatedly discovered, I had one character too many. This superfluous character having been removed, light immediately flooded in on a canvas that had been so long irremediably dark, and in a mere three weeks the story was extracted from the womb it had apparently been so reluctant to leave. "The path of art endlessly difficult" indeed.'

The Triple Echo was made into a film, starring Oliver Reed and Glenda Jackson; the première was held in November 1972.

On 29 August 1969, after a friendship of fifty years, Bates again turned to his old schoolmaster, Edmund Kirby, for more advice. This time he was seeking guidance on ballistics – the use of the shot-gun by Alice Charlesworth in the story (pp 79–80).

A 110   THE BLOSSOMING WORLD   1971
An Autobiography
Volume Two

A 110a First English edition

H.E. BATES | THE | BLOSSOMING | WORLD | An Autobiography | VOLUME TWO | Illustrated by John Ward | (publisher's device) | LONDON | MICHAEL JOSEPH

Collation: (A)-K^8 L^4 M^8 184 pp, consisting of half-title, ALSO BY H.E. BATES on verso, pp (1–2); title-page, notices of publication, copyright and reservation of rights, ISBN 7181 0795 0, printer's and binder's imprint on verso, pp (3–4); text, including illustrations, pp 5–(182); blank pp (183–184).

Binding: 8vo, 5$\frac{7}{8}$ x 9 ins. Dark-brown cloth; author's name and title lettered along spine and divided by a star, all in gold; publisher's name at foot of spine in gold; top edges dyed orange; fore and lower edges cut; orange end papers illustrated in black.

Dust jacket designed by John Ward; pictorial illustration in colour overall; lettered on front cover and spine in black.

Price: £2.50 net. 50s. Published October 1971.

Set and printed in Great Britain by Tonbridge Printers Ltd., Peach Hall Works, Tonbridge, Kent, in Baskerville eleven on thirteen point, and bound by James Burn at Esher, Surrey.

Notes: Illustrations by John Ward. In colour on dust jacket and in black on both end papers; also on pp 6, (9, full-page), (13 full-page), 15, 33, 36, 38, 40, 55, 59, 65, 70, 72, 73, 75, 77, 78, 87, 92, 94, 100, 103, 105, (107, full-page), 109, 113, 115, 116, (119, full-page), 122, (124 full-page), 128, 132, 145, 150, 152, 154, 159, 164, 169, 173, (182).

The author was paid an outright fee of £5,000 for volume and serial rights.

The manuscript is owned by the Bates family.

A 110b First American edition 1971

THE | BLOSSOMING | WORLD | An Autobiography | VOLUME TWO | H.E. BATES | Illustrated by John Ward | UNIVERSITY OF MISSOURI PRESS | COLUMBIA

Collation: (A-K)^8 (L)^4 (M)^8 184 pp, consisting of half-title, verso blank, pp (1–2); title-page, notices of first publication in Great Britain and of copyright, American publisher's imprint, ISBN 0-8262-0106-7 and Library of Congress Catalog Card No. 71-149009, note of manufacture in United States of America on verso, pp (3–4); text, pp 5–(182); blank pp (183–184).

Binding: 8vo, 5$\frac{7}{8}$ x 8$\frac{7}{8}$ ins. Dark-blue cloth; lettered along spine in gold; all edges cut; blue end papers.

Pictorial dust jacket in colour designed by John Ward. Blue-grey, illustrations and lettering in black.

Price: $6.50

Manufactured in The United States of America

A 111   DULCIMA   1971

H.E. BATES | (single ornamental rule) | Dulcima | (publisher's device) | PENGUIN BOOKS | IN ASSOCIATION WITH | MICHAEL JOSEPH

Collation: (A.-1)-D.-4^{12} 96 pp, consisting of publisher's name, half-title and biographical note, verso blank, pp (1–2); title-page, publisher's imprint, note of publications containing 'Dulcima', maker's and printer's imprint, note of conditions of sale, pp (3–4); dedication 'To W. SOMERSET MAUGHAM', verso blank, pp (5–6); text, pp 7–(90); publisher's advertisement, verso blank, pp (91–92); publisher's list of books by Laurie Lee, L.P. Hartley and H.E. Bates, pp (93–96).

Binding: 8vo, 4$\frac{3}{8}$ x 7$\frac{1}{8}$ ins. Paper covers; front cover illustrated in colour with a scene from the EMI film production, with white and blue lettering and publisher's device in orange, black and white; back cover lettered in blue and white with publisher's device in orange, black and white; orange spine with lettering and publisher's device in black and white.

Price: United Kingdom 20p. Australia $0.70. New Zealand $0.70. South Africa R0.50. Canada $0.85

Fiction ISBN 0 14 00.3380 7
Made and printed in Great Britain by Hazell Watson & Viney Ltd., Aylesbury,
Bucks. Set in Linotype Juliana.

Notes: 'Dulcima' was one of three novellas first published as a collection in *The Nature of Love* (A 79).
In 1972 EMI Film Productions released the film version of 'Dulcima', starring Carol White and John Mills, with Stuart Wilson. It was adapted for the screen and directed also by Frank Nesbitt, produced by Basil Rayburn.

A 112   A LOVE OF FLOWERS   1971

A Love of Flowers | H.E. BATES | Illustrations by Pauline Ellison | MICHAEL JOSEPH

Collation: (A-E)^{16} 160 pp, consisting of half-title, ALSO BY H.E. BATES on verso, pp (1-2); recto blank, frontispiece, pp (3-4); title-page, notices of publication, copyright and reservation of rights, ISBN 7181 0575 3, printer's and binder's imprint on verso, pp (5-6); Preface, pp 7-10; fly title, verso blank, pp (11-12); text, including illustrations, pp 13-155 (blank pages, pp (32) and (60); Index, pp 156-160.

Binding: 8vo, $5\frac{3}{4}$ x $8\frac{3}{4}$ ins. Dark brown boards; lettered on spine in gold with three ornamental designs in black; all edges cut; fawn end papers.
Dust jacket; front cover and spine carries photograph in colour of the author's home and garden at Little Chart by Iain Macmillan; lettering on front cover and along spine in white; back cover white with reviews of *The Vanished World* in black.

Price: £2 net. 40s. Published June 1971. 5,759 copies were sold.
Photoset and printed in Great Britain by BAS Printers Limited, Wallop, Hampshire, in Apollo twelve on fourteen point and bound by James Burn at Esher, Surrey.

Notes: Illustrations by Pauline Ellison in black and white: frontispiece, p (4) and pp 13, 14, 15, (17, full-page), 20, 21, 23, 25, 26, 27, 29, 36, 38, 39, 41, 42, 44, 46, (47, full-page), 49, (51, full-page), 53, 55, 56, (58, full-page), (65, full-page), 66, (69, full-page), 73, (78, full-page), (79, full-page), 98, 99, 105, 113, 115, 117, 118, 119, 121, (123, full-page), 124, 127, 128, 133, 135, 136, 137, 138, 139, 148, 149, 150, 155.
Publisher's Note: 'In achieving a long-cherished ambition to write a gardening book H.E. Bates has taken for his starting-point a serious illness that overtook him in 1966, when serious illness threatened for a time to end not only his career as a writer but all activities in the way of gardening, his major source of recreation.
'Happily these fears were unfounded. Nevertheless he feels strongly that eventual recovery had as much to do with the therapeutic value of his garden as with medicine. This book is therefore not merely one of gardening advice, though it is essentially sound and practical, describing as it does a host of plants, exotic as well as hardy, long-loved as well as uncommon, which the author grows in his garden in the heart of Kent. It is also highly personal and perhaps, in parts, controversial. In

embracing the entire garden year, from the first winter crocuses in December to the last glimpse of roses in November, it is an aesthetic as well as instructive testament, full of enthusiasm, good sense, good humour, much horticultural knowledge and an unashamed joy in the miracle of leaf, flower and earth.'

The manuscript is owned by the Bates family.

A 113   THE SONG OF THE WREN   1972

THE SONG OF THE WREN | by | H.E. BATES | (publisher's device) | London | MICHAEL JOSEPH

Collation: (A)-D^{16} E^4 E^{16} 168 pp, consisting of half-title, ALSO BY H.E. BATES on verso, pp (1–2); title-page, notices of publication, copyright and reservation of rights, ISBN 7181 1012 9, printer's, paper supplier's and binder's imprint on verso, pp (3–4); (Contents), verso blank, pp (5–6); fly title, The Song of the Wren, verso blank, pp (7–8); text, pp 9–17; blank page, p (18); fly title, The Dam, verso blank, pp (19–20); text, pp 21–58; fly title, The Man Who Loved Squirrels, verso blank, pp (59–60); text, pp 61–133; blank page, p (134); fly title, The Tiger Moth, verso blank, pp (135–136); text, pp 137–155; blank page, p (156); fly title, Oh! Sweeter Than The Berry, verso blank, pp (157–158), text, pp 159–168.

Binding: 8vo, 5 x 7$\frac{3}{4}$ ins. Deep-orange boards; lettered along spine in gold; all edges cut; white end papers.

White dust jacket designed and front cover illustrated in colour by Joanna Carey. All lettering in black.

Price: £1.90 net. Published 30 May 1972. A total of 7,620 copies were sold.

Set and printed in Great Britain by Tonbridge Printers Ltd., Peach Hall Works, Tonbridge, Kent, in Bembo twelve on fourteen point, on paper supplied by P.F. Bingham Ltd., and bound by Dorstel Press, Harlow, Essex.

Contents: The Song of the Wren - The Dam - The Man Who Loved Squirrels - The Tiger Moth - Oh! Sweeter than the Berry

Notes: The manuscript is owned by the Bates family.

A 114   THE WORLD IN RIPENESS   1972
An Autobiography
Volume Three

H.E. BATES | THE | WORLD | IN RIPENESS | An Autobiography | VOLUME THREE | Illustrated by John Ward | (publisher's device) | LONDON | MICHAEL JOSEPH

Collation: (A)-E-(F)-H⁸ I⁴ K⁸ 152 pp, consisting of half-title, ALSO BY H.E. BATES on verso, pp (1–2); (an additional buff-coloured leaf bound in here, recto blank, full-page illustration of the author in black as a frontispiece); title-page, notices of publication, copyright and reservation of rights, acknowledgements for quotation from R.F. Delderfield's *Overture for Beginners*, printer's, paper supplier's and binder's imprint on verso, pp (3–4); text, including illustrations, pp 5–152.

Binding: 8vo, 5⅞ x 9 ins. Dark-green cloth; author's name and title lettered along spine and divided by a star, all in gold; publisher's name lettered at foot of spine in gold; top edges dyed yellow; fore and lower edges cut; buff end papers illustrated in black.
    Dust jacket designed by John Ward; pictorial illustration in colour overall; lettered on front cover and on spine in black.
    ISBN 7181 1028 5 (printed only on dust jacket).

Price: £3.00 net. Published September 1972
    Set and printed in Great Britain by Tonbridge Printers Ltd., Peach Hall Works, Tonbridge, Kent, in Baskerville eleven on thirteen point on paper supplied by P.F. Bingham Ltd., and bound by James Burn at Esher, Surrey.

Notes: Illustrations by John Ward: on both end papers and a frontispiece on the additional buff-coloured leaf bound in before the title-page, and on pp 5, 6, 8, 10, 12, 14, 25, 26, 40, (45, full-page), 47, 49, 50, 52, 53, 54, 59, 62, 63, 65, 68, 71, (75, full-page), (81, full-page), 83, 88, 90, 92, (94, full-page), (96, full-page), 103, 106, 117, 118, 121, 126, 129, 131, 133, 145, 146, (149, full-page).
    The manuscript is owned by the Bates family.
    The author was paid an outright fee of £5,000 for volume and serial rights.
    The first American edition was published in 1972 by the University of Missouri Press, Columbia.

A 115   A FOUNTAIN OF FLOWERS   1974

published posthumously

A Fountain of Flowers | H.E. BATES | Colour Plates by Patrick Matthews | MICHAEL JOSEPH

Collation: (A-F)⁸ 96 pp + (16 pp colour plates bound in) consisting of blank leaf pasted down to form front end paper, pp (1–2); recto blank, ALSO BY H.E. BATES on verso, pp (3–4); half-title, verso blank, pp (5–6); title-page, notices of publication, copyright, reservation of rights, ISBN 0 7181 1158 3, printer's and binder's imprint on verso, pp (7–8); Preface, pp 9–11; text, pp 12–91; blank page, p (92); blank leaf, pp (93–94); blank leaf pasted down to form back end paper, pp (95–96).

Binding: 8vo, 6⅛ x 9¼ ins. Dark brown boards; author's name and title lettered along spine in gold; publisher's name lettered at foot of spine in gold; all edges cut; no separate end papers.

Dust jacket with colour photograph on front cover and spine by Patrick Matthews (spelt 'Mathews' on front flap); lettering on front cover and along spine in black; publisher's name at foot of spine in white; reviews of *A Love of Flowers* on back cover in black with title in blue.

Price: £3.25 net. A total of 3,672 copies were sold.

Printed in Great Britain by Redwood Burn Limited, Trowbridge and Esher and bound by Dorstel Press, Harlow.

Notes: Colour plates by Patrick Matthews: four full-page, between pp 24–25; two, opposite p 32; two, opposite p 33; two full-page and four others between pp 40–41; two, opposite p 48; two, opposite p 49; two, opposite p 64; two, opposite p 65; four, opposite p 80; six, opposite p 81.

Publisher's Note 'H.E. Bates, who completed this book shortly before his death in 1974, wrote more than half a hundred books: novels, short stories, autobiography, essays and criticism. Through all of them runs the thread of his love of the land, of gardens and of all beautiful things that can be grown.

'*A Fountain of Flowers* is a long, very personal essay on the pleasures and adventures of the author's own gardening life. He had a questing eye for a new plant, a new idea, a great love of colour, and a talent for achieving it in his Kentish garden through all the twelve months of the year.'

A 116   THE GRAPES OF PARADISE   1974
Eight Novellas

H.E. Bates | The Grapes of Paradise | Eight Novellas | Penguin Books | in association with Michael Joseph

Collation: (G.P.-1) G.P.-16^{10} 320 pp, consisting of publisher, half-title and biographical note, verso blank, pp (1–2); title-page, publisher's imprint, note of previous publications, notice of copyright, printer's imprint, conditions of sale on verso, pp (3–4); Contents, verso blank, pp (5–6); text, pp 7–(316); publisher's advertisement and device, verso blank, pp (317–318); short list of other books by H.E. Bates, pp (319–320).

Binding: 8vo, 4$\frac{3}{8}$ x 7$\frac{1}{8}$ ins. Paper covers; front cover illustrated with photograph in colour by Elisabeth Novick, lettering in white and publisher's device in orange, black and white; cream spine with author's name, ISBN number and publisher's device in black; back cover black with lettering in white and publisher's device in orange, black and white; all edges cut; no end papers.

Price: United Kingdom 90p : Canada $2.50

ISBN 0 14 00.3820 5. Made and printed in Great Britain by Hazell Watson & Viney Ltd, Aylesbury, Bucks. Set in Monotype Times.

Contents: Death of a Huntsman - Night Run to the West - Summer in Salander - The Queen of Spain Fritillary - An Aspidistra in Babylon - A Month by the Lake - A Prospect of Orchards - The Grapes of Paradise

Notes: The same title, *The Grapes of Paradise*, was given to the American edition of *An Aspidistra in Babylon* (A 89) which contained the four novellas: An Aspidistra in Babylon, A Month by the Lake, A Prospect of Orchards, The Grapes of Paradise. The first four short novels in the Contents above were first published as a collection in *Death of a Huntsman* in England and as *Summer in Salander* in America (A 83a and b).

A 117   THE GOOD CORN and other stories   1974

LONGMAN IMPRINT BOOKS | The Good Corn | and other stories by | H.E. Bates | selected and edited by | Geoffrey Halson, M.A. | Head of the English Department at Hounsdown School | (publisher's device) | Longman

Collation: (A-F)^{16} (G)^8 x + 198 pp, consisting of half-title, titles of Longman Imprint Books and Companion LP Records on verso, pp (i–ii); title-page, publisher's imprints, notices of copyright and publication, ISBN 0 582 23335 6, Acknowledgements, filmsetter's and printer's imprint on verso, pp (iii–iv); Contents, verso blank, pp (v–vi); Editor's Introduction, pp vii–ix; blank p (x); text, pp 1–151; Note on the stories, points for discussion and suggestions for further reading, pp 152–185; Other writings by H.E. Bates, pp 186–191; List of books recommended, pp 192–194; two blank leaves, pp (195–198).

Binding: 8vo, 4$\frac{3}{4}$ x 7$\frac{1}{2}$ ins. Paper covers illustrating pastoral scene in orange and pink; title, publisher's imprint and author's name lettered in black within black-lined oval design on front and back cover; title and author's name lettered along spine in black on white background followed by publisher's imprint in white on black background; all edges cut; no end papers.
   The publishers state that 5,000+ copies of the book had been sold when it went out of print in 1984.
   Filmset in Hong Kong by T.P. Graphic Arts Services. Printed in Hong Kong by Yu Luen Offset Printing Factory Limited.

Contents: Editor's Introduction; The Stories: Love in a Wych Elm - Let's Play Soldiers - Every Bullet Has Its Billet - The Station - Château Bougainvillaca - Time to Kill - The Loved One - The Ox - The Good Corn - Mr Penfold - The Maker of Coffins - The Little Jeweller - Where the Cloud Breaks - Colonel Julian - Note on the stories, points for discussion and suggestions for further reading - Other writings by H.E. Bates - List of books recommended.

A 118   H.E. BATES   1975

H.E. Bates | edited by | ALAN CATTELL | HARRAP | (publisher's device) | LONDON

Collation: (A-F)^{16} 192 pp, consisting of THE PEGASUS LIBRARY with half-title, frontispiece, pp (1–2); title-page, notices of publication, copyright and reservation of rights, ISBN 0 245 52744 3, photosetter's, printer's and binder's imprint on verso, pp (3–4); Contents, The Pegasus Library titles and acknowledgements on verso, pp (5–6); Introduction, verso blank, pp (7–8); text, pp 9–171; For Discussion, pp 172–178; H.E. Bates - His Life, pp 179–182; H.E. Bates - His Work, pp 183–188; Further Reading, pp 189–190; Bibliography, pp (191)–192.

Binding: 8vo, 4¾ x 7 ins. Moss-green limp linen covers with design in brown incorporating publisher's device; The Pegasus Library in white and author's name in black on front cover; The Pegasus Library in white with Harrap and ISBN number in black on back cover; title lettered along spine in black; all edges cut; no end papers.

Photoset by North Herts Photosetters Ltd., Stevenage, printed by Redwood Burn Limited, Trowbridge and Esher and bound at the Pitman Press, Bath.

Contents: Introduction - How Vainly Men Themselves Amaze - Nina - And No Birds Sing - The Earth - Let's Play Soldiers - The Revelation - Queenie White - Squiff - A Threshing Day for Esther - A Couple of Fools - The Frontier - For Discussion - H.E. Bates : His Life - H.E. Bates : His Work - Further Reading - Bibliography

Notes: The frontispiece is a drawing of the author by John Ward.

A 119   THE POISON LADIES   1976
& OTHER STORIES

Literature for Life Series | General Editor : Kenyon Calthrop | THE POISON LADIES | & OTHER STORIES | H.E. Bates | Selected by Mike Poulton with an introduction by | John L. Foster | Illustrated by Kathy Wyatt | (publisher's device) WHEATON a member of the Pergamon group

Collation: (T.P.L.-A)-T.P.L.-G^8 viii + 104 pp, consisting of recto blank, frontispiece, pp (i–ii); title-page, publisher's imprints, notice of copyright, acknowledgements, reservation of rights, notice of First edition, printer's imprint ISBN 0 08 020546 1 on verso, pp (iii–iv); Contents, verso blank, pp (v–vi); Introduction, pp (vii–viii); text, pp 1–104.

Binding: 8vo, 5¾ x 8¼ ins. Limp linen covers; colour photography of Susan Fleetwood on front cover with lettering in white and yellow; greenish-buff back cover and spine lettered in black; all edges cut; no end papers.

No dust jacket.

Price: £1.75. 7,500 copies were printed. Printed in Great Britain by A. Wheaton & Co., Exeter.

Contents: The Poison Ladies - The Cowslip Field - The Watercress Girl - Great Uncle Crow - Harvest Moon - The Ox - Cut and Come Again - The Mower - Where the Cloud Breaks - The Queen of Spain Fritillary - The Beauty of the Dead

Notes: Illustration by Kathy Wyatt is full-page frontispiece, p (ii).
Photograph on front cover from Granada Television's production of *The Watercress Girl* (A 88), Country Matters series.

A 120   THE YELLOW MEADS   1976
             OF ASPHODEL

THE YELLOW MEADS | OF ASPHODEL | by | H.E. BATES | (publisher's device) | LONDON | MICHAEL JOSEPH

Collation: (A)-D^{16} 128 pp, consisting of half-title, ALSO BY H.E. BATES on verso, pp (1–2); title-page, notices of publication and copyright, reservation of rights, ISBN 0 7181 1499 X, printer's and binder's imprint on verso, pp (3–4); (Contents), verso blank, pp (5–6); fly title, The Proposal, verso blank, pp (7–8); text, pp 9–18; fly title, The Yellow Meads of Asphodel, verso blank, pp (19–20); text, pp 21–40 (three stars at foot of pp 33 and 38); fly title, A Taste of Blood, verso blank, pp (41–42); text, pp 43–59 (three stars at foot of p 53); blank page, p (60); fly title, The Love Letters of Miss Maitland, verso blank, pp (61–62); text, pp 63–80 (three stars at foot of p 72); fly title, The Lap of Luxury, verso blank, pp (81–82); text, pp 83–103; blank page, p (104); fly title, Loss of Pride, verso blank, pp 105–106; text, pp 107–114; fly title, The House by the River, verso blank, pp (115–116); text, pp 117–127; blank p (128).

Binding: 8vo, 4⅞ x 7¾ ins. Dark green boards; lettering of author's name and title along spine in gold; publisher's name in gold at foot of spine; all edges cut; white end papers.
White dust jacket with overall floral illustration in green and yellow by Richard Reid; front cover and spine lettered in black.

Price: £3.50 net. Published August 1976. A total of 5,306 copies were sold
Printed in Great Britain by Hollen Press Ltd at Slough and bound by Dorstel Press at Harlow.

Contents: The Proposal - The Yellow Meads of Asphodel - A Taste of Blood - The Love Letters of Miss Maitland - The Lap of Luxury - Loss of Pride - The House by the River

Notes: *Publisher's note:* 'The last and posthumous collection of stories by H.E. Bates contains seven works which between them exemplify most facets of his talent. Here is a story about Uncle Silas, the forerunner of the fabulously successful Pop Larkin series; a story of Miss Shuttleworth, H.E. Bates's last great comic invention, whose portrait he would certainly have developed had he lived; stories set in the Midlands, and in the sunlight and exotic flora of his beloved south of France; and a modern tale of young hooligans on the road. Nothing of service life, or of the south seas, but a wide range for all that, and one to remind readers of a great storyteller.'
The Yellow Meads of Asphodel (A 121) was published as a single story in a limited edition of 350 copies in August 1976 to celebrate the fortieth anniversary of Michael Joseph Limited, 52 Bedford Square, London WC1.

A 121   THE YELLOW MEADS OF   1976
**   ASPHODEL (the single story)**

H.E. Bates | THE YELLOW MEADS | OF ASPHODEL | WITH DRAWINGS
BY | JOHN WARD | (drawing in brown) | MICHAEL JOSEPH : LONDON

Collation: (A)-D⁴ 32 pp, consisting of half-title, verso blank, pp (1–2); title-page,
notice of limitation and publication, printer's, paper supplier's and binder's imprint,
notice of copyright on verso, pp (3–4); blank p (5); full page drawing, p (6); text,
pp 7–(32).

Binding: 8vo, 5 x 7¾ ins. Brown cloth; floral decoration in gold within blind
stamped circle at right-hand corner of front cover; lettering with two designs along
spine in gold on dark brown strip; all edges cut; azure blue end papers.
        Glassine wrapper. Published August 1976.
        This edition was limited to 350 copies on the occasion of the fortieth anniversary
of Michael Joseph Limited, 52 Bedford Square, London WC1. It was set and printed
in Great Britain in Caslon 12 on 13 point type by Western Printing Services, on
paper supplied by P.F. Bingham Limited and bound by Redwood Burn.

Notes: Drawings by John Ward: in brown on title-page, p (3), repeated in black
and white at p 30, in black and white at pp (6, full-page), 7, 8, 9, 10, 13, 14, 16,
17, (20), 22, 23, 25, (27, full-page), 30, (32).
        'The Yellow Meads of Asphodel' was one of a collection of seven stories published
by Michael Joseph in August 1976 (A 120). Copies were sent out with a slip reading:
'This edition of one of the last stories written by H.E. Bates comes to you with the
compliments of the Directors of Michael Joseph Limited on the occasion of the firm's
fortieth anniversary.'

A 122   THE BEST OF H.E. BATES   1980
**   A Selection of Novels and Short Stories**

The Best of H.E. Bates | A Selection of Novels and Short Stories | (publisher's
device) | LONDON | MICHAEL JOSEPH

Collation: (A-U)¹⁶ (vi) + 634 pp, consisting of half-title, BOOKS BY H.E.
BATES on verso, pp (i–ii); title-page, notices of publication and copyright, reservation of rights, ISBN 0 7181 1943 6, printer's and binder's imprint on verso, pp
(iii–iv); Contents, verso blank, pp (v–vi); text, pp (1)–634, (blank pp (374), (516),
(546), (566), (572).

Binding: 8vo, 5¼ x 8½ ins. Dark-blue cloth; lettering, with ornament and publisher's device on spine in gold; blue and white headband; all edges cut; white end
papers.
        Dust jacket designed by Graham Rogers; front cover and spine illustrated with
pastoral scene in colour and lettered in black; back cover white with portrait of the
author and a note on H.E. Bates from *The Times Literary Supplement* in black.

Price: £6.95 net. A total of 31,201 copies were sold.
Printed and bound by Donnelley & Sons, Co., Chicago, Illinois, USA.

Contents: Fair Stood the Wind for France - The Purple Plain - The Darling Buds of May - The Triple Echo - The Four Beauties - The Simple Life - The Bedfordshire Clanger - The Major of Hussars - The Wild Cherry Tree - The Little Farm - Great Uncle Crow

Notes: The title *The Best of H.E. Bates* had been given in 1963 to the American edition of the English edition of *Seven by Five* (see A 98).

A 123   PERFICK, PERFICK!   1985

H.E. BATES | PERFICK, PERFICK! | The Story of the Larkin Family | THE DARLING BUDS OF MAY | A BREATH OF FRENCH AIR | WHEN THE GREEN WOODS LAUGH | OH! TO BE IN ENGLAND | A LITTLE OF WHAT YOU FANCY | (publisher's device) | Michael Joseph | London

Collation: 584 pp, consisting of half-title, BOOKS BY H.E. BATES on verso, pp (1–2); title-page, notices of first publication, copyright and reservation of rights, British Library Cataloguing in Publication Data, printer's and binder's imprint on verso, pp (3–4); CONTENTS, verso blank, pp (5–6); fly title, THE DARLING BUDS OF MAY, verso blank, pp (7–8); text, pp 9–(116); fly title, A BREATH OF FRENCH AIR, verso blank, pp (117–118); text, pp 119–(225); blank page, p (226); fly title, WHEN THE GREEN WOODS LAUGH; stanza from BLAKE: Songs of Innocence on verso, pp (227–228); text, pp 229–325; blank page, p (326); fly title, OH! TO BE IN ENGLAND, dedication on verso, pp (327–328); text, pp 329–428; fly title, A LITTLE OF WHAT YOU FANCY, verso blank, pp (429–430); text pp 431–(582); blank pp (583–584).

Binding: 8vo, $5\frac{1}{2}$ x $8\frac{1}{2}$ ins. Dark-green boards; author and title lettered along spine with publisher at foot, all in silver; all edges cut; cream end papers.
Dust jacket designed by Graham Rogers with coloured illustration and black lettering on front cover and spine. Back cover white with Reviews of the Larkin Novels in black.

Price: £12.95 net. A total of 8,076 copies were sold.
British Library Cataloguing in Publication Data: Bates, H.E. Perfick, Perfick! I. Title 823'.914(F) PR6003.A965
Printed and bound in Great Britain by Billing & Sons Ltd., London and Worcester.

Contents: The Darling Buds of May - A Breath of French Air - When the Green Woods Laugh - Oh! To Be in England - A Little of What You Fancy

A 124   A MONTH BY THE LAKE   1987
& OTHER STORIES

H.E. BATES | (short rule) | A MONTH BY THE LAKE | & OTHER STORIES | (ornament) | INTRODUCTION BY ANTHONY BURGESS | (publisher's device) | (long rule) | A NEW DIRECTIONS BOOK

Collation: (A-G^{16}) (xii) + 212 pp, consisting of half-title, verso blank, pp (i–ii); title-page, notices of copyright, reservation of rights, Editor's Note, notices of manufacture and publication, Library of Congress Cataloging-in-Publication Data, publisher's imprint on verso, pp (iii–iv); CONTENTS, verso blank, p v–(vi); H.E. BATES - AN INTRODUCTION (Anthony Burgess), pp vii–x; fly title, A MONTH BY THE LAKE & OTHER STORIES, verso blank, pp (xi–xii); text, pp 1–209; Biographical Note 'ABOUT H.E. BATES', p (210); a list of 'MORE REVIVED MODERN CLASSICS', pp (211–212).

Binding: 8vo, $5\frac{1}{4}$ x $7\frac{7}{8}$ ins. Green cloth with cream headband; lettered along spine with publisher's device in gold; all edges cut; white end papers.
   White dust jacket designed by Hermann Strohbach. Illustration of fruit-laden tree on front cover in green. Lettered on front cover and spine in red and black with publisher's devices in red. Photograph of the author by Baron on back cover with a note on the author by David Garnett in black.

Price: $17.95
   A paperbook was published simultaneously (price $8.95). The design on front cover of dust jacket was repeated on front of paper cover in black.
   The first printing was 2,000 clothbound; 5,000 paperbound.
   Library of Congress Cataloging-in-Publication Data Bates, H.E. (Herbert Ernest), 1905–1974. A month by the lake and other stories. (New Directions paperbook; 645) I. Title. PR6003.A965A6 1987 823'.912 87-5680 ISBN 0-8112-1035-9 ISBN 0-8112-1036-7 (pbk.)
   Manufactured in America and published for James Laughlin by New Directions Publishing Corporation 80 Eigth* Avenue, New York 10011.
   *printing error on p (iv)

Contents: Introduction - A Month by the Lake - The Flame - Time - Sergeant Carmichael - It's Just The Way It Is - The Flag - Elaine - Country Society - The Evolution of Saxby - The Maker of Coffins - The Cowslip Field - Death and the Cherry Tree - The Butterfly - Where the Cloud Breaks - Mrs. Eglantine - The Chords of Youth - The Song of the Wren
   (At the end of each story the date when it was first collected is given.)

Editor's Note p (iv): 'Following the title story, "A Month by the Lake", first published in 1964, the stories proceed in chronological order, covering the years 1926–1972. Thanks are due to the author's widow and his son, Richard Bates, who have approved this selection, and to Professor Dennis Vannatta, author of a critical study on Bates (Twayne Publishers and G.K. Hall, 1983), for his advice. This too is the place to gratefully acknowledge the help of my New Directions colleague Laurie Callahan. - G.J.O.'

A 125   A PARTY FOR THE GIRLS   1988
SIX STORIES

H.E. BATES | (short rule) | A PARTY FOR THE GIRLS | (short rule) | SIX STORIES | (ornament) | (publisher's device) | (long rule) | A NEW DIRECTIONS BOOK

Collation: (A–H^{16}) (vi) + 250 pp, consisting of half-title, ALSO BY H.E. BATES on verso, pp (i–ii); title-page, notices of copyright, reservation of rights, manufacture and publication, Library of Congress Cataloging-in-Publication Data, publisher's imprint on verso, pp (iii–iv); CONTENTS, verso blank, pp v–(vi); fly title, A PARTY FOR THE GIRLS, verso blank, pp (1–2); text, pp 3–243; blank page, p (244); Biographical note 'ABOUT H.E. BATES' p (245); blank p (246); two blank leaves, pp (247–250).

Binding: 8vo, $5\frac{1}{4}$ x $7\frac{7}{8}$ ins. Mauve cloth with scarlet headband; lettered along spine with publisher's device in gold; all edges cut; white end papers.
   White dust jacket designed by Hermann Strohback. Floral illustration on front cover in mauve. Front cover and spine lettered in red and black with publisher's devices in red. Photograph of the author by Baron on back cover with notes on the author and publisher's imprint in black.

Price: $21.95
   A paperbook was published simultaneously (price $10.95). Design on front cover of dust jacket above was repeated on front of paper cover in black (New Directions paperbook 653).
   The first printing was 1,500 clothbound; 4,000 paperbound.
   Library of Congress Cataloging-in-Publication Data Bates, H.E. (Herbert Ernest), 1905–1974. A party for the girls: six stories / by H.E. Bates. (A New Directions Book) p. cm.-(Revived modern classics) ISBN 0-8112-1050-2. ISBN 0-8112-1051-0 (pbk) I. Title II. Series. PR6003.A965P3 1988 87-26874 823'.912-dc19 CIP
   Manufactured in America and published for James Laughlin by New Directions Publishing Corporation 80 Eighth Avenue, New York 10011.

Contents: A Party for the Girls - The Mill - Summer in Salander - A Great Day for Bonzo - Death of a Huntsman - White Wind

Notes: The ornament on the title-page is repeated before the beginning of each story.

A 126   ELEPHANT'S NEST IN A   1989
RHUBARB TREE

H.E. BATES | ELEPHANT'S NEST | IN A RHUBARB TREE | & OTHER STORIES | (ornament) | (publisher's device) | (long rule) | A NEW DIREC-TIONS BOOK

Collation: (A-0)^8 (viii) + 216 pp, consisting of A REVIVED MODERN CLAS-
SIC, long rule, half-title, ALSO BY H.E. BATES on verso, pp (i–ii); title-page,
notices of copyright, reservation of rights, manufacture and publication, Library
of Congress Cataloging-in-Publication Data, publisher's imprint on verso, pp (iii–
iv); CONTENTS, verso blank, pp v–(vi); fly title, ELEPHANT'S NEST IN A
RHUBARB TREE, verso blank, pp (vii–viii); text, pp 1–206; ABOUT H.E. BATES,
verso blank, pp (207–208); MORE REVIVED MODERN CLASSICS, pp (209–210);
three blank leaves, pp (211–216).

Binding: 8vo, $5\frac{1}{4}$ x $7\frac{7}{8}$ ins. Maroon cloth with yellow headband; lettered along
spine with publisher's device in gold; all edges cut; cream end papers.
  White dust jacket designed by Hermann Strohbach. On front cover floral illustration in brown, lettering in red and black with device in red, lettered along spine
in black with publisher's device in red, on back cover in red, brown and black, with
publisher's advertisements for A MONTH BY THE LAKE & OTHER STORIES
and A PARTY FOR THE GIRLS Also by H.E. Bates.

Price: $17.95
  A paperback edition was published simultaneously (price $10.95). Design on
front cover of dust jacket was repeated on front of paperback cover in black. (New
Directions paperbook 669).
  The first printing was 1,500 clothbound; 4,000 paperback.
  Library of Congress Cataloging-in-Publication Data: Bates H.E. (Herbert
Ernest). 1905–1974. Elephant's Nest in a rhubarb tree & other stories/H.E. Bates.
p. cm. ISBN 0-8112-1087-1. ISBN 0-8112-1088-X (pbk.) I. Title. PR6003 A965E45
1989. 823.912-dc19 88-38040 CIP

Contents: Elephant's Nest in a Rhubarb Tree - The Captain - Italian Haircut
- The Little Jeweller - Château Bougainvillaea - The Disinherited - The Greatest
People on Earth[1] - The Major of Hussars - Thelma - Go, Lovely Rose - The Kimono
- Love in a Wych Elm - Let's Play Soldiers - Great Uncle Crow - The Watercress
Girl - Cococut Radio - The Trespasser

Notes: The ornament on the title-page is repeated at the beginning of each story.
  Manufactured in America on acid free paper and published for James Laughlin
by New Directions Publishing Corporation, 80 Eighth Avenue, New York 10011.

---

[1] The title should be The Greatest People in the World (correct in text).

B
Short stories and novellas

B1 A Waddler

1.1	2 March 1926	*Manchester Guardian*

B2 The Flame

2.1	27 March 1926	*The Nation*, London, xxxviii, pp 892-3
2.2	1928	*Day's End and Other Stories* (A 6)
2.3	1934	*Thirty Tales* (A 21)
2.4	1963	*Seven by Five/The Best of H.E. Bates* (A 98a and 98b)
2.5	1987	*A Month by the Lake & Other Stories* (A 124)
	See	*The Vanished World* (A 107) pp 161-2
		The Blossoming World (A 110) pp 19, 63

B3 The Lesson

3.1	1 June 1926	*Manchester Guardian*
3.2	1928	*Day's End and Other Stories* (A 6)

B4 The Laugh

4.1	16 July 1926	*New Leader*, London, xiii, 40, p 10

B5 The Mother

5.1	7 August 1926	*Manchester Guardian*
5.2	1928	*Day's End and Other Stories* (A 6)
5.3	1933	*Capajon: Fifty-four Short Stories published 1921-1933 by Jonathan Cape,* Introduction by Edward Garnett. London: Jonathan Cape. pp 91-3

		(The book contained fifty-three stories.)
5.4	1934	*Thirty Tales* (A 21)
5.5	1937	*Fifty-Three Short Stories*, Selected, with an Introduction by Edward Garnett, pp 91-3. London: Jonathan Cape (A reissue of *Capajon* B 5.3 above, this time with the correct number of fifty-three stories.)

B6 Two Candles

6.1	Summer 1926	*Now and Then*, No.20. London: Jonathan Cape pp 21-6
6.2	1928	*Day's End and Other Stories* (A 6)
6.3	1934	*Thirty Tales* (A 21)

B7 The Idiot

7.1	23 October 1926	*New Statesman*, London, xxviii, pp 43-4
7.2	1928	*Day's End and Other Stories* (A 6)
7.3	1934	*Thirty Tales* (A 21)

See *The Vanished World* (A 107) p 179

B8 The Birthday

8.1	30 October 1926	*The Nation*, London, xl, pp 144-5
8.2	1928	*Day's End and Other Stories* (A 6)
8.3	1934	*Thirty Tales* (A 21)

B9 The Holiday

9.1	1 January 1927	*New Statesman*, London, xxviii, pp 363-4
9.2	1928	*Day's End and Other Stories* (A 6)
9.3	1934	*Thirty Tales* (A 21)

B10 In View of the Fact That

10.1	1927	*The Spring Song and In View of the Fact That* (A 5)

B11 The Spring Song

11.1	1927	*The Spring Song and In View of the Fact That* (A 5)
11.2	Spring 1927	*The New Coterie:* A quarterly of literature

		and art. London: E. Archer, Number Five, pp 8-14
		As in B 11.1 the frontispiece is a drawing of the
		author by William Roberts.
11.3	1928	*Day's End and Other Stories* (A 6)
11.4	1934	*Thirty Tales* (A 21)
11.5	March 1935	*Argosy*, viii, 106, pp 104-6
11.6	May 1952	*Argosy*, xiii, 5, pp 79-84 as 'Spring Song'

B12 Fear

12.1	26 March 1927	*Nation and Athenaeum*, London, xl, pp 891-2
12.2	1927	*The Best Short Stories of 1927*, with an Irish
		supplement, Ed. Edward J. O'Brien, pp 44-8
		New York: Dodd, Mead
12.3	1928	*The Best Short Stories of 1927*
		First Series: English, Ed. Edward J. O'Brien,
		pp 56-60 London: Jonathan Cape
12.4	1928	*Day's End and Other Stories* (A 6)
12.5	1933	*Capajon: Fifty-four short stories*
		published 1921-1933 by Jonathan Cape,
		Introduction by Edward Garnett, London: Jonathan
		Cape, pp 93-8 (See Note to B 5.3)
12.6	1934	*Thirty Tales* (A 21)
12.7	November 1934	*Argosy*, xvi, 102, pp 100-2
12.8	1937	*Fifty-three Short Stories,* Selected, with an
		Introduction by Edward Garnett, London:
		Jonathan Cape, pp 93-8 (see Note to B 5.5)
	See *The Blossoming World* (A 110) p 63	

B13 The Easter Blessing

13.1	March-May 1927	*The Bermondsey Book,* London, iv, 2, pp 60-65
13.2	1928	*Day's End and Other Stories* (A 6)
13.3	1934	*Seven Years' Harvest.* An Anthology of the
		Bermondsey Book, 1923-1930, compiled by Sidney
		Gutman, London: Heinemann, pp 240-46
13.4	1938	*Country Tales* (A 30)
13.5	1940	*Country Tales* (A 36)

B14 The Baker's Wife

14.1	April 1927	*Humanist,* London, iv, 4, pp 169-72
14.2	1928	*Day's End and Other Stories* (A 6)
14.3	1934	*Thirty Tales* (A 21)

B15 Never

15.1	26 June 1927	*New Statesman*, London, xxvii, pp 291-3
15.2	1928	*Day's End and Other Stories* (A 6)
15.3	1938	*Country Tales* (A 30)
15.4	1940	*Country Tales* (A 36)
15.5	1981	*The Oxford Book of Short Stories*, chosen by V.S. Pritchett, Oxford University Press, pp 391-4

B16 The Shepherd

| 16.1 | 27 August 1927 | *The Nation*, London, xli, pp 691-3 |
| 16.2 | 1928 | *Day's End and Other Stories* (A 6) |

B17 The Dove

| 17.1 | 6 October 1927 | *Manchester Guardian* |
| 17.2 | 1928 | *Day's End and Other Stories* (A 6) |

See *The Blossoming World* (A 110) p 58

B18 Blossoms

18.1	31 Dec 1927	*The Nation*, London, xlii, pp 511-3
18.2	1928	*Day's End and Other Stories* (A 6)
18.3	1934	*Thirty Tales* (A 21)

B19 Harvest

19.1	December 1927	*The New Adelphi*, London, i, 2, pp 109-12
19.2	1928	*Day's End and Other Stories* (A 6)
19.3	July 1933	*Capajon: Fifty-four Short Stories published 1921-1933 by Jonathan Cape*. Introduction by Edward Garnett, London: Jonathan Cape, pp 98-103 (see Note to B 5.3)
19.4	1934	*Thirty Tales* (A 21)
19.5	1937	*Fifty-three Short Stories*, Selected, with an Introduction by Edward Garnett, London: Jonathan Cape, pp 98-103 (see Note to B 5.5)

B20 Fishing

20.1	3 February 1928	*Manchester Guardian*
20.2	1928	*Day's End and Other Stories* (A 6)
20.3	1934	*Thirty Tales* (A 21)
20.4	1965	*Best Fishing Stories*, Ed. with Introduction by John Moore, London: Faber & Faber, pp 49-52

B21 The White Mare

(later published as 'Lanko's White Mare') (B 38)
21.1   May 1928   *London Mercury*, London, xviii, pp 22-9

B22 Parrot

22.1   26 May 1928   *T.P.'s Weekly*, London, p 137

B23 The Voyage

23.1   March-May 1928 *The Bermondsey Book*, London, v, 2, pp 51-6
23.2   1928   *Day's End and Other Stories* (A 6)
23.3   1934   *Thirty Tales* (A 21)

B24 The Father

24.1   June 1928   *The New Adelphi*, London, i, 4, pp 329-32
24.2   1928   *Day's End and Other Stories* (A 6)
24.3   1934   *Thirty Tales* (A 21)

B25 The Barge

25.1   1928   *Day's End and Other Stories* (A 6)

B26 Day's End

26.1   1928   *Day's End and Other Stories* (A 6)

B27 The Fuel-Gatherers

27.1   1928   *Day's End and Other Stories* (A 6)
27.2   1934   *Thirty Tales* (A 21)

B28 Gone Away

28.1   1928   *Day's End and Other Stories* (A 6)

B29 Nina

29.1   1928   *Day's End and Other Stories* (A 6)
29.2   Autumn 1928   *Now and Then*, London, No.29, pp 33-7
29.3   1975   *H.E. Bates* (A 118)

B30   The Schoolmistress

| 30.1 | 1928 | *Day's End and Other Stories* (A 6) |
| 30.2 | 1934 | *Thirty Tales* (A 21) |

B31   A Tinker's Donkey

31.1	9 Nov 1928	*Manchester Guardian*
31.2	1929	*Seven Tales and Alexander* (A 8)
31.3	1934	*Thirty Tales* (A 21)
31.4	1940	*Stories for Girls,* chosen by Kathleen Lines, London: Faber and Faber, pp 11-15
31.5	1951	*Twenty Tales* (A 71)

B32   The Child

32.1	December 1928	*The Criterion,* London, viii, 31, pp 215-9
32.2	Summer 1929	*Now and Then,* London, No.32, pp 41-4
32.3	1929	*Seven Tales and Alexander* (A 8)
32.4	1929	*Best Short Stories of 1929,* Ed. Edward J. O'Brien, London: Jonathan Cape, No.1. pp 42-6
32.5	1929	*Best Short Stories of 1929,* with an Irish Supplement, New York: Dodd, Mead, pp 35-9
32.6	1934	*Thirty Tales* (A 21)
32.7	1938	*An Anthology of Modern Short Stories* Ed. J.W. Marriott, London: Nelson, pp 139-45

B33   A Comic Actor

33.1	29 June 1929	*New Statesman and Nation,* London, xxxiii, pp 366-8
33.2	1929	*Seven Tales and Alexander* (A 8)
33.3	1930	*Best Short Stories of 1930,* Ed. Edward J. O'Brien, 1st Series, English, London: Jonathan Cape, pp 40-49
33.4	1930	*Best Short Stories of 1930,* with an Irish and Colonial Supplement, New York: Dodd, Mead, pp 24-32
33.5	November 1931	*Argosy,* x, 66, pp 63-6
33.6	1934	*Thirty Tales* (A 21)

B34   The Barber

| 34.1 | 20 July 1929 | *New Statesman and Nation,* London, xxxiii, pp 468-70 |

34.2	1929	*Seven Tales and Alexander* (A 8)
34.3	1934	*Thirty Tales* (A 21)
34.4	1951	*Twenty Tales* (A 71)

B35 Pensioned Off

| 35.1 | September - November 1929 | *New Adelphi,* London, iii, 1, pp 55-7 |

B36 Alexander

36.1	1929	*Seven Tales and Alexander* (A 8)
36.2	1934	*Thirty Tales* (A 21)
36.3	1939	*Modern Short Stories,* Ed. John Hadfield, London: J.M. Dent, (Everyman's Library No. 954) pp 273-330
36.4	1951	*Twenty Tales* (A 71)

B37 The King Who Lived on Air - A Child's Tale

| 37.1 | 1929 | *Seven Tales and Alexander* (A 8) |

B38 Lanko's White Mare

38.1	1929	*Seven Tales and Alexander* (A 8)
38.2	1934	*Thirty Tales* (A 21)
38.3	1951	*Twenty Tales* (A 71)

For first publication see 'The White Mare' (B 21) and author's note in
Seven Tales and Alexander (A 8) concerning considerable changes to the story.

B39 The Peach-Tree: A Fantasy

| 39.1 | 1929 | *Seven Tales and Alexander* (A 8) |

B40 Sheep

40.1	January 1930	*The Window,* a quarterly magazine Eds, Eric Partridge and Bertram Ratcliffe, London; privately published by Eric Partridge. i, 1, pp 2-8
40.2	1932	*The Black Boxer Tales* (A 14)
40.3	1949	*The Bride Comes to Evensford And Other Tales* (A 63)

B41   The Hessian Prisoner

41.1	1930	*The Hessian Prisoner* (A 10)
41.2	March 1931	*Fortnightly Review*, London, cxxxv, 135, pp 374-88
41.3	1932	*The Black Boxer Tales* (A 14)
41.4	1932	*The Furnival Book of Short Stories* London; Joiner and Steele, pp 35-54
41.5	1934	*Thirty Tales* (A 21)
41.6	1949	*The Bride Comes to Evensford And Other Tales* (A 63)

See   *The Vanished World* (A 107) p 95

B42   A Love Story

42.1	3 April 1930	*Everyman*, London; J.M. Dent & Sons, iii, 62, pp 295-6
42.2	Winter 1930	*Now and Then*, London, No.37, pp 41-4
42.3	1932	*The Black Boxer Tales* (A 14)
42.4	1934	*Thirty Tales* (A 21)
42.5	January 1935	*Argosy*, viii, 104, pp 25-6
42.6	1949	*The Bride Comes to Evensford And Other Tales* (A 63)

B43   A Threshing Day for Esther

43.1	11 October 1930	*John O'London's Weekly*, London, xxiv, 599, pp 5, 6, 8, 9
43.2	1932	*The Black Boxer Tales* (A 14)
43.3	1933	*Capajon: Fifty-four Short Stories published 1921-1933 by Jonathan Cape*, Introduction by Edward Garnett, London; Jonathan Cape, pp 103-17 (See Note to B 5.3)
43.4	1934	*Thirty Tales* (A 21)
43.5	1937	*Fifty-three Short Stories*, Selected, with an Introduction by Edward Garnett; London: Jonathan Cape, pp 103-17 (See Note to B 5.5)
43.6	1949	*The Bride Comes to Evensford And Other Tales* (A 63)
43.7	1951	*Selected Short Stories of H.E. Bates* (A 70)
43.8	1975	*H.E. Bates* (A 118)

The story was also published as *A Threshing Day* in a limited edition by W. & G. Foyle Ltd in July 1931 (A 12; B 48)

B44   Charlotte Esmond

44.1	October 1930	*The Criterion*, London, x, 38, pp 55-74
44.2	1932	*The Black Boxer Tales* (A 14)
44.3	1934	*Thirty Tales* (A 21)
44.4	1949	*The Bride Comes to Evensford And Other Tales* (A 63)

The story was also published as *Mrs. Esmond's Life* in a limited edition
by E. Lahr in 1931 (A 13; B 54)

B45   The Tree

| 45.1 | 1930 | *The Tree* (A 9) |

B46   Country Sale

| 46.1 | January 1931 | *Fortnightly Review*, London, cxxxv, pp 107-14 |

B47   On The Road

47.1	28 Feb 1931	*New Statesman and Nation*, i, Supplement vii-x
47.2	Winter 1931	*Now and Then*, Jonathan Cape, London, No.40, pp 26-9
47.3	1932	*The Best Short Stories of 1931*, Ed. Edward J. O'Brien, London: Jonathan Cape, pp 15-21; New York; Dodd, Mead, pp 3-8
47.4	1932	*The Black Boxer Tales* (A 14)
47.5	1934	*Thirty Tales* (A 21)
47.6	1948	*Turnstile One: A Literary Miscellany from The New Statesman and Nation*, Ed. V.S. Pritchett, London: Turnstile Press Ltd, pp 33-7
47.7	1949	*The Bride Comes to Evensford and Other Tales* (A 63)
47.8	November 1950	*Argosy*, xi, 11, pp 135-9

B48   A Threshing Day

| 48.1 | 1931 | *A Threshing Day* (A 12) |

Also published as 'A Threshing Day for Esther', see B43

B49   Death in Spring

| 49.1 | 29 August 1931 | *John O'London's Weekly*, London, xxv, 645, pp 713-14 |

49.2	1932	*The Black Boxer Tales* (A 14)
49.3	1934	*Thirty Tales* (A 21)
49.4	1938	*Country Tales* (A 30)
49.5	1940	*Country Tales* (A 36)
49.6	1949	*The Bride Comes to Evensford And Other Tales* (A 63)
49.7	1949	*English Country Short Stories,* Ed. R. Lewin, London: Elek, pp 211-19
49.8	1951	*Selected Short Stories of H.E. Bates* (A 70)

B50 The Mower

50.1	September 1931	*This Quarter*, Paris, iv, 1, pp 37-9
50.2	1932	*The Black Boxer Tales* (A 14)
50.3	1934	*Thirty Tales* (A 21)
50.4	1936	*Modern Short Stories of the Open Air*, Ed. John Hadfield, London: J.M. Dent, pp 2-15, republished in 1951 by the Country Book Club, London
50.5	1937	*Selected Modern Short Stories*, selected by Alan Steele, Penguin Books, pp 11-31
50.6	February 1943	*Argosy*, iv, 1, pp 29-37
50.7	1949	*The Bride Comes to Evensford And Other Tales* (A 63)
50.8	1951	*Selected Short Stories of H.E. Bates* (A 70)
50.9	1961	*Short Story Study*, a critical anthology compiled by A.J. Smith (University College, Swansea) and W.H. Mason (Manchester Grammar School) London: Edward Arnold
50.10	1963	*Seven by Five/The Best of H.E. Bates* (A 98a/98b)
50.11	1976	*The Poison Ladies and Other Stories* (A 119)

B51 A Flower Piece

51.1	10 October 1931	*New Statesman and Nation,* ii, 33 (new series), Supplement pp v-vi
51.2	1932	*The Black Boxer Tales* (A 14)
51.3	1932	*The Best Short Stories of 1932*, First Series, English, Ed. Edward J. O'Brien, London. Jonathan Cape, pp 38-43; New York: Dodd, Mead, pp 24-9
51.4	1934	*Thirty Tales* (A 21)
51.5	1949	*The Bride Comes to Evensford And Other Tales* (A 63)
51.6	1951	*Selected Short Stories of H.E. Bates* (A 70)

| 51.7 | 1963 | *Seven by Five/The Best of H.E. Bates* (A 98a/98b) |

B52   The Russian Dancer

52.1	14 Nov 1931	*John O'London's Weekly*, xxvi, 656, pp 213-14
52.2	1932	*The Black Boxer Tales* (A 14)
52.3	1949	*The Bride Comes to Evensford And Other Tales* (A 63)

B53   The Black Boxer

53.1	3, 10, 17 December 1931	*Everyman*, London: J.M. Dent, vi, 149-51
53.2	1932	*The Black Boxer Tales* (A 14)
53.3	1938	*Country Tales* (A 30)
53.4	1940	*Country Tales* (A 36)
53.5	1949	*The Bride Comes to Evensford And Other Tales* (A 63)

B54   Mrs. Esmond's Life

| 54.1 | 1931 | *Mrs. Esmond's Life* (A 13) |

The story was first published as 'Charlotte Esmond' (B44)

B55   Sally Go Round the Moon

55.1	1932	*Sally Go Round the Moon* (A 15)
55.2	1934	*The Woman Who Had Imagination and Other Stories* (A 20)
55.3	1935	*New English Short Stories*, Ed. Edward J. O'Brien, London: Jonathan Cape (Florin Books), 1935 pp 13-34
55.4	1938	*Country Tales* (A 30)
55.5	1940	*Country Tales* (A 36)

B56   The Man from Jamaica

| 56.1 | 2 April 1932 | *John O'London's Weekly*, xxvii, 677, pp 5-6 |
| 56.2 | 1933 | *The House with the Apricot and Two Other Tales* (A 19) |

B57   A German Idyll

57.1	1932	*A German Idyll* (A 16)
57.2	1934	*The Woman Who Had Imagination and Other Stories* (A 20)
57.3	1947	*Thirty-One Selected Tales* (A 60)
57.4	1957	*Selected Stories* (A 84)

B58   Time

58.1	20 August 1932	*New Statesman and Nation*, iv, 78, pp 205-6
58.2	April 1933	*Story*, Story Magazine Inc. New York, ii, 12, pp 79-83
58.3	1933	*The Best Short Stories of 1933* Ed. Edward J. O'Brien, First Series. English. London, Jonathan Cape, pp 29-35
58.4	1933	*The Best British Short Stories 1933* Ed. Edward J. O'Brien, Boston and New York; Houghton Mifflin, pp 11-15
58.5	1934	*The Woman Who Had Imagination and Other Stories* (A 20)
58.6	1936	*Short Stories by Modern Writers* Ed. R.W. Jepson, London: Longmans, pp 202-9
58.7	1938	*Country Tales* (A 30)
58.8	1940	*Country Tales* (A 36)
58.9	1963	*Seven by Five/The Best of H.E. Bates* (A 98a/98b)
58.10	1987	*A Month by the Lake and Other Stories* (A 124)

B59   Innocence

59.1	27 August 1932	*John O'London's Weekly.* xxvii, 698, p 753
59.2	1933	*Full Score*, Ed. F. Armstrong, Rich and Cowan, London, pp 269-73
59.3	1934	*The Woman Who Had Imagination and Other Stories* (A 20)
59.4	1938	*Country Tales* (A 30)
59.5	1940	*Country Tales* (A 36)

B60   The Gleaner

60.1	5 Nov 1932	*New Statesman and Nation* iv, pp 545-6
60.2	Spring 1933	*Now and Then*, London, No.44, pp 18-20
60.3	1934	*The Woman Who Had Imagination and Other Stories* (A 20)

60.4	1934	*The Best Short Stories of 1934*
		Ed. Edward J. O'Brien,
		English and American, London,
		Jonathan Cape, pp 17-22
60.5	1934	*The Best British Short Stories 1934*
		Ed. Edward J. O'Brien, Boston and
		New York: Houghton Mifflin pp 3-7
60.6	1935	*Then and Now*, London: Jonathan Cape,
		pp 97-102 (with a drawing by Rowland Hilder)
60.7	1938	*Country Tales* (A 30)
60.8	1940	*Country Tales* (A 36)

B61 The Country Doctor

| 61.1 | 1932 | *The Story Without An End and* |
| | | *The Country Doctor* (A 18) |

B62 The Story Without An End

62.1	1932	*The Story Without An End and The Country*
		Doctor (A 18)
62.2	September 1933	*London Mercury*, xxviii, 167, pp 396-407
62.3	1934	*The Woman Who Had Imagination and Other*
		Stories (A 20)
62.4	1938	*Country Tales* (A 30)
62.5	1940	*Country Tales* (A 36)
62.6	April 1943	*Argosy*, iv, 3, pp 65-78

B63 A Little War

63.1	1933	*Charles Wain*: a Miscellany of Short Stories
		collected by W.L.H., London; Mallison Publishing,
		pp 11-20. A limited edition of 95 copies was also
		published in 1933, signed by all eighteen
		contributors, with a frontispiece by Nina Hamnett
63.2	1933	*New Clarion* London, iv, 79, pp 6, 12

B64 The Pink Cart

64.1	18 Feb 1933	*John O'London's Weekly*, xxviii, 723, pp 789-90
64.2	1933	*The House with the Apricot and Two Other*
		Tales (A 19)
64.3	1935	*Cut and Come Again* (A 25)
64.4	1938	*Country Tales* (A 30)
64.5	1940	*Country Tales* (A 36)

B65   The Lily

65.1	22 Feb 1933	*The Listener*, London, ix, 215, pp 306-07
65.2	1934	*The Woman Who Had Imagination and Other Stories* (A 20)
65.3	1939	*My Uncle Silas* (A 35)
65.4	June 1941	*Argosy*, ii, 17, pp 85-90
65.5	1943	*W. Somerset Maugham's Introduction to Modern English and American Literature*, Blakiston Co., Philadelphia, PA

B66   Obadiah

66.1	1 April 1933	*New Clarion*, London, p 325

B67   The House with the Apricot

67.1	1933	*The House with the Apricot and Two Other Tales* (A 19)
67.2	1935	*Cut and Come Again* (A 25)
67.3	1938	*Country Tales* (A 30)
67.4	1940	*Country Tales* (A 36)

B68   For the Dead

68.1	30 Dec 1933	*New Statesman and Nation*, vi, p 869
68.2	1934	*The Woman Who Had Imagination and Other Stories* (A 20)
68.3	1947	*Thirty-One Selected Tales* (A 60)

B69   Harvest Moon

69.1	20 January 1934	*New Statesman and Nation*, vii, pp 84-5
69.2	1935	*Cut and Come Again* (A 25)
69.3	1938	*Country Tales* (A 30)
69.4	1940	*Country Tales* (A 36)
69.5	October 1948	*Courier*, London, xi, 4, pp 89-94
69.6	1957	*Selected Stories* (A 84)
69.7	1976	*The Poison Ladies and Other Stories* (A 119)

B70   The Woman Who Had Imagination

70.1	1934	*The Woman Who Had Imagination and Other Stories* (A 20)

70.2	1938	*Country Tales* (A 30)
70.3	1940	*Country Tales* (A 36)
70.4	1956	*Modern English Short Stories*, Second series Ed. Derek Hudson, London: Oxford University Press, pp 167-98

B71 The Wedding

71.1	1934	*The Woman Who Had Imagination and Other Stories* (A 20)
71.2	1939	*My Uncle Silas* (A 35)
71.3	April 1942	*Argosy*, iii 3, pp 41-8
71.4	1969	*Best Country Stories*, Ed. Ruth Tomlin, London: Faber and Faber, pp 85-94

See *The Vanished World* (A 107) p 61

B72 The Waterfall

72.1	1934	*The Woman Who Had Imagination and Other Stories* (A 20)
72.2	1938	*Country Tales* (A 30)
72.3	1940	*Country Tales* (A 36)

B73 Millenium Also Ran

| 73.1 | 1934 | *The Woman Who Had Imagination and Other Stories* (A 20) |
| 73.2 | 1947 | *Thirty-One Selected Tales* (A 60) |

B74 The Brothers

74.1	1934	*The Woman Who Had Imagination and Other Stories* (A 20)
74.2	1938	*Country Tales* (A 30)
74.3	1940	*Country Tales* (A 36)

B75 Death of Uncle Silas

| 75.1 | 1934 | *The Woman Who Had Imagination and Other Stories* (A 20) |
| 75.2 | 1939 | As 'The Death of Uncle Silas' in *My Uncle Silas* (A 35) |

B76 The Bath

76.1   March 1934   *Lovat Dickson's Magazine*, London,
                              ii, 3, pp 292-302
76.2   1935   *Modern Short Stories*, London, Lovat
                              Dickson and Thompson, pp 272-82
76.3   1935   *Cut and Come Again* (A 25)
76.4   1938   *Country Tales* (A 30)
76.5   1940   *Country Tales* (A 36)
76.6   1951   *Modern Short Stories* (second series)
                              Ed. A.J. Merson, London: Macmillan, pp 23-33

B77 The Revelation

77.1   Summer 1934   *John O'London's Weekly*, xxxi, 793, pp 405-6
77.2   1935   *Cut and Come Again* (A 25)
77.3   1939   *Modern English Short Stories*, First Series,
                              Ed. Phyllis M. Jones, World's Classics, Oxford
                              University Press, pp 341-50
77.4   1939   *My Uncle Silas* (A 35)
77.5   May 1942   *Argosy*, iii, 4, pp 109-14
77.6   January 1949   *Courier*, London, xii, 1, pp 83-9
77.7   1975   *H.E. Bates*, (A 118)
77.8   1985   *The Best Love Stories*, London: Hamlyn,
                              pp 570-75

B78 The Spriv

78.1   7 July 1934   *John O'London's Weekly*, xxxi, 795,
                              pp 529, 530, 534

B79 The Plough

79.1   29 August 1934   *The Listener*, London, xii, 294 pp 376-7
79.2   1935   *Cut and Come Again* (A 25)
79.3   1938   *Country Tales* (A 30)
79.4   1940   *Country Tales* (A 36)

B80 Waiting Room

80.1   13 October 1934   *New Statesman and Nation*, London,
                              viii, 190, pp 469-70
80.2   1935   *Cut and Come Again* (A 25)
80.3   1938   *Country Tales* (A 30)
80.4   1940   *Country Tales* (A 36)
80.5   1951   *Selected Short Stories of H.E. Bates* (A 70)

B81 The Mad Woman

81.1 November 1934 *Lovat Dickson's Magazine*, iii, 5, pp 568-76

B82 The Hedge

82.1 12 Dec 1934 *The Listener*, London, xii, 309, pp 1001-2

B83 The Duet

83.1 1935   *The Duet* (A 24)
83.2 November 1940 *Argosy*, i, 10 (new series), pp 43-50

B84 Beauty's Daughters

84.1 1935   *Cut and Come Again* (A 25)
84.2 1935   *The Best Short Stories of 1935*, English
          and American, Ed. Edward J. O'Brien, London:
          Jonathan Cape, pp 28-44
84.3 1935   *The Best British Short Stories* 1935,
          Ed. Edward J. O'Brien, Boston and New York:
          Houghton Mifflin, pp 13-27
84.4 1938   *Country Tales* (A 30)
84.5 1940   *Country Tales* (A 36)
84.6 1951   *Selected Short Stories of H.E. Bates* (A 70)

B85 Cut and Come Again

85.1 1935   *Cut and Come Again* (A 25)
85.2 1938   *Country Tales* (A 30)
85.3 1940   *Country Tales* (A 36)
85.4 November 1941 *Argosy* ii, 22, pp 19-24
85.5 1957   *Selected Stories* (A 84)
85.6 1976   *The Poison Ladies and Other Stories* (A 119)
85.7 1985   *Best Love Stories*, London: Hamlyn, pp 576-81

B86 The Irishman

86.1 1935   *Cut and Come Again* (A 25)
86.2 1947   *Thirty-One Selected Tales* (A 60)

B87 Jonah and Bruno

87.1 1935   *Cut and Come Again* (A 25)
87.2 1938   *Country Tales* (A 30)
87.3 1940   *Country Tales* (A 36)

B88 Little Fish

88.1	1935	*Cut and Come Again* (A 25)
88.2	1938	*Country Tales* (A 30)
88.3	1940	*Country Tales* (A 36)

B89 The Mill

89.1	1935	*Cut and Come Again* (A 25)
89.2	1936	*The Best Short Stories of 1936, English and American*, Ed. Edward J.O'Brien. London: Jonathan Cape, pp 17-59; Boston & New York: Houghton Mifflin
89.3	1938	*Country Tales* (A 30)
89.4	1940	*Country Tales* (A 36)
89.5	1951	*Selected Short Stories of H.E. Bates* (A 70)
89.6	1957	*Selected Stories* (A84)
89.7	1963	*Seven by Five/The Best of H.E. Bates* (A 98a/98b)
89.8	1988	*A Party for the Girls - Six Stories* (A 125)

See   *The Blossoming World* (A 110) pp 86, 87, 123

B90 The Station

90.1	1935	*Cut and Come Again* (A 25)
90.2	1938	*Country Tales* (A 30)
90.3	1940	*Country Tales* (A 36)
90.4	October 1941	*Argosy*, ii, 21, pp 43-51
90.5	September 1948	*Courier*, London, xi, 3, pp 86-96
90.6	1951	*Selected Short Stories of H.E. Bates* (A 70)
90.7	1957	*Selected Stories* (A 84)
90.8	1963	*Seven by Five/The Best of H.E. Bates* (A 98a/98b)
90.9	January 1964	*Argosy*, xxv, 1, pp 35-43
90.10	1974	*The Good Corn and other stories* (A 117)

B91 The Grace Note

| 91.1 | May 1936 | *Fortnightly Review*, 145, pp 541-7 |
| 91.2 | 1936 | *Hotch Potch*, Ed. John Brophy, The Council of the Royal Liverpool Children's Hospital, pp 11-19 |

B92 Italian Haircut

92.1	20 June 1936	*John O'London's Weekly*, (Summer number) xxxv, 897, pp 404, 408
92.2	1937	*Something Short and Sweet* (A 28)
92.3	Jan-Jun 1938	*Lilliput II*, London, Ed. Stefan Lorant, pp 445-9

92.4	1938	*Country Tales* (A 30)
92.5	1940	*Country Tales* (A 36)
92.6	1951	*Twenty Tales* (A 71)
92.7	1989	*Elephant's Nest in a Rhubarb Tree &* *Other Stories* (A 126)

B93 Cloudburst

93.1	15 August 1936	*John O'London's Weekly*, xxxv, 905, pp 693-4 as 'Cloud Burst'
93.2	1937	*Something Short and Sweet* (A 28)
93.3	1937	*The Best British Short Stories 1937*, Ed. Edward J. O'Brien, New York: Houghton Mifflin pp 17-24
93.4	26 Jan 1938	*Daily Express*, London, p 4
93.5	1938	*Country Tales* (A 30)
93.6	1940	*Country Tales* (A 36)
93.7	1947	*Country Life* A Prose and Verse Anthology of Country Life in Great Britain, Selected and edited by A.F. Scott, London: Macmillan, pp 214-22
93.8	1951	*Twenty Tales* (A 71)

B94 Finger Wet, Finger Dry

94.1	9 October 1936	*John O'London's Weekly*, xxxvi, 913, pp 43-4
94.2	January 1937	*Story*, Story Magazine Inc., New York, x, 54, pp 9-13
94.3	1937	*The Best Short Stories of 1937*, English and American, Ed. Edward J. O'Brien, London: Jonathan Cape, pp 33-8
94.4	1937	*Something Short and Sweet* (A 28)
94.5	1939	*My Uncle Silas* (A 35)
94.6	March 1942	*Argosy*, iii, 2, pp 75-9

B95 The Man Who Loved Cats

95.1	March 1937	*New Statesman and Nation*, xiii, pp 406-7
95.2	1937	*Something Short and Sweet* (A 28)
95.3	1947	*Thirty-One Selected Tales* (A 60)

B96 Purchase's Living Wonders

| 96.1 | 1937 | *Something Short and Sweet* (A 28) |
| 96.2 | 1951 | *Twenty Tales* (A 71) |

B97 Something Short and Sweet

97.1	1937	*Something Short and Sweet* (A 28)
97.2	1947	*Thirty-One Selected Tales* (A 60)

B98 The Captain

98.1	1937	*Something Short and Sweet* (A 28)
98.2	1940	*Country Tales* (A 36)
98.3	1951	*Twenty Tales* (A 71)
98.4	1989	*Elephant's Nest in a Rhubarb Tree &* *Other Stories* (A 126)

B99 The Palace

99.1	1937	*Something Short and Sweet* (A 28)
99.2	1938	*Country Tales* (A 30)

B100 The Kimono

100.1	1937	*Something Short and Sweet* (A 28)
100.2	1938	*Country Tales* (A 30)
100.3	1940	*Country Tales* (A 36)
100.4	(1940)	*Missing from their Homes*, London Hutchinson, pp 109-31
100.5	1951	*Twenty Tales* (A 71)
100.6	1957	*Selected Stories* (A 84)
100.7	1963	*Seven by Five/The Best of H.E. Bates* (A 98a/98b)
100.8	1985	*The Best Love Stories*, London: Hamlyn, pp 556-69
100.9	1989	*Elephant's Nest in a Rhubarb Tree &* *Other Stories* (A 126)

B101 Mister Livingstone

101.1	1937	*Something Short and Sweet* (A 28)
101.2	1947	*Thirty-One Selected Tales* (A 60)

B102 The Case of Miss Lomas

102.1	1937	*Something Short and Sweet* (A 28)
102.2	1951	*Twenty Tales* (A 71)

B103   The Sow and Silas

103.1	1937	*Something Short and Sweet* (A 28)
103.2	1939	*My Uncle Silas* (A 35)
103.3	September 1942	*Argosy*, iii, 8, pp 83-8
103.4	1951	*Selected Short Stories of H.E. Bates* (A 70)

B104   The Landlady

104.1	1937	*Something Short and Sweet* (A 28)
104.2	1938	*Country Tales* (A 30)
104.3	1940	*Country Tales* (A 36)
104.4	1951	*Twenty Tales* (A 71)

B105   No Country

105.1	1937	*Something Short and Sweet* (A 28)
105.2	1947	*Thirty-One Selected Tales* (A 60)

B106   Breeze Anstey

106.1	1937	*Something Short and Sweet* (A 28)
106.2	1938	*Country Tales* (A 30)
106.3	1940	*Country Tales* (A 36)
106.4	1951	*Twenty Tales* (A 71)
106.5	1957	*Selected Stories* (A 84)
106.6	1963	*Seven by Five/The Best of H.E. Bates* (A 98a/98b)

B107   Spring Snow

107.1	1937	*Something Short and Sweet* (A 28)
107.2	1937	*Penguin Parade I*, Denys Kilham Roberts, Penguin Books Ltd, pp 107-14
107.3	1947	*Thirty-One Selected Tales* (A 60)

B108   Perhaps We Shall Meet Again...

108.1	January 1938	*Fortnightly Review*, 149, pp 66-71
108.2	1939	*The Flying Goat* (A 34)
108.3	1951	*Twenty Tales* (A 71)

B109   The Blind

109.1	7 January 1938	*The Spectator*, London, 160, 5715, pp 13-14
109.2	1939	*The Flying Goat* (A 34)
109.3	1947	*Thirty-One Selected Tales* (A 60)

B110   A Funny Thing

110.1	28 Feb 1938	*Daily Express*, London, p 18
110.2	1938	*The Best Short Stories of 1938*, Ed. Edward J. O'Brien, London: Jonathan Cape, pp 39-45
110.3	1939	*The Flying Goat* (A 34)
110.4	1939	*My Uncle Silas* (A 35)
110.5	February 1942	*Argosy*, iii, 1, pp 81-5

B111   Château Bougainvillaea

111.1	22 April 1938	*John O'London's Weekly*, xxxiv, 993, pp 109-110
111.2	January 1939	*Atlantic Monthly*, Boston, Mass., 163, pp 82-87
111.3	1939	*The Flying Goat* (A 34)
111.4	1947	*Thirty-One Selected Tales* (A 60)
111.5	1951	*Selected Short Stories of H.E. Bates* (A 70)
111.6	1957	*Selected Stories* (A 84)
111.7	1974	*The Good Corn and other stories* (A 117)
111.8	1989	*Elephant's Nest in a Rhubarb Tree & Other Stories* (A 126)

B112   The Machine

112.1	5 August 1938	*John O'London's Weekly*, xxxiv, 1008, pp 657-8
112.2	1939	*The Flying Goat* (A 34)
112.3	1939	*Under Thirty*, an Anthology edited by M. Harrison, Rich and Cowan, London, pp 29-33 (the story introduced by the author's autobiographical note)
112.4	1947	*Thirty-One Selected Tales* (A 60)

B113   The Dog and Mr. Morency

113.1	28 October 1938	*John O'London's Weekly*, xl, 1020, pp 169-70
113.2	1939	*The Flying Goat* (A 34)
113.3	1947	*Thirty-One Selected Tales* (A 60)

B114   The Ox

114.1	March 1939	*Atlantic Monthly*, Boston, Mass., 163, pp 391-401
114.2	1939	*The Flying Goat* (A 34)
114.3	1939	*The Best Short Stories of 1939*, English and American Ed. Edward J. O'Brien, London; Jonathan Cape, pp 21-41
114.4	1939	*The Best British Short Stories*, Ed.

		Edward J. O'Brien, Boston: Houghton Mifflin
114.5	1947	*Thirty-One Selected Tales* (A 60)
114.6	1951	*Selected Short Stories of H.E. Bates* (A 70)
114.7	1957	*Selected Stories* (A 84)
114.8	1963	*Seven by Five/The Best of H.E. Bates* (A 98a/98b)
114.9	1974	*The Good Corn and other stories* (A 117)
114.10	1976	*The Poison Ladies and Other Stories* (A 119)
	See	*The Blossoming World* (A 110) p 138

B115 Elephant's Nest in a Rhubarb Tree

115.1	14 April 1939	*John O'London's Weekly*, xli, 1044, pp 69-70
115.2	1939	*The Flying Goat* (A 34)
115.3	1947	*Thirty-One Selected Tales* (A 60)
115.4	1989	*Elephant's Nest in a Rhubarb Tree &* *Other Stories* (A 126)

B116 I Am Not Myself

116.1	1939	*I Am Not Myself* (A 33)
116.2	September 1939	*Atlantic Monthly*, Boston, Mass., 164 pp 344-53
116.3	1939	*The Flying Goat* (A 34)
116.4	1947	*Thirty-One Selected Tales* (A 60)
116.5	1951	*Selected Short Stories of H.E. Bates* (A 70)
116.6	1957	*Selected Stories* (A 84)

B117 The White Pony

117.1	1939	*The Flying Goat* (A 34)
117.2	1947	*Thirty-One Selected Tales* (A 60)

B118 Every Bullet Has Its Billet

118.1	1939	*The Flying Goat* (A 34)
118.2	1947	*Thirty-One Selected Tales* (A 60)
118.3	1974	*The Good Corn and other stories* (A 117)

B119 The Ship

119.1	1939	*The Flying Goat* (A 34)
119.2	1947	*Thirty-One Selected Tales* (A 60)

B120   The Flying Goat

120.1   1939   *The Flying Goat* (A 34)
120.2   1951   *Twenty Tales* (A 71)

B121   The Late Public Figure

121.1   1939   *The Flying Goat* (A 34)
121.2   1951   *Twenty Tales* (A 71)

B122   Shot Actress - Full Story

122.1   1939   *The Flying Goat* (A 34)
122.2   1951   *Twenty Tales* (A 71)
122.3   1963   *Short Stories of Our Time*, Ed. Douglas Barnes,
                         London: Harrap
122.4   1968   *Best Theatre Stories*, Ed. Guy Slater, London:
                         Faber and Faber, pp 71-82

B123   The Wreath

123.1   1939   *The Flying Goat* (A 34)
123.2   1947   *Thirty-One Selected Tales* (A 60)

B124   The Shooting Party

124.1   1939   *My Uncle Silas* (A 35)

B125   Silas the Good

125.1   1939   *My Uncle Silas* (A 35)

B126   A Happy Man

126.1   1939   *My Uncle Silas* (A 35)
126.2   November 1939 *Lilliput*, London, v, 5, pp 501-4

B127   Silas and Goliath

127.1   1939   *My Uncle Silas* (A 35)

B128   A Silas Idyll

128.1	1939	*My Uncle Silas* (A 35)
128.2	December 1942	*Argosy*, iii, 11, pp 97-9
128.3	1971	*Fair Stood the Wind for France* together with two short stories, Ed. Geoffrey Halson, London: Longman, pp 297-300

B129   The Race

129.1	1939	*My Uncle Silas* (A 35)

Published later as 'My Uncle the Tortoise' (B 174)

B130   The Return

130.1	1939	*My Uncle Silas* (A 35)

B131   Old

131.1	7 December 1939	*The Listener*, London, xxii, 569, pp 1135-6, with one illustration
131.2	1940	*The Beauty of the Dead and Other Stories* (A 38)
131.3	1944	*The Toc H Gift Book*, London: Frederick Muller, pp 215-21
131.4	1951	*Twenty Tales* (A 71)

B132   Fuchsia

132.1	22 Dec 1939	*The Spectator*, clxiii, pp 896-7
132.2	1940	*The Beauty of the Dead and Other Stories* (A 38)
132.3	1947	*Thirty-One Selected Tales* (A 60)

B133   The Beauty of the Dead

133.1	December 1939	*Fortnightly Review*, London, clii, 146, pp 655-64
133.2	1940	*The Beauty of the Dead and Other Stories* (A 38)
133.3	1941	*The Beauty of the Dead and One Other Short Story* (A 39)
133.4	1947	*Thirty-One Selected Tales* (A 60)
133.5	1951	*Selected Short Stories of H.E. Bates* (A 70)
133.6	1957	*Selected Stories* (A 84)
133.7	1976	*The Poison Ladies and Other Short Stories* (A 119)

B134 The Bridge

134.1	January 1940	*Horizon*, London, i, 1, pp 31-50
134.2	1940	*The Beauty of the Dead and Other Stories* (A 38)
134.3	1941	*The Beauty of the Dead and One Other Story* (A 39)
134.4	1941	*The Best Short Stories of 1940*, English and American, Ed. Edward J. O'Brien, London: Jonathan Cape, pp 39-58
134.5	1941	*The Best British Short Stories 1940*, Ed. Edward J. O'Brien, Boston, Mass.: Houghton Mifflin
134.6	December 1946	*Good Housekeeping*, London, 123, pp 36-7
134.7	1947	*Thirty-One Selected Tales* (A 60)
134.8	1951	*Selected Short Stories of H.E. Bates* (A 70)
134.9	1957	*Selected Stories* (A 84)

B135 The Earth

135.1	January 1940	*Atlantic Monthly*, Boston, Mass., 165, pp 95-100
135.2	1940	*The Beauty of the Dead and Other Stories* (A 38)
135.3	1947	*Thirty-One Selected Tales* (A 60)
135.4	1948	*Seven Masterpiece Stories*, Ed. Harold Herd, London: Fleet Publications (The Writer's Library), pp 135-45
135.5	1951	*Selected Short Stories of H.E. Bates* (A 70)
135.6	1957	*Selected Stories* (A 84)
135.7	1975	*H.E. Bates* (A 118)

B136 Mr. Penfold

136.1	January 1940	*Harper's Magazine*, New York, clxxx, pp 140-46
136.2	1940	*The Beauty of the Dead and Other Stories* (A 38)
136.3	1947	*Thirty-One Selected Tales* (A 60)
136.4	1951	*Selected Short Stories of H.E. Bates* (A 70)
136.5	1957	*Selected Stories* (A 84)
136.6	1974	*The Good Corn and Other Stories* (A 117)

B137 The Little Jeweller

137.1	April 1940	*Life and Letters To-Day* (continuing the *London Mercury and Bookman*), London, xxv, 32, pp 42-65
137.2	1940	*The Beauty of the Dead and Other Stories* (A 38)
137.3	1947	*Thirty-One Selected Tales* (A 60)
137.4	1974	*The Good Corn and Other Stories* (A 117)
137.5	1989	*Elephant's Nest in a Rhubarb Tree & Other Stories* (A 126)

B138 Time to Kill

138.1	May 1940	*Fortnightly Review*, London, 153, pp 530-38
138.2	1940	*The Beauty of the Dead and Other Stories* (A 38)
138.3	1947	*Thirty-One Selected Tales* (A 60)
138.4	1974	*The Good Corn and Other Stories* (A 117)

B139 The Ferry

| 139.1 | 1940 | *The Beauty of the Dead and Other Stories* (A38) |
| 139.2 | 1947 | *Thirty-One Selected Tales* (A 60) |

B140 The Loved One

140.1	1940	*The Beauty of the Dead and Other Stories* (A 38)
140.2	1947	*Thirty-One Selected Tales* (A 60)
140.3	1951	*Selected Short Stories of H.E. Bates* (A 70)
140.4	1957	*Selected Stories* (A 84)
140.5	1974	*The Good Corn and Other Stories* (A 117)

B141 The Banjo

| 141.1 | 1940 | *The Beauty of the Dead and Other Stories* (A 38) |
| 141.2 | 1947 | *Thirty-One Selected Tales* (A 60) |

B142 A Scandalous Woman

142.1	1940	*The Beauty of the Dead and Other Stories* (A 38)
142.2	Winter 1940-41	*Kingdom Come* (founded in war-time Oxford, incorporating 'Bolero' and 'Light and Dark'), Eds. John Waller and Miles Vaughan Williams, Oxford University Press, ii, 2, (sixth number) pp 45-7
142.3	1951	*Twenty Tales* (A 71)

B143 Love Is Not Love

143.1	1940	*The Beauty of the Dead and Other Stories* (A38)
143.2	1947	*Thirty-One Selected Tales* (A 60)
143.3	1957	*Selected Stories* (A 84)

B144 Quartette

| 144.1 | 1940 | *The Beauty of the Dead and Other Stories* (A38) |
| 144.2 | 1951 | *Twenty Tales* (A 71) |

B145   The Goat and the Stars

| 145.1 | 1940 | *The Beauty of the Dead and Other Stories* (A 38) |
| 145.2 | 1951 | *Twenty Tales* (A 71) |

B146   Fishers

| 146.1 | 16 January 1941 | *The Listener*, London, xxv, 627, pp 91-2 |
| 146.2 | 1944 | *Best Broadcast Stories*, Ed. Hilton Brown, London: Faber and Faber, pp 99-106 |

B147   The Park

147.1	June 1941	*Life and Letters Today*, London, xxix, 46, pp 227-46
147.2	1945	*Stories of the Forties*, Eds. Reginald Moore and Woodrow Wyatt, London: Nicholson and Watson, Volume I, pp 219-32
147.3	1951	*Colonel Julian and Other Stories* (A 68)

B148   The Little Farm

148.1	1941	*The Saturday Book*, 1941-1942, Ed. Leonard Russell, London: Hutchinson, pp 172-211 (with three wood engravings by Agnes Miller Parker)
148.2	1951	*Colonel Julian and Other Stories* (A 68)
148.3	1980	*The Best of H.E. Bates* (A 122)

B149   It's Just the Way It Is

149.1	2 February 1942	*News Chronicle*, London, p 2
149.2	1942	*The Greatest People in the World and Other Stories* (A41)
149.3	1943	*There's Something In The Air* (A 45)
149.4	1944	*Something in the Air* (A 52)
149.5	1952	*The Stories of Flying Officer 'X'* (A 77)
149.6	1953	*The Flying Omnibus*, Ed. Paul Jensen, London: Cassell, pp 204-8
149.7	1987	*A Month by the Lake & Other Stories* (A 124)

See *The World in Ripeness* (A 114) p 126

B150   It's Never in the Papers

| 150.1 | 9 Feb 1942 | *News Chronicle*, London, p 2 |
| 150.2 | 4 Sept 1942 | *Forum* (Jerusalem Radio Magazine) vii, p 2 |

150.3	1942	*The Greatest People in the World and Other Stories* (A 41)
150.4	1943	*There's Something In The Air* (A 45)
150.5	1944	*Something In The Air* (A 52)
150.6	1952	*The Stories of Flying Officer 'X'* (A 77)

B151 O'Callaghan's Girl

151.1	16 Feb 1942	*News Chronicle*, London, p 2
151.2	21 August 1942	*Forum* (Jerusalem Radio Magazine), p 2
151.3	1943	*There's Something In The Air* (A 45)

B152 The Sun Rises Twice

152.1	23 Feb 1942	*News Chronicle*, London, p 2
152.2	June 1942	*Argosy*, iii, 5, pp 11-15
152.3	18 Sept 1942	*Forum* (Jerusalem Radio Magazine), p 4
152.4	1942	*The Greatest People in the World and Other Stories* (A 41)
152.5	1943	*There's Something In The Air* (A 45)
152.6	1944	*Something In The Air* (A 52)
152.7	1952	*The Stories of Flying Officer 'X'* (A 77)
152.8	1960	*Recent Short Stories*, selected by E.L. Black, London: Odhams Press, pp 202-10

See *The World in Ripeness* (A 114) p 18

B153 Macintyre's Magna Charta

| 153.1 | 2 March 1942 | *News Chronicle*, London, p 2 |
| 153.2 | 1943 | *There's Something In The Air* (A 45) |

B154 K For Kitty

154.1	9 March 1942	*News Chronicle*, London, p 2
154.2	1942	*The Greatest People in the World and Other Stories* (A 41)
154.3	16 October 1942	*Forum* (Jerusalem Radio Magazine), p 4
154.4	1943	*There's Something In The Air* (A 45)
154.5	1944	*Something In The Air* (A 52)
154.6	1952	*The Stories of Flying Officer 'X'* (A 77)

B155 The Beginning Of Things

| 155.1 | 22 April 1942 | *News Chronicle*, London, p 2 |
| 155.2 | July 1942 | *Argosy*, iii, 6, pp 97-100 |

155.3	1943	*There's Something In The Air* (A 45)
155.4	1943	*How Sleep The Brave and Other Stories* (A 47)
155.5	1944	*Something In The Air* (A 52)
155.6	1952	*The Stories of Flying Officer 'X'* (A 77)

B156 Croix de Guerre

156.1	11 May 1942	*News Chronicle*, London, p 2
156.2	August 1942	*Argosy*, iii, 7, pp 39-42
156.3	1943	*How Sleep the Brave and Other Stories* (A 47)
156.4	1944	*Something In The Air* (A 52)
156.5	1952	*The Stories of Flying Officer 'X'* (A 77)

B157 The Disinherited

157.1	18 May 1942	*News Chronicle*, London, p 2
157.2	September 1942.	*Argosy*, iii, 8, pp 3-6
157.3	1943	*There's Something In The Air* (A 45)
157.4	1943	*How Sleep the Brave and Other Stories* (A 47)
157.5	1944	*Something in the Air* (A 52)
157.6	1952	*The Stories of Flying Officer 'X'* (A 77)
157.7	1982	*Short Stories from the Second World War*, Oxford University Press, pp 89-92
157.8	1985	*The Best War Stories*, London: Hamlyn, pp 385-8
157.9	1989	*Elephant's Nest in a Rhubarb Tree & Other Stories* (A 126)

B158 Yours Is The Earth

158.1	3 June 1942	*News Chronicle*, London, p 2
158.2	1943	*There's Something In The Air* (A 45)
158.3	1943	*How Sleep the Brave and Other Stories* (A 47)
158.4	1944	*Something in the Air* (A 52)
158.5	1952	*The Stories of Flying Officer 'X'* (A 77)
158.6	1971	*Fair Stood the Wind for France with two short stories*, Ed. Geoffrey Halson, London: Longman, pp 291-4

B159 Here We Go Again

| 159.1 | July 1942 | *Lilliput*, London, xi, 1, Issue No.61, pp 6-8 |
| 159.2 | 1943 | *There's Something In The Air* (A 45) |

B160   The Young Man from Kalgoorlie

160.1	1942	*The Greatest People in the World and Other Stories* (A 41)
160.2	1943	*There's Something In The Air* (A 45)
160.3	1944	*Something in the Air* (A 52)
160.4	1952	*The Stories of Flying Officer 'X'* (A 77)
160.5	1956	*Best Flying Stories*, Ed. J.W.R. Taylor, London: Faber and Faber, pp 180-93
160.6	1956	*The Harrap Book of Short Stories*, Ed. J.C. Bullocke, London: Harrap, pp 180-93
160.7	1958	*Twelve Modern Short Stories*, Eds. E.E. Allen and A.T. Mason, London: E. Arnold, pp 105-19
	See	*The World in Ripeness* (A 114) pp 19, 126

B161   No Trouble At All

161.1	1942	*The Greatest People in the World and Other Stories* (A 41)
161.2	1943	*There's Something In The Air* (A 45)
161.3	1944	*Something in the Air* (A 52)
161.4	1952	*The Stories of Flying Officer 'X'* (A 77)
161.5	1982	*Short Stories from the Second World War*, Oxford University Press, pp 93-8

B162   A Personal War

162.1	1942	*The Greatest People in the World and Other Stories* (A 41)
162.2	1943	*There's Something In The Air* (A 45)
162.3	1944	*Something in the Air* (A 52)
162.4	1952	*The Stories of Flying Officer 'X'* (A 77)

B163   The Greatest People in the World

163.1	1942	*The Greatest People in the World and Other Stories* (A 41)
163.2	1943	*There's Something in the Air* (A 45)
163.3	July 1944	*Argosy*, v, 6, pp 3-10
163.4	1944	*Something in the Air* (A 52)
163.5	1952	*The Stories of Flying Officer 'X'* (A 77)
163.6	1989	*Elephant's Nest in a Rhubarb Tree & Other Stories* (A 126) (title wrongly printed on Contents page as 'The Greatest People on Earth' but correctly in text)

B164   There's No Future In It

164.1	1942	*The Greatest People in the World and Other Stories* (A 41)
164.2	30 October 1942	As 'There Is No Future In It' in *Forum*, (Jerusalem Radio Magazine), p 4
164.3	February 1943	*The American Federationist*, Washington D C, Volume 50, pp 28-9
164.4	1943	*There's Something In The Air* (A 45)
164.5	1944	*Something in the Air* (A 52)
164.6	1952	*The Stories of Flying Officer 'X'* (A 77)

B165   The Bride Comes to Evensford

165.1	1942	*The 1943 Saturday Book*, Ed. Leonard Russell, London: Hutchinson, pp 147-89
165.2	1943	*The Bride Comes to Evensford* (A 44)
165.3	1949	*The Bride Comes to Evensford And Other Tales* (A 63)

B166   Sergeant Carmichael

166.1	1942	*The 1943 Saturday Book*, Ed. Leonard Russell, London: Hutchinson, pp 204-16
166.2	November 1942	*Royal Air Force Journal*, London, No.1. pp 7-12 (illustrated with one photograph and one drawing)
166.3	1943	*There's Something in the Air* (A 45)
166.4	10 April 1944	*Senior Scholastic*, New York: Scholastic Inc, Volume 44, p 21
166.5	1946	*Slipstream: a Royal Air Force anthology*, Eds. Squadron Leader R. Raymond and Squadron Leader David Langdon. London: Eyre and Spottiswoode, pp 70-6
166.6	1952	*The Stories of Flying Officer 'X'* (A 77)
166.7	1958	*Contemporary Short Stories*, Ed. E.R. Wood, London: Blackie, pp 7-26
166.8	1987	*A Month by the Lake & Other Stories* (A 124)

B167   Happy Christmas Nastashya

167.1	December 1942	*Royal Air Force Journal*, London. No.2 pp 20-22 (with one illustration)

B168 Li Tale

168.1   1943   *There's Something in the Air* (A 45)

B169 Sorry, No Saccharine

169.1   1943   *There's Something in the Air* (A 45)

B170 Morning Victory

170.1   1943   *There's Something in the Air* (A 45)
170.2   1943   *Bugle Blast: An anthology from the Services*,
                                     Eds. Jack Aistrop and Reginald Moore, London:
                                     George Allen & Unwin, pp 101-4

B171 Free Choice, Free World

171.1   1943   *There's Something in the Air* (A 45)
171.2   1946   *Slipstream: A Royal Air Force anthology*,
                                     Eds. Squadron Leader R. Raymond and Squadron
                                     Leader David Langdon, London: Eyre and
                                     Spottiswoode, pp 52-5
171.3   1952   *The Stories of Flying Officer 'X'* (A 77)

B172 There's Something in the Air

172.1   1943   *There's Something in the Air* (A 45)
172.2   1943   *How Sleep the Brave and Other Stories* (A 47)
172.3   1944   *Something in the Air* (A 52)
172.4   1952   *The Stories of Flying Officer 'X'* (A 77)

B173 The Bell

173.1   4 June 1943   *Jerusalem Radio Forum* (Airgraph Digest) p 4
173.2   1946   *Slipstream: A Royal Air Force anthology*, Eds.
                                     Squadron Leader R. Raymond and Squadron
                                     Leader David Langdon. London:
                                     Eyre and Spottiswoode, pp 220-23
173.3   1952   *The Stories of Flying Officer 'X'* (A 77)

B174 My Uncle the Tortoise

174.1   June 1943   *Argosy*, iv, 5, pp 73-6
First published as 'The Race', see B 129

B175   How Sleep the Brave

175.1	1943	*How Sleep the Brave and Other Stories* (A 47)
175.2	1944	*Something in the Air* (A 52)
175.3	1952	*The Stories of Flying Officer 'X'* (A 77)

B176   The Risk

175.1   1943   *Wings of War: An illustrated R.A.F. anthology,*
                  Ed. F. Alan Walbank, London: Batsford, pp 139-40
From 'The Greatest People in the World' (B 163)

B177a   The Three Thousand and One Hours of Sergeant Kostek

177a.1   1943   *English Story* (Fourth Series), Ed. Woodrow
                  Wyatt, London: Collins, pp 86-9
177a.2   1965   *Forty Short Short Stories*, selected by J.C. Reid,
                  London: Edward Arnold, pp 24-8

B177b   From this Time Forward

177b.1   1943   *Printer's Pie – A Miscellany by Leading
                  Writers*, Ed. Leonard Russell,
                  London: Hutchinson, pp 41–6
                  (with one illustration by Laurence
                  Scarfe)

B178   Joe Johnson

177.1   1944   *Best Broadcast Stories*, Ed. Hilton Brown,
                  London: Faber, pp 107-18
178.2   1951   *Colonel Julian and Other Stories* (A 68)

B179   Colonel Motley

179.1   February 1945   *Atlantic Monthly*, Boston, Mass., clxxv,
                         pp 88-92
Published in England as 'Colonel Julian' (B 180)

B180   Colonel Julian

180.1   August 1945   *Life and Letters Today*, London, xlvi, pp 110-21
180.2   1951   *Colonel Julian and Other Stories* (A 68)
180.3   1960   *The Faber Book of Stories*, chosen by Kathleen

		Lines, London: Faber and Faber, pp 291-302
180.4	1963	*Seven by Five/The Best of H.E. Bates* (A 98a/98b)
180.5	1974	*The Good Corn and Other Stories* (A 117)

B181   Time-Expired

181.1	1945	*Voices on the Green*, Eds. A.R.J. Wise and Reginald Smith, London: Michael Joseph Ltd, pp 45-54
181.2	1946	*Little Reviews Anthology*, Ed. Denys Val Baker, London: Eyre & Spottiswoode, pp 10-18
181.3	1951	*Colonel Julian and Other Stories* (A 68)
181.4	1956	*Aspects of the Short Story*, Eds. E.L. Black and J.P. Parry, London: John Murray, pp 103-13

B182   The Cruise of the Breadwinner

182.1	23 March 1946	*The Saturday Evening Post*, Philadelphia, Pa.
182.2	April 1946	*The Cornhill Magazine*, London, 967, pp 3-40
182.3	1946	*Twelve Modern Short Novels*, London: Odhams Press, pp 469-511 (with two decorations by B. S. Biro)
182.4	1946	*The Cruise of the Breadwinner* (A 56)
182.5	1951	*The Cruise of the Breadwinner & Dear Life* (A 69)
182.6	1957	*The Cruise of the Breadwinner and Dear Life*, London: Transworld Publishers (Corgi Books T 414) pp (7)-73
182.7	1962	*The Saturday Evening Post Reader of Sea Stories*, Ed. Day Edgar, New York: Doubleday, pp 274-310
182.8	1965	*Six Stories*, Selected with an introduction by H.E. Bates, Oxford University Press (World's Classics No. 604), pp 208-64

B183   Mrs. Vincent

| 183.1 | August 1946 | *Atlantic Monthly*, Boston, Mass., clxxviii, pp 110-13 |
| 183.2 | 1951 | *Colonel Julian and Other Stories* (A 68) |

B184   Verdict from the Heart

| 184.1 | 5 July 1947 | *Saturday Evening Post*, Philadelphia, Pa, pp 18-19 |

B185   The Major of Hussars

185.1	November 1947	*The Saturday Book*, Seventh Year, Ed. Leonard Russell, London: Hutchinson, pp 170-84 (with illustrations by Leonard Scarfe)
185.2	1949	*Pick of To-Day's Short Stories*, 1st Series, Ed. John Pudney, London: Odhams Press, pp 1-18
185.3	1951	*Colonel Julian and Other Stories* (A 68)
185.4	1963	*Seven by Five/The Best of H.E. Bates* (A 98a/98b)
185.5	1980	*The Best of H.E. Bates* (A 122)
185.6	1989	*Elephant's Nest in a Rhubarb Tree & Other Stories* (A 126)

B186   The Bedfordshire Clanger

186.1	September 1949	*Argosy*, x, 9, pp 49-53
186.2	1951	*Colonel Julian and Other Stories* (A 68)
186.3	1957	*Sugar for the Horse* (A 85)
186.4	1980	*The Best of H.E. Bates* (A 122)

B187   Dear Life

187.1	November 1949 (in America) February 1950 (in England)	*Dear Life* (A 64)
187.2	1951	*The Cruise of the Breadwinner & Dear Life* (A 69)
187.3	1957	*The Cruise of the Breadwinner and Dear Life*, London: Transworld Publishers (Corgi Books T 414), pp 75-188

B188   Love Me Little, Love Me Long

| 188.1 | May 1950 | *Argosy*, xi, 5, pp 39-44 |
| 188.2 | 1968 | *The Wild Cherry Tree* (A 106) |

B189   The Frontier

189.1	1950	*Pick of To-Day's Short Stories*, Second Series, Ed. John Pudney, London: Odhams Press, pp 31-51
189.2	December 1950	*Argosy*, xi, 12, pp 139-59
189.3	1951	*Colonel Julian and Other Stories* (A 68)
189.4	1963	*Seven by Five/The Best of H.E. Bates*

		(A 98a/98b)
189.5	1975	*H.E. Bates* (A 118)

B190   A Song to Remember

190.1   28 Dec 1950   *Woman's Own Magazine*, London
Published later as 'A Christmas Song' (B 196)

B191   Sugar for the Horse

191.1	February 1951	*Argosy*, xii, 2, pp 5-10
191.2	1951	*Colonel Julian and Other Stories* (A 68)
191.3	1957	*Sugar for the Horse* (A 85)
191.4	1962	*Tauchnitz Book of English Short Stories*, (New Series 119), Stuttgart: Bernard Tauchnitz Verlag, pp 7-17

B192   No More The Nightingales

| 192.1 | April 1951 | *Argosy*, xii, 4, pp 19-26 |
| 192.2 | 1951 | *Colonel Julian and Other Stories* (A 68) |

B193   The Lighthouse

193.1	May 1951	*Argosy*, xii, 5, pp 97-112
193.2	1951	*Colonel Julian and Other Stories* (A 68)
193.3	1963	*Seven by Five/The Best of H.E. Bates* (A 98a/98b)

B194   A Girl Called Peter

194.1	1951	*Colonel Julian and Other Stories* (A 68)
194.2	August 1951	*Argosy*, xii, 8, pp 113-21
194.3	September 1951	*Atlantic Monthly*, Boston, Mass., lxxxviii, pp 47-51

B195   The Flag

195.1	1951	*Colonel Julian and Other Stories* (A 68)
195.2	1963	*Seven by Five/The Best of H.E. Bates* (A 98a/98b)
195.3	1987	*A Month by the Lake & Other Stories* (A 124)

B196   A Christmas Song

196.1   1951   *Colonel Julian and Other Stories* (A 68)
196.2   1963   *Seven by Five/The Best of H.E. Bates*
                             (A 98a/98b)
First published as 'A Song to Remember' (B 190)

B197   The Snow Line

197.1   October 1951   *The Saturday Book* (Eleventh Year),
                             Ed. Leonard Russell, London: Hutchinson,
                             pp 225-46 (illustrated by Malvina Cheek)
197.2   1961   *Now Sleeps the Crimson Petal and Other Stories/*
                             The Enchantress and Other Stories
                             (A 91a/91b)

B198   The Grass God

198.1   1951   *The Grass God* (A 72)
198.2   1953   *The Nature of Love* (A 79)

B199   For Valour

199.1   Winter 1951-52   *Modern Reading* (incorporating Books
                             and Authors), Ed. Reginald Moore, London:
                             Modern Reading, No. 20, pp 19-24
                             (with one illustration)

B200   The Delicate Nature

200.1   July 1952   *Argosy*, xiii, 7, pp 111-42
200.2   1953   *The Nature of Love* (A 79)

B201   Across the Bay

201.1   November 1952   *Argosy*, xiii, 11, pp 4-22
201.2   1955   *The Daffodil Sky* (A 81)
201.3   1963   *Seven by Five/The Best of H.E. Bates*
                             (A 98a/98b)

B202   The Evolution of Saxby

202.1   Jan–Feb 1953   *Lilliput*, London, xxxii, 2, Issue No.188, pp 65-80
202.2   1955   *The Daffodil Sky* (A 81)
202.3   1963   *Seven by Five/The Best of H.E. Bates*
                             (A 98a/98b)
202.4   1987   *A Month by the Lake & Other Stories* (A 124)

B203   The Far Journey

203.1   9 February 1953 *Evening News*, London, p 7 (with one illustration)
Later published as 'The Far Distant Journey' (B 248)

B204   Chaff in the Wind

204.1	20 April 1953	*Evening News*, London, p 6 (with one illustration)
204.2	1953	*Pick of To-Day's Short Stories:* 4, Ed. John Pudney, London: Putnam, pp 6-13
204.3	October 1954	*Argosy*, xv, 10, pp 45-50
204.4	1955	*The Daffodil Sky* (A 81)
204.5	1963	*Seven by Five/The Best of H.E. Bates* (A 98a/98b)

B205   The Treasure Game

205.1	July 1953	*The Atlantic Monthly*, Boston, Mass., pp 57-60
205.2	1955	*The Daffodil Sky* (A 81)

B206   Cherry Ripe

206.1	August 1953	*Argosy*, xiv, 8, pp 39-46

B207   Elaine

207.1	3 Sept 1953	*Evening News*, London, p 9
207.2	1955	*The Daffodil Sky* (A 81)
207.3	1963	*Seven by Five/The Best of H.E. Bates* (A 98a/98b)
207.4	1987	*A Month by the Lake & Other Stories* (A 124)

B208   Go, Lovely Rose

208.1	27 October 1953	*Evening News*, London, p 7 (with one illustration)
208.2	1955	*The Daffodil Sky* (A 81)
208.3	1963	*Seven by Five/The Best of H.E. Bates* (A 98a/98b)
208.4	16 Sept 1972	*Woman*, London lxxi, 1839, pp 44-6, 54
208.5	1974	*Breaking Away*, An anthology edited by Michael Marland, London: Longman Group, pp 12-18
208.6	1989	*Elephant's Nest in a Rhubarb Tree & Other Stories* (A 126)

B209   The Watercress Girl

209.1	November 1953	*Mademoiselle*, New York, 38, pp 88-9
209.2	August 1954	*Argosy*, xv, 8, pp 5-16, as 'Watercress Girl'
209.3	1959	*The Watercress Girl and Other Stories* (A 88)
209.4	1963	*Seven by Five/The Best of H.E. Bates* (A 98a/98b)
209.5	1976	*The Poison Ladies and Other Stories* (A 119)
209.6	1989	*Elephant's Nest in a Rhubarb Tree & Other Stories* (A 126)

B210a   Dulcima

210a.1	1953	*The Nature of Love* (A 79)
210a.2	Jul-Aug 1953	*Lilliput*, London, xxxiii, 2, pp 56-88
210a.3	1971	*Dulcima* (A 111)

B210b   A man in the house

210b.1	20 March 1954	*John Bull*, London, vc, 2491, pp (7)–9, 36–37, 39, illustrated by Henry Seabright

B211   The Yellow Crab

211.1	Summer 1954	*The Cornhill*, London, No. 1000, pp 303-20
211.2	November 1959	*Argosy*, xx, 10, pp 45-60
211.3	1961	*Now Sleeps the Crimson Petal and Other Stories/ The Enchantress and Other Stories* (A 91a/91b)

B212   Love in a Wych Elm

212.1	1954	*Woman's Own*, London
212.2	September 1959	*Argosy*, xx, 8, pp 67-75
212.3	1959	*The Watercress Girl and Other Stories* (A 88)
212.4	1963	*Seven by Five/The Best of H.E. Bates* (A 98a/98b)
212.5	1974	*The Good Corn and Other Stories* (A 117)
212.6	24 August 1985	*Woman's Realm*, London, pp 14 (full-page illustration in colour), pp (15), 20,22
212.7	1989	*Elephant's Nest in a Rhubarb Tree & Other Stories* (A 126)

B213   Roman Figures

213.1	August 1955	*Argosy*, xvi, 8, pp 5-14
213.2	1955	*The Daffodil Sky* (A 81)

B214   Summer in Salander

214.1	September 1955	*Argosy*, xvi, 9, pp 26-55
214.2	1957	*Death of a Huntsman/Summer in Salander* (A 83a/83b)
214.3	1974	*The Grapes of Paradise* (A 116)
214.4	1988	*A Party for the Girls* (A 125)

B215   The Lotus Land

215.1	17 October 1955	*Evening Standard*, London, p 19 The first story in a series, *'Tales of Tahiti'*, illustrated by A.R. Whitear
215.2	1964	*The Fabulous Mrs V* (A 99)

B216   The Ginger-Lily Girl

216.1	18 October 1955	*Evening Standard*, London, p 19 The second story in *'Tales of Tahiti'*, illustrated by A.R. Whitear
216.2	1964	*The Fabulous Mrs V* (A 99)

B217   Mrs. Eglantine

217.1	19 October 1955	*Evening Standard*, London, p23 The third story in *'Tales of Tahiti'*
217.2	1961	*Now Sleeps the Crimson Petal and Other Stories/ The Enchantress and Other Stories* (A 91a/91b)
217.3	1963	*Seven by Five/The Best of H.E. Bates* (A 98a/98b)
217.4	1987	*A Month by the Lake & Other Stories* (A 124)
	See	*The World in Ripeness* (A 114) p 144

B218   The Sugar Train

218.1	20 October 1955	*Evening Standard*, London, p 19 The fourth story in *'Tales of Tahiti'*, illustrated by A.R. Whitear

B219   The Laughing Princess

219.1   21 October 1955 *Evening Standard*, London, p 19
                              The fifth story in *'Tales of Tahiti'*
                              illustrated by A.R. Whitear

B220   Coconut Radio

220.1   22 October 1955 *Evening Standard*, London, p 11
                              The sixth and final story in *'Tales of Tahiti'*.
                              Illustrated by A.R. Whitear
220.2   1965   *The Wedding Party* (A 102)
220.3   1989   *Elephant's Nest in a Rhubarb Tree &*
                             Other Stories (A 126)

B221   The Good Corn

221.1   October 1955   *Argosy*, xvi, 10, pp 32-42
221.2   1955   *The Daffodil Sky* (A 81)
221.3   1963   *Seven by Five/The Best of H.E. Bates*
                             (A 98a/98b)
221.4   1974   *The Good Corn and Other Stories* (A 117)

B222   The Daffodil Sky

222.1   1955   *The Daffodil Sky* (A 81)
222.2   1963   *Seven by Five/The Best of H.E. Bates*
                             (A 98a/98b)

B223   Country Society

223.1   1955   *The Daffodil Sky* (A 81)
223.2   1963   *Seven by Five/The Best of H.E. Bates*
                             (A 98a/98b)
223.3   1987   *A Month by the Lake & Other Stories* (A 124)

B224   The Maker of Coffins

224.1   1955   *The Daffodil Sky* (A 81)
224.2   1963   *Seven by Five/The Best of H.E. Bates*
                             (A 98a/98b)
224.3   1974   *The Good Corn and Other Stories* (A 117)
224.4   1987   *A Month by the Lake & Other Stories* (A 124)

B225   The Small Portion

| 225.1 | 1955 | *The Daffodil Sky* (A 81) |
| 225.2 | 1973 | *An Overpraised Season,* Ten stories selected by Charlotte Zolotow, New York: Harper & Row Inc.; 1974 London: The Bodley Head, pp 145-57 |

B226   The Common Denominator

| 226.1 | 1955 | *The Daffodil Sky* (A 81) |

B227   A Place in the Heart

| 227.1 | 1955 | *The Daffodil Sky* (A 81) |

B228   Third View on the Reichenbach

| 228.1 | 1955 | *The Daffodil Sky* (A 81) |

B229   The Double Thumb

| 229.1 | 13 August 1956 | *Evening Standard,* London, p 13 (with one illustration) |
| 229.2 | 1957 | *Sugar for the Horse* (A 85) |

B230   The Singing Pig

| 230.1 | 14 August 1956 | *Evening Standard,* London, p 13 (with one illustration) |
| 230.2 | 1957 | *Sugar for the Horse* (A 85) |

B231   The Eating Match

| 231.1 | 15 August 1956 | *Evening Standard,* London, p 13 (with one illustration) |
| 231.2 | 1957 | *Sugar for the Horse* (A 85) |

B232   The 'Widder'

| 232.1 | 16 August 1956 | *Evening Standard,* London, p 13 |
| 232.2 | 1957 | *Sugar for the Horse* (A 85) |

B233   The Little Fishes

233.1	17 August 1956	*Evening Standard*, London, p 13 (with one illustration)
233.2	1957	*Sugar for the Horse* (A 85)
233.3	1963	*Country Bunch: A collection by Miss Read*, London: Michael Joseph, pp 249-55 (illustrated by Andrew Dobbs)
233.4	1965	*Best Fishing Stories*, Edited with an Introduction by John Moore, London: Faber & Faber, pp 85 - 91
233.5	1974	*Great British Short Stories*, selected by the editors of Reader's Digest, with an Introduction by J.B. Priestley, London: Reader's Digest Association, pp 61-5 (with one illustration by Elizabeth Trimby)

B234   Aunt Tibby

234.1	18 August 1956	*Evening Standard*, London, p 9
234.2	1957	*Sugar for the Horse* (A 85)

B235   The Queen of Spain Fritillary

235.1	September 1956	*Argosy*, xvii, 9, pp 30-51
235.2	1957	*Death of a Huntsman/Summer in Salander* (A 83a/83b)
235.3	1974	*The Grapes of Paradise* (A 116)
235.4	1976	*The Poison Ladies and Other Stories* (A 119)

B236a   Queenie White

236a.1	January 1957	*Argosy*, xviii, 1, pp 51-7
236a.2	1957	*Sugar for the Horse* (A 85)
236a.3	1975	*H.E. Bates* (A 118)

B236b   The White Wand

236b.1	2, 9 March 1957	*John Bull*, London, ci, 2644, pp 9–11 30, 32–3, 35, 37; 2645, pp 34–8. Illustrated by Zelinski. Following this serialisation, changes were made in the story.
236b.2	1968	*The Four Beauties* (A 104)
236b.3	1988	*A Party for the Girls* (A 125)

B237   Death of a Huntsman

237.1	April 1957	*Argosy*, xviii, 4, pp 104-43 (decoration by Owen Ward)
237.2	1957	*Death of a Huntsman/Summer in Salander* (A 83a/83b)
237.3	1974	*The Grapes of Paradise* (A 116)
237.4	1988	*A Party for the Girls* (A 125)

B238   A Great Day for Bonzo

238.1	October 1957	*Argosy*, xviii, 10, pp 102-43
238.2	1959	*The Watercress Girl and Other Stories* (A 88)
238.3	1988	*A Party for the Girls* (A 125)

B239   Night Run to the West

| 239.1 | 1957 | *Death of a Huntsman/Summer in Salander* (A 83a/83b) |
| 239.2 | 1974 | *The Grapes of Paradise* (A 116) |

B240   The Blue Feather

| 240.1 | 1957 | *Sugar for the Horse* (A 85) |

B241   The Foxes

| 241.1 | 1957 | *Sugar for the Horse* (A 85) |

B242   The Fire Eaters

| 242.1 | 1957 | *Sugar for the Horse* (A 85) |
| 242.2 | 18 Nov 1951 | *Sunday Dispatch*, p. 2 (with one illustration) |

B243   A Prospect of Orchards

243.1	Winter 1957	*The Cornhill*, London, clxix, 1014, pp 394-421
243.2	1960	*An Aspidistra in Babylon/The Grapes of Paradise* (A 89a/89b)
243.3	1974	*The Grapes of Paradise* (A 116)

B244   Now Sleeps the Crimson Petal

244.1	January 1958	*Argosy*, xix, 1, pp 26-42
244.2	1961	*Now Sleeps the Crimson Petal and Other Stories/ The Enchantress and Other Stories* (A 91a/91b)
244.3	1963	*Seven by Five/The Best of H.E. Bates* (A 98a/98b)

B245   Summer Enchantress

245.1	April 1958	*Argosy* xix, 4, pp 56-76

B246   Let's Play Soldiers

246.1	December 1958	*Argosy*, xix, 12, pp 66-75
246.2	1959	*The Watercress Girl and Other Stories* (A 88)
246.3	1963	*Seven by Five/The Best of H.E. Bates* (A 98a/98b)
246.4	1974	*The Good Corn and Other Stories* (A 117)
246.5	1975	*H.E. Bates* (A 118)
246.6	1989	*Elephant's Nest in a Rhubarb Tree & Other Stories* (A 126)

B247   The Cowslip Field

247.1	1959	*The Watercress Girl and Other Stories* (A 88)
247.2	July 1960	*The Flower Grower*, Albany, USA: Williams Press, xlvii, pp 47-51
247.3	1963	*Seven by Five/The Best of H.E. Bates* (A 98a/98b)
247.4	1976	*The Poison Ladies and Other Stories* (A 119)
247.5	1987	*A Month by the Lake & Other Stories* (A 124)

B248   The Far Distant Journey

248.1	1959	*The Watercress Girl and Other Stories* (A 88)

First published as 'The Far Journey' (B 203)

B249   The Pemberton Thrush

249.1	1959	*The Watercress Girl and Other Stories* (A 88)
249.2	May 1959	*Argosy*, xx, 5, pp 59-67, as 'Pemberton Thrush'

B250   Death and the Cherry Tree

250.1	1959	*The Watercress Girl and Other Stories* (A 88)
250.2	1968	*Through the Green Woods*, Ed. Stan Barstow, Leeds: E.J. Arnold, pp 9-16
250.3	1987	*A Month by the Lake & Other Stories* (A 124)

B251   The Butterfly

251.1	1959	*The Watercress Girl and Other Stories* (A 88)
251.2	1987	*A Month by the Lake & Other Stories* (A 124)

B252   The House with the Grapevine

252.1	1959	*The Watercress Girl and Other Stories* (A 88)

B253   Great Uncle Crow

253.1	1959	*The Watercress Girl and Other Stories* (A 88)
253.2	1963	*Seven by Five/The Best of H.E. Bates* (A 98a/98b)
253.3	April 1969	*Trident*, First issue of British European Airways in-flight magazine, London: IPC Magazines Ltd for British European Airways
253.4	1976	*The Poison Ladies and Other Stories* (A 119)
253.5	1980	*The Best of H.E. Bates* (A 122)
253.6	1989	*Elephant's Nest in a Rhubarb Tree & Other Stories* (A 126)

B254   Source of the World

254.1	1959	*The Watercress Girl and Other Stories* (A 88)

B255   The Poison Ladies

255.1	1959	*The Watercress Girl and Other Stories* (A 88)
255.2	1976	*The Poison Ladies and Other Stories* (A 119)

B256   An Aspidistra in Babylon

256.1	11 July 1959	*Woman's Own*, London
256.2	1960	*An Aspidistra in Babylon/The Grapes of Paradise* (A 89a/89b)
256.3	1974	*The Grapes of Paradise* (A 116)

See *The World in Ripeness* (A 114) p 124

B257 Lost Ball

257.1	Autumn 1959	*The Cornhill Magazine*, London, clxxi, pp 20-27
257.2	1961	*Now Sleeps the Crimson Petal and Other Stories/ The Enchantress and Other Stories* (A 91a/91b)
257.3	1963	*Seven by Five/The Best of H.E. Bates* (A 98a/98b)

B258 The Day of the Tortoise

258.1	September 1960	*Argosy* xxi, 9, pp 106-43 (illustrated by Mary Dinsdale)
258.2	1961	*The Day of the Tortoise* (A 92)

B259 Shandy Lil

259.1	October 1960	*Argosy*, xxi, 10, pp 47-52
258.2	1965	*The Wedding Party* (A 102)

B260 The Courtship

260.1	25 Dec 1960	*Sunday Express*, London, p 6
260.2	1961	*Pick of Today's Short Stories*, 12, Ed. John Pudney, London: Putnam, pp 47-57
260.3	1965	*The Wedding Party* (A 102)

B261 A Month by the Lake

261.1	1960	*An Aspidistra in Babylon/The Grapes of Paradise* (A 89a/89b)
261.2	1974	*The Grapes of Paradise* (A 116)
261.3	1987	*A Month by the Lake & Other Stories* (A 124)

B262 The Grapes of Paradise

262.1	10, 17 March 1956	*John Bull*, London, ic, 2593, pp 9-13, 36-38, 41; 2594, pp 26-29, 36-38, 40-43, 45
262.2	1960	*An Aspidistra in Babylon/The Grapes of Paradise* (A 89a/89b)
262.3	1974	*The Grapes of Paradise* (A 116)

B263 The Place Where Shady Lay

263.1   January 1961   *Argosy*, xxii, 1, pp 64-70
263.2   1961   *Now Sleeps the Crimson Petal and Other Stories/*
                         The Enchantress and Other Stories
                         (A 91a/91b)

B264 Silas on the Wagon

264.1   January 1961   *Argosy*, xxii, 1, pp 71-5

B265 The Diamond Hair-Pin

265.1   March 1961   *Modern Woman*, London
265.2   1964   *The Fabulous Mrs V* (A 99)

B266 Where the Cloud Breaks

266.1   March 1961   *Woman's Own*, London
266.2   1961   *Now Sleeps the Crimson Petal and Other Stories/*
                         The Enchantress and Other Stories
                         (A 91a/91b)
266.3   1963   *Seven by Five/The Best of H.E. Bates*
                         (A 98a/98b)
266.4   1974   *The Good Corn and Other Stories* (A 117)
266.5   1976   *The Poison Ladies and Other Stories* (A 119)
266.6   1987   *A Month by the Lake & Other Stories* (A 124)
Published in America as 'Misunderstanding' (B 272)
      See *The World in Ripeness* (A 114) p 124

B267 The Enchantress

267.1   1961   *Now Sleeps the Crimson Petal and Other Stories/*
                         The Enchantress and Other Stories
                         (A 91a/91b)
267.2   1963   *Seven by Five/The Best of H.E. Bates*
                         (A 98a/98b)

B268 Daughters of the Village

268.1   1961   *Now Sleeps the Crimson Petal and Other Stories/*
                         The Enchantress and Other Stories
                         (A 91a/91b)

B269   Thelma

269.1   1961   *Now Sleeps the Crimson Petal and Other Stories/*
                            The Enchantress and Other Stories
                            (A 91a/91b)
269.2   1963   *Seven by Five/The Best of H.E. Bates*
                            (A 98a/98b)
269.3   1989   *Elephant's Nest in a Rhubarb Tree &*
                            Other Stories (A 126)

B270   The Spring Hat

270.1   1961   *Now Sleeps the Crimson Petal and Other Stories/*
                            The Enchantress and Other Stories
                            (A 91a/91b)

B271   An Island Princess

271.1   1961   *Now Sleeps the Crimson Petal and Other Stories/*
                            The Enchantress and Other Stories
                            (A 91a/91b)

B272   Misunderstanding

272.1   8 July 1961   *Saturday Evening Post*, Philadelphia, Pa.,
                            ccxxxiv, p 24. Published in England as 'Where the
                            Cloud Breaks' (B 266)

B273   The Ring of Truth

273.1   July 1961   *Argosy*, xxii, 7, pp 114-43
273.2   1962   *The Golden Oriole* (A 94)

B274   Trespassers Beware

274.1   10 Feb 1962   *The Saturday Evening Post*,
                            Philadelphia, Pa., ccxxv, pp 30-31

B275   The Quiet Girl

275.1   February 1962   *Argosy* xxiii, 2, pp 108-35 (illustrated by Biro)
275.2   1962   *The Golden Oriole* (A 94)

B276   The Trespasser

| 276.1 | August 1962 | *Argosy*, xxiii, 8, pp 2-14 |
| 276.2 | 1964 | *The Fabulous Mrs V* (A 99) |
| 276.3 | 1989 | *Elephant's Nest in a Rhubarb Tree &*
Other Stories (A 126) |

B277   The Golden Oriole

| 277.1 | 1962 | *The Golden Oriole* (A 94) |

See *The World in Ripeness* (A 114) p 124

B278   Mr Featherstone Takes a Ride

| 278.1 | 1962 | *The Golden Oriole* (A 94) |

See *The World in Ripeness* (A 114) p 144

B279   The World is Too Much With Us

| 279.1 | 1962 | *The Golden Oriole* (A 94) |

B280   The Old Eternal

| 280.1 | January 1963 | *Argosy*, xxiv, 1, pp 4-13 |
| 280.2 | 1965 | *The Wedding Party* (A 102) |

B281   Captain Poop-Deck's Paradise

| 281.1 | March 1963 | *Argosy*, xxiv, 3, pp 4-13 |
| 281.2 | 1963 | *Pick of To-day's Short Stories*: 14, Ed. John
Pudney, London: Eyre & Spottiswoode, pp 11-23 |
| 281.3 | 1965 | *The Wedding Party* (A 102) |

B282   The Fabulous Mrs V

| 282.1 | April 1963 | *Woman's Own*, London |
| 282.2 | 1964 | *The Fabulous Mrs V* (A 99) |

B283   The Cat who Sang

| 283.1 | June 1963 | *Argosy*, xxiv, 6, pp 28-37
(illustrated by Jennetta Vise) |
| 283.2 | 1964 | *The Fabulous Mrs V* (A 99) |

B284   And No Birds Sing

284.1	1964	*The Fabulous Mrs V* (A 99)
284.2	1975	*H.E. Bates* (A 118)
284.3	1989	*Elephant's Nest in a Rhubarb Tree & Other Stories* (A 126)

B285   A Couple of Fools

285.1	1964	*The Fabulous Mrs V* (A 99)
285.2	1975	*H.E. Bates* (A 118)

B286   Afternoon at the Château

286.1	1964	*The Fabulous Mrs V* (A 99)

B287   A Party for the Girls

287.1	1964	*The Fabulous Mrs V* (A 99)
287.2	1988	*A Party for the Girls* (A 125)

B288   A Dream of Fair Women

288.1	11964	*The Fabulous Mrs V* (A 99)

B289   A Nice Friendly Atmosphere

289.1	1964	*The Fabulous Mrs V* (A 99)

B290   The Winter Sound

290.1	1965	*The Wedding Party* (A 102)

B291   The Wedding Party

291.1	1965	*The Wedding Party* (A 102)

B292   Early One Morning

292.1	1965	*The Wedding Party* (A 102)

B293 Squiff

| 293.1 | 1965 | *The Wedding Party* (A 102) |
| 293.2 | 1975 | *H.E. Bates* (A 118) |

B294 The Primrose Place

| 294.1 | 1965 | *The Wedding Party* (A 102) |

B295 The Sun of December

| 295.1 | 1965 | *The Wedding Party* (A 102) |

B296 A Teetotal Tale

| 296.1 | 1965 | *The Wedding Party* (A 102) |

B297 The Picnic

| 297.1 | 1965 | *The Wedding Party* (A 102) |

B298 Sands of Time

| 298.1 | 12 March 1966 | *Woman's Own*, London, pp 36-8, 41, 88 91, 93, 94, 96 |

Published later as 'How Vainly Men Themselves Amaze' (B 308)

B299 The Four Beauties

299.1	23, 30 April 1966	*Woman's Own*, London
299.2	1968	*The Four Beauties* (A 104)
299.3	1980	*The Best of H.E. Bates* (A 122)

B300 Some Other Spring

300.1	July 1966	*Argosy*, xxvii, 7, pp 122-43 (illustrated by Margaret Theakston)
300.2	1968	*The Wild Cherry Tree* (A 106)
300.3	1989	*Elephant's Nest in a Rhubarb Tree & Other Stories* (A 126)

B301   The Simple Life

301.1	September 1967	*Argosy*, xxviii, 9, pp 50-70
		(one illustration by Margaret Theakston)
301.2	1968	*The Four Beauties* (A 104)
301.3	1980	*The Best of H.E. Bates* (A 122)

B302   The Chords of Youth

302.1	1968	*The Four Beauties* (A 104)
302.2	1987	*A Month by the Lake & Other Stories* (A 124)

B303   The Wild Cherry Tree

303.1	11 May 1968	*Woman's Own*, London, pp 20, 23, 86, 88, 90
303.2	1968	*The Wild Cherry Tree* (A 106)
303.3	1980	*The Best of H.E. Bates* (A 122)
303.4	25 Sept 1982	*Woman's Own*, London pp 16-19, 21, 23

B304   In the Middle of Nowhere

304.1	July 1968	*Argosy*, xxix, 7, pp 32-45 (one illustration
		by David Knight)
304.2	1968	*The Wild Cherry Tree* (A 106) as
		'The Middle of Nowhere'

B305   Halibut Jones

305.1	1968	*The Wild Cherry Tree* (A 106)

B306   The World Upside-Down

306.1	1968	*The Wild Cherry Tree* (A 106)
306.2	1989	*Elephant's Nest in a Rhubarb Tree &*
		Other Stories (A 126)

B307   How Vainly Men Themselves Amaze

307.1	1968	*The Wild Cherry Tree* (A 106)
307.2	1975	*H.E. Bates* (A 118)

First published as 'Sands of Time' (B 298)

B308   The First Day of Christmas

308.1   1968   *The Wild Cherry Tree* (A 106)

B309   The Black Magnolia

309.1   1968   *The Wild Cherry Tree* (A 106)

B310   Same Time, Same Place

310.1   1968   *The Wild Cherry Tree* (A 106)

B311   The Triple Echo

311.1   1970   *The Triple Echo* (A 109)
311.2   1980   *The Best of H.E. Bates* (A 122)

B312   The Man Who Loved Squirrels

312.1   May 1971   *Argosy*, xxxii, 4, pp 96-124
312.2   1972   *The Song of the Wren* (A 113)

B313   The Song of the Wren

313.1   1972   *The Song of the Wren* (A 113)
313.2   1987   *A Month by the Lake & Other Stories* (A 124)

B314   The Dam

314.1   1972   *The Song of the Wren* (A 113)

B315   The Tiger Moth

315.1   1972   *The Song of the Wren* (A 113)

B316   Oh! Sweeter than the Berry

316.1   1972   *The Song of the Wren* (A 113)

B317   The Proposal

317.1   5 April 1974   *Daily Telegraph Magazine*, London,
                                pp 63, 66, 70
317.2   1976   *The Yellow Meads of Asphodel* (A 120)

B318   The Yellow Meads of Asphodel

318.1   1976   *The Yellow Meads of Asphodel* (A 120)
318.2   1976   *The Yellow Meads of Asphodel* (A 121)
                          This publication is a single story in a limited
                          edition of 350 copies to celebrate the fortieth
                          anniversary of Michael Joseph Ltd.

B319   A Taste of Blood

319.1   1976   *The Yellow Meads of Asphodel* (A 120)

B320   The Love Letters of Miss Maitland

320.1   1976   *The Yellow Meads of Asphodel* (A 120)

B321   The Lap of Luxury

321.1   1976   *The Yellow Meads of Asphodel* (A 120)

B322   Loss of Pride

322.1   1976   *The Yellow Meads of Asphodel* (A 120)

B323   The House by the River

323.1   1976   *The Yellow Meads of Asphodel* (A 120)

C

Essays, articles, commentaries introductions

C1 Northamptonshire Men of Letters
No.1 John Clare the Peasant Poet (1793-1864)

1.1   December 1921   *Kettering Grammar School Magazine*,
                               Sixth Issue, pp 11-12

C2 At the Sign of the Rainbow
2.1   13 August–   *The Reminder* - An Illustrated Weekly,
            19 November   T. Beaty Hart Ltd. Kettering, i, 24-38
            1924   These weekly columns written under the pseudonym
                               'Boy Blue', consisted mainly of events and
                               commentaries on life in his home town of Rushden.
                               Bates was then nineteen years of age and employed
                               locally as a clerk in the office of a firm of
                               leather merchants.

C3 Stephen Crane: A Neglected Genius
3.1   October 1931   *The Bookman*, Book Society Ltd, London, lxxxi, 81,
                               pp 10-11

C4 A Note on D.H. Lawrence
4.1   30 July 1932   *New Clarion*, London, i, 8, p 174

C5 A Cotswold Day
5.1   27 August 1932   *New Clarion*, i, 12, p 271

C6 England Living and England Dead
6.1   10 Sept 1932   *New Clarion*, i, 14, p 319

C7 A Traveller in Little Things (on W.H. Hudson)
7.1   15 October 1932 *New Clarion*, i, 19, p 439

**C8 The Man who Half-made Christmas
(on Charles Dickens)**
8.1   3 December 1932 *New Clarion*, i, 26, p 606

C9 'Foreword' (A Terrible Day)
9.1   (1932)   *A Terrible Day* by David Garnett, William
                            Jackson, Furnival Books, London. No.9, pp 7-10

C10 George Moore
10.1   11 Feb 1933   *New Clarion*, ii, 36, p 193

C11 Lament for a Lost Poet (on John Galsworthy)
11.1   25 Feb 1933   *New Clarion*, ii, 38, p 229

C12 Crime by Blossoms
12.1   27 May 1933   *New Statesman and Nation*, viii, 183, pp 684-5

C13 London's Doorstep (Off the Highway in Kent)
13.1   10 June 1933   *New Clarion*, p 4

C14 My Cottage That Was a Barn
14.1   July 1933   *The Countryman*, London, 7, No.2, pp 357-60

C15 Mushroom Time
15.1   6 October 1933 *The Spectator*, London, cli, p 439

C16 A Kentish Portrait
16.1   28 October 1933 *New Statesman and Nation*, pp 513-14

C17   My Beginning

17.1   1933   *Ten Contemporaries: Notes towards their*
                          Definitive Bibliography (Second Series),
                          John Gawsworth (T.I.F. Armstrong), with
                          a prefatory word by P.H. Muir. Joiner and
                          Steele Ltd, London, pp 17-22; followed by
                          a bibliography, pp 23-36 (the edition limited to
                          1,000 copies).
17.2   January 1947   *Literary Digest*, London, i, 4, pp 10-11

C18   Season of Catkins

18.1   23 Feb 1934   *The Spectator*, London, clii, p 268

C19   A Note on the English Short Story

19.1   February 1934   *Lovat Dickson's Magazine*, London, pp 145-8

C20   The Lace-makers

20.1   28 April 1934   *New Statesman and Nation*, vii, p 637
20.2   1937   *Down the River* (A 29)

C21   A Midland Portrait

21.1   7 July 1934   *New Statesman and Nation*, viii, 176,
                          New Series, pp 12-13

C22   A Country Pub

22.1   25 August 1934 *New Statesman and Nation*, viii, 183,
                          pp 237-8

C23   December Spring

23.1   7 December 1934 *The Spectator*, cliii, pp 873-4

C24   Grammar School (Kettering)

24.1   1934   *The Old School: Essays by divers hands*,
                          Ed. Graham Greene, London: Jonathan Cape,
                          pp 21-3
See *The Vanished World* (A 107) pp 77, 81, 102

C25   The Ouse and the Nen

25.1   1934   *English Country: Fifteen essays by various*
                                    authors, edited with an introduction
                                    by H.J. Massingham. London: Wishart & Co.,
                                    pp 3-17

C26   The Snows of Spring

26.1   1 February 1935   *The Spectator*, cliv, 5562, pp 160-61
26.2   1936   *Through the Woods* (A 27) As 'Snows of Spring'
(Considerable changes were made from the text published in *The Spectator*)

C27   March Buds

27.1   22 March 1935   *The Spectator*, cliv, 5569, pp 472-3

C28   My Poacher

28.1   April 1935   *The Countryman*, London, xi, 1, pp 122-3

C29   Country Life

29.1   26 April 1935 - 24 October 1941 *The Spectator*
              26 April - 10 May 1935, cliv, 5574-6
              20 December - 27 December 1935, clv, 5608-9
              3 January - 14 February 1936, clvi, 5610-16
              22 January - 29 January 1937, clviii, 5665-66
              12 February - 26 March 1937, clviii, 5668-74
              18 February - 1 April 1938, clx, 5721-27
              17 February - 24 March 1939, clxii, 5773-78
              31 May 1940 - 28 June 1940, clxiv, 5840-44
              5 July 1940 - 26 July 1940, clxv, 5845-48
              8 November - 29 November 1940, clxv, 5863-66
              13 December - 27 December 1940, clxv, 5868-70
              3 January - 21 March 1941, clxvi, 5871-82
              4 April - 27 June 1941, clxvi, 5884-96
              4 July - 29 August 1941, clxvi, 5897-905
              12 September - 24 October 1941, clxvi, 5907-13
A selection of the notes was published by Penguin Books in 1943 (A 46)
See *The Blossoming World* (A 110) pp 81, 174-6

C30   Wild Trees in Blossom

30.1   17 May 1935   *The Spectator*, cliv, 5577, pp 832-3

C31   Chelsea (on the Chelsea Flower Show)
31.1   25 May 1935   *New Statesman and Nation*, ix, 222, p 749

C32   Flowers and Faces
32.1   1935   *Flowers and Faces* (A 23)

C33   Why I Live in the Country
33.1   January 1936   *The Countryman*, xii, 2, pp 494-9

C34   Spring Gardens
34.1   20 March 1936   *The Spectator*, clvi, 5621, pp 509-10

C35   The Novelist's Ear
35.1   March 1936   *Fortnightly Review*, London, cxlv, pp 277-82

C36   The Other Chelsea
(on the Chelsea Flower Show)
C36.1   23 May 1936   *New Statesman and Nation*, xi, 274
(new series), p 802

C37   A Poacher's Life
C37.1   May 1936   *An Anthology of Modern Nature Writing*,
Ed. Henry Williamson, Modern Anthologies No.6,
London: Thomas Nelson and Sons Ltd., pp 260-69
From *The Poacher* (A 22)

C38   May in the Woods
38.1   June 1936   *Fortnightly Review*, London, cxlv, pp 721-4

C39   Poaching Days
39.1   5 Sept 1936   *John O'London's Weekly*, London, xxxv, 908, p 791

C40   The Wood in April
40.1   1936   *Through the Woods* (A 27)

C41 The Other Wood
41.1   1936   *Through the Woods* (A 27)

C42 Trees in Flower
42.1   1936   *Through the Woods* (A 27)

C43 Flowers and Foxes
43.1   1936   *Through the Woods* (A 27)

C44 Oaks and Nightingales
44.1   1936   *Through the Woods* (A 27)

C45 The Villain
45.1   1936   *Through the Woods* (A 27)

C46 Woods and Hills
46.1   1936   *Through the Woods* (A 27)

C47 The Height of Summer
47.1   1936   *Through the Woods* (A 27)

C48 Woods and the Sea
48.1   1936   *Through the Woods* (A 27)

C49 Poachers and Mushrooms
49.1   1936   *Through the Woods* (A 27)

C50 The Heart of Autumn
50.1   1936   *Through the Woods* (A 27)
50.2   1941   (part) *The House of Tranquility: an anthology
                        for to-day*, selected and edited by Arthur
                        Stanley, London: Eyre & Spottiswoode, pp 204-5

C51 Winter Gale and Winter Spring
51.1   1936   *Through the Woods* (A 27)

C52 Primroses and Catkins
52.1   1936   *Through the Woods* (A 27)

C53 The Darling Buds of March
53.1   1936   *Through the Woods* (A 27)
Part of this essay was published in 1941 as 'Buds of March' (C 87)

C54 The Circle is Turned
54.1   1936   *Through the Woods* (A 27)

C55 Crafts of Old England
55.1   4 Dec 1936   *John O'London's Weekly*, Special illustrated
                                  supplement, pp i-viii, bound between pp 426-7

C56 Thomas Hardy and Joseph Conrad
56.1   1936   *The English Novelists: A survey of the novel by
                                  twenty contemporary novelists*, Ed. Derek
                                  Verschoyle, London: Chatto and Windus: pp 229-44

C57 The Twin Rivers
57.1   1937   *Down the River* (A 29)

C58 A Boy's Brook
58.1   1937   *Down the River* (A 29)

C59 The First River
59.1   1937   *Down the River* (A 29)

C60 Fish and Fishermen
60.1   1937   *Down the River* (A 29)

C61 The Flood
61.1   1937   *Down the River* (A 29)

C62 The Frost
62.1   1937   *Down the River* (A 29)

C63 The Second River
63.1   1937   *Down the River* (A 29)

C64 Water Flowers and Water Creatures
64.1   1937   *Down the River* (A 29)

C65 Flowers of Childhood
65.1   1937   *Down the River* (A 29)

C66 The Water-Mill
66.1   1937   *Down the River* (A 29)

C67 Otters and Men
67.1   1937   *Down the River* (A 29)
67.2   1947   *Otters and Men* (A 58) (an abridgement, published
                            as a pamphlet by the National Society
                            for the Abolition of Cruel Sports)

C68 The Rivers of England
68.1   1937   *Down the River* (A 29)

C69a Down to the Sea
69a.1   1937   *Down the River* (A 29)

C69b The English Forest
69b.1   1937   *Romantic Britain*, Ed. Tom Stephenson, London:
                            Odhams Press, pp 227-36 (illustrated
                            with 10 photographs)

C69c Lilies and Coal
69c.1   February 1938   *My Garden: An intimate magazine
                            for garden lovers*, edited and owned
                            by Theo A. Stephens, Weldons Ltd, London,
                            pp 163-7

C70   Ought Victorians To Speak Of "The Good Old Days"?
70.1   18 March 1938   *John O'London's Weekly*, xxxviii, 988, p 982

C71   Spring Sowing
71.1   31 March 1939   *The Spectator*, clxii, 5779, pp 525-6

C72   Where I Work
72.1   Spring 1939   *Now and Then*,London, No. 62, p 7

C73   Birds and Seeds
73.1   27 October 1939 *The Spectator*, clxiii, p 280

C74   An Autobiographical Note
74.1   1939   *Under Thirty: an anthology*, Ed. M. Harrison, London: Rich & Cowan (The short story, 'The Machine' (B 112.3) introduced by the author)

C75   The Hedge Chequerwork
75.1   1939   *The English Countryside: a survey of its chief features*, Ed. and introduced by H.J. Massingham, London: B.T. Batsford, pp 39-54

C76   'Who Prop, In These Bad Days, My Mind?'
76.1   April 1940   *The Countryman*, xxi, 1, pp 30-31

C77   Fellow Passengers
77.1   18 October 1940 *The Spectator*, clxv, pp 386-7

C78   October Lake
78.1   1 November 1940 *The Spectator*, clxv, p 439

C79   Country Parliament
79.1   January 1941   *Life and Letters Today*, London, xxviii, 41, pp 198-204

C80 The Rural School
80.1   April-June 1941   *The Countryman*, xxiii, 1, pp 19-20

C81 O More Than Happy Countryman
81.1   24 May 1941   *The Field*, London, pp 644-6
81.2   1943   *O More Than Happy Countryman* (A 48)
81.3   1949   *The Country Heart* (A 62)
81.4   1985   *The Happy Countryman*, London: Robinson
                              Publishing, pp 93-104

C82 The Poacher at Work
82.1   1941   *The English Scene*, Edited and arranged by
                              F. Alan Walbank, London: B.T. Batsford Ltd.,
                              pp 156-8 (an excerpt from *The Poacher*
                              (A 22))

C83 Rutland: The Toy County
83.1   7 June 1941   *Country Life*, London, lxxxix, pp 494-6

C84 A Note on Saroyan
84.1   September 1941   *Modern Reading*, Ed. Reginald Moore, London:
                              Staples Books, pp 27-30 (see also *The Modern
                              Short Story* (A 40), Chapter VIII,
                              pp 187-92)

C85 Artichokes and Asparagus
85.1   October 1941   *Life and Letters Today*, London, xxxi, 50, pp 4-21

C86 Sea Days, Sea Flowers
86.1   October 1941   *The Saturday Book, 1941-1942*, Ed. Leonard
                              Russell, London: Hutchinson, pp 16-32
                              (Border and ornamental initial engraved
                              by Albert E. Barlow. Five wood engravings
                              by Agnes Miller Parker.)
86.2   1943   *O More Than Happy Countryman* (A 48)
86.3   1949   *The Country Heart* (A 62)
86.4   1985   *The Happy Countryman*, London: Robinson
                              Publishing, pp 20-8

C87 Buds of March
87.1   1941   *The House of Tranquility: An Anthology for today,*
                                 Selected and arranged by Arthur Stanley, London:
                                 Eyre & Spottiswoode, pp 203-4 (an excerpt from
                                 'The Darling Buds of March' (C53.1))

C88 The Man in Action
88.1   September 1942   *Flying and Popular Aviation,* Chicago, xxxi,
                                 3, pp 130-3, 222-5, 230 (with photographs of a
                                 Spitfire and its crew)
88.2   1985   *The Spitfire Log,* A 50th-anniversary tribute to
                                 the world's most famous fighter plane, compiled
                                 by Peter Haining, London: Souvenir Press,
                                 pp 88-93 (with a cartoon drawn in August 1940
                                 by Russell Brockbank and photographs from
                                 Flying and Popular Aviation above)

C89 Animals - All the Year Round
(a commentary)
89.1   October 1942   *The 1943 Saturday Book,* Ed. Leonard Russell,
                                 London: Hutchinson, pp 241-52 (with twelve
                                 engravings by Agnes Miller Parker)

C90 Sudden Spring
90.1   1942   *In the Heart of the Country* (A 42)
90.2   1949   *The Country Heart* (A 62)

C91 Fisherman's Luck
91.1   1942   *In the Heart of the Country* (A 42)
91.2   1949   *The Country Heart* (A 62)

C92 Overture to Summer
92.1   1942   *In the Heart of the Country* (A 42)
92.2   1949   *The Country Heart* (A 62)

C93 Fruit Blossom Time
93.1   1942   *In the Heart of the Country* (A 42)
93.2   1949   *The Country Heart* (A 62)

C94 "Clouded August Thorn"
94.1   1942   *In the Heart of the Country* (A 42)
94.2   1949   *The Country Heart* (A 62)

C95 Strange Battlefields
95.1   1942   *In the Heart of the Country* (A 42)
95.2   1949   *The Country Heart* (A 62)

C96 The Great Snow
96.1   1942   *In the Heart of the Country* (A 42)
96.2   1949   *The Country Heart* (A 62)

C97 A Summer Spring
97.1   1942   *In the Heart of the Country* (A 42)
97.2   1949   *The Country Heart* (A 62)

C98 "...Bring Forth May Flowers"
98.1   1942   *In the Heart of the Country* (A 42)
98.2   1949   *The Country Heart* (A 62)

C99 Victorian Garden
99.1   1942   *In the Heart of the Country* (A 42)
99.2   1949   *The Country Heart* (A 62)
99.3   1960   *Mother's Bedside Book*, Ed. Eric
                      Duthie, London: Heinemann; an excerpt,
                      pp 326-30

C100 Wealden Beauty
100.1   1942   *In the Heart of the Country* (A 42)
100.2   1949   *The Country Heart* (A 62)

C101 The Strangeness of Fish
101.1   1942   *In the Heart of the Country* (A 42)
101.2   1949   *The Country Heart* (A 62)

C102 The Parish Pump
102.1   1942   *In the Heart of the Country* (A 42)
102.2   1949   *The Country Heart* (A 62)

C103   Flowers and Downland
103.1   1942   *In the Heart of the Country* (A 42)
103.2   1949   *The Country Heart* (A 62)

C104   The English Countryside
104.1   1942   *The English Spirit*, Ed. Anthony Weymouth,
                         London: George Allen & Unwin Ltd, pp 35-9
Originally broadcast as a talk in the BBC Empire Service

C105   Men Who Fly Above Fear
105.1   5 Sept 1943   *New York Times Magazine*, New York, pp 8-9

C106   Et Decorum Est Pro Patria Mori
106.1   1943   *O More Than Happy Countryman* (A 48)
106.2   1949   *The Country Heart* (A 62)
106.3   1985   *The Happy Countryman*, London: Robinson
                         Publishing, pp 7-13

C107   The Great House
107.1   1943   *O More Than Happy Countryman* (A 48)
107.2   1949   *The Country Heart* (A 62)
107.3   1985   *The Happy Countryman*, London: Robinson
                         Publishing, pp 14-19

C108   Mr. Pimpkins
108.1   1943   *O More Than Happy Countryman* (A 48)
108.2   1949   *The Country Heart* A 62)
108.3   1985   *The Happy Countryman*, London: Robinson
                         Publishing, pp 29-37

C109   The Future Garden
109.1   1943   *O More Than Happy Countryman* (A 48)
109.2   1949   *The Country Heart* (A 62)
109.3   1985   *The Happy Countryman*, London: Robinson
                         Publishing, pp 38-52

C110   The Garden on Leave
110.1   1943   *O More Than Happy Countryman* (A 48)
110.2   1949   *The Country Heart* (A 62)
110.3   1985   *The Happy Countryman*, London: Robinson
                         Publishing, pp 53-8

C111   The New Country

111.1	1943	*O More Than Happy Countryman* (A 48)
111.2	1949	*The Country Heart* (A 62)
111.3	1985	*The Happy Countryman*, London: Robinson Publishing. pp 59-71

C112   The Old Tradition

112.1	1943	*O More than Happy Countryman* (A 48)
112.2	1949	*The Country Heart* (A 62)
112.3	1985	*The Happy Countryman*, London: Robinson Publishing, pp 72-9

C113   The Green Hedges

113.1	1943	*O More Than Happy Countryman* (A 48)
113.2	1949	*The Country Heart* (A 62)
113.3	1985	*The Happy Countryman*, London: Robinson Publishing, pp 80-92

C114   The Battle of Britain 1940

114.1	September 1944	*Royal Air Force Journal*, London, ii, 9, pp 298-300, with one illustration from an oil painting by John Armstrong
114.2	1946	*Slipstream: A Royal Air Force anthology* Edited by Squadron Leader R. Raymond and Squadron Leader David Langdon, London: Eyre & Spottiswoode, pp 5-7

C115   Tomorrow : The Country

115.1	October 1944	*The Saturday Book*, 4, Ed. Leonard Russell, London: Hutchinson, pp 65-72

C116   My Grandfather's Farm

116.1	October 1944	*Royal Air Force Journal*, London. ii, 10, pp 344-6 with one drawing by Corporal C.E. Pierce
116.2	1946	*Slipstream, A Royal Air Force anthology* Ed. Squadron Leader R. Raymond and Squadron Leader David Langdon, London: Eyre & Spottiswoode, pp 105-110

C117 The Rate for the Job
117.1 Autumn 1944 *The Author*, London, pp 19-21

C118 Introduction
118.1 1944 *The W.A.A.F. in Action*, London: Adam and Charles Black in collaboration with the Air Ministry, pp 7-12

C119 Three Days to Calcutta
119.1 18 August 1945 *Christian Science Monitor*, (Weekly Magazine Section), Boston, Mass., pp 7,18

C120 They Have Left the Farm
120.1 December 1945 *Royal Air Force Journal*, London, iii, 12, pp 456-8, with one drawing by Sergeant T. Gourdie
This article is a sequel to 'My Grandfather's Farm' (C 116)

C121 Greetings from our Readers
121.1 Spring 1947 *The Countryman*, xxxv, 1, p 14

C122 So This Is SPAIN TODAY
122.1 8 November 1948 *News Chronicle*, London

C123 Concerning Authors' Cottages (1. H.E. Bates)
123.1 1948 *The Countryman Book*, a selection of articles and illustrations from *The Countryman*, made by J.W. Robertson Scott, CH. London: Odhams Press Ltd, pp 121-3

C124 Railway Flowers
124.1 7 August 1949 *Sunday Times*, London
124.2 1952 *The Country of White Clover* (A 74)

C125 Introduction: Yesterday
    Epilogue: Tomorrow
125.1 1949 *The Country Heart* (A 62)

C126 My Best Novel
126.1   January 1950   *My Best Novel* (a guide to the writings
                                of twelve novelists), Islington Public Libraries,
                                London, p 1.

C127 Introduction: The Englishman's Spring
127.1   1950   *In England Now, Spring*, London: Avalon Press,
                                pp 8-11

C128 Exhilarating
128.1   1950   *Spice of Life*, compiled by J. Thurston
                                Thrower, London: Burke Publishing, p 44, one
                                illustration by Dennis Mallet

C129 The less I like poetry
129.1   1950   *Spice of Life*, compiled by J. Thurston Thrower,
                                London: Burke Publishing, p 89

C130 Foreword
130.1   1950   *Pointillists and their Period*, Redfern
                                Gallery, London, pp (3-4)

C131 Kent
131.1   December 1951   *Country Fair*, London, i, 6, (County
                                Supplement No.6) pp 81-8

C132 Night Light
132.1   April 1952   *Woman's Journal*, London, pp 36-7; 129-30

C133 Twenty-Five Years
133.1   Spring 1952   *The Countryman*, xlv, 1, pp 33-9
143.2   1962   *The Countryman Anthology*, Ed. John Cripps,
                                London: A. Baker, pp 11-20

C134 Journey to Spring
134.1   1952   *The Country of White Clover* (A 74)

C135   The Country of White Clover
135.1   1952   *The Country of White Clover* (A 74)

C136   A Piece of England
136.1   1952   *The Country of White Clover* (A 74)

C137   Trees and Men
137.1   1952   *The Country of White Clover* (A 74)
137.2   July 1956   *The Atlantic Monthly*, Boston, Mass.
                               cxcviii, pp 75-9

C138   Union Rustic
138.1   1952   *The Country of White Clover* (A 74)

C139   The Face of Summer
139.1   1952   *The Country of White Clover* (A 74)

C140   The Show
140.1   1952   *The Country of White Clover* (A 74)

C141   All Summer in a Day
141.1   1952   *The Country of White Clover* (A 74)

C142   The New Hodge
142.1   1952   *The Country of White Clover* (A 74)

C143   Sea and September
143.1   1952   *The Country of White Clover* (A 74)

C144   The Turn of the Year
144.1   1952   *The Country of White Clover* (A 74)

C145   Kent Is My County
145.1   19 July 1952   *Illustrated Magazine*, Odhams Press
                               Ltd, London. pp 22-5

C146 The New Writer's Cramp
146.1   4 August 1952   *Daily Telegraph*, London

C147 What Future for the Young Writer?
147.1   18 Dec 1952   *Daily Telegraph*, London

C148 A Welcome to the Book Window
148.1   Christmas 1952   *Book Window*, No.1, pp i-iv

C149 Escape (Commentary)
149.1   1952   *Escape – or Die*, Authentic stories of the
                               R.A.F. Escaping Society by Paul Brickhill,
                               London: Evans Brothers, pp 11-15

C150 Bahamian Flower Show
150.1   31 May 1953   *Sunday Times*, London. Two drawings
                               by John Minton

C151 What I'd Like to Show the World
151.1   31 May 1953   *Sunday Express*, London

C152 Jealousy
152.1   16 August 1953 *Sunday Express*, London, p 2

C153 Past Masters
153.1   25 October 1953 *Sunday Times*, London, p 6
                               One illustration by Andrew H. Freeth

C154 The Blackpool Miracle
(on the Football Association Challenge Cup Final, 2 May 1953)
154.1   1953   *The F.A. Book for Boys*. Number Six.
                               London: Naldrett Press, pp 31-7. With ten
                               photographs

C155 Foreword
155.1   1953   *The Reader's Digest Omnibus*, London,
                               pp ix-xii

C156   Lost World of Fancy

156.1   27 March 1954   *Everybody's Weekly*, London,
                                     pp 24-5, 46. Illustrations by Reg Gray

C157   Back Home

157.1   16 May 1954   *Sunday Express*, London

C158   Don't Blame the Author - He Reflects Today

158.1   9 August 1954   *Daily Mail*, London

C159   Witch-Hunt in the Book Shops

159.1   19 Nov 1954   *Evening News*, London

C160   Foreword

160.1   Foreword in catalogue to exhibition "Plaisirs
                                     de l'époque 1900", 7 December 1954-8 January
                                     1955, Redfern Gallery, London. 3 pp, with
                                     illustrations

C161   Introduction

161.1   1954   *The Lovers' Pocketbook (Les amoureux de Peynet)*,
                                     Raymond Peynet, edited by Kaye Webb,
                                     London: Perpetua Ltd, pp (1-3)

C162   Why I Wrote That Book

162.1   2 April 1955   *Everybody's Weekly*, London, p 25

C163   Corinthian-Casuals v Bishop Auckland 1956

163.1   8 April 1956   *Sunday Times*, London
163.2   1962   *The Footballer's Companion*, Ed. Brian
                                     Glanville, London: Eyre & Spottiswoode,
                                     pp 204-7

C164   Foreword

164.1   1956   *Pick of To-day's Short Stories 7*,
                                     Ed. John Pudney, London: Putnam, pp 9-13

C165 Landscape Lost
165.1   22 Nov 1957   *The Spectator*, cic, p 668

C166 Introduction
166.1   1957   *Green Mansions* by W.H. Hudson, London:
                            Collins, pp 11-16

C167 Shoemakers Remembered
167.1   1957   *The Book of Leisure*, Ed. John Pudney,
                            London: Odhams Press, pp 116-26 (illustrated
                            by David Knight)

C168 Candle for Spring
168.1   28 March 1958   *The Spectator*, cc, 200, p 387

C169 Manchester United - a tribute
169.1   1958-59   *The Football Association Year Book*,
                            London: The Football Association, pp 55-8
169.2   1961   *The Footballer's Fireside Book*,
                            London: Heinemann Ltd, pp 119-22
169.3   1962   *The Footballer's Companion*, London:
                            Eyre & Spottiswoode, pp 11 435-8

C170 'When the Cinemagoer complains that - "It Isn't Like the Book" - Who's To Blame?'
170.1   May 1959   *Films and Filming*, London, p 7

C171 Introduction
171.1   1959   *The Beach of Falesà* by Robert Louis
                            Stevenson, London: The Folio Society, pp 9-18

C172 Hemingway's Short Stories
172.1   1961   *Hemingway and His Critics: An international
                            anthology*, Ed.C.H. Baker, New York: Hill and
                            Wang
An excerpt from *The Modern Short Story* (A 40)

C173 Easy Exotics
173.1   1963   *A Book of Gardens*, Ed. James Turner, with
                              illustrations by Gay Galsworthy, London:
                              Cassell, pp 3-12

C174 A Tribute to J.W. Robertson Scott
174.1   Summer 1963   *The Countryman*, London. lx, 2 pp 382-3

C175 40 Years A Writer
175.1   14 May 1965   *Weekend Telegraph*, London, pp 47, 49, 51-2

C176 Introduction
176.1   1965   *Six Stories by various authors*, Selected
                              by H.E. Bates, London: Oxford University Press.
                              World's Classics No.604 pp (vii)-xvii

C177 A Rabbit Remembers
177.1   1965   *Cricket Bag – a miscellany for the twelfth man*
                              ... Ed. Leslie Frewin, London: Macdonald,
                              pp 107-10

C178 Undersoil Heating for Sub-Tropical Treasures (Gardens of Ideas)
(on the garden of Loelia Duchess of Westminster)
178.1   1 March 1968   *Daily Telegraph Magazine*, London, 178,
                              pp 30-32

C179 Growing 4,400 Alpines in Birmingham (Gardens of Ideas)
(on the garden of Roy Elliott)
179.1   15 March 1968   *Daily Telegraph Magazine*, London, 180, pp 52-4

C180 Conservatory Revived (Gardens of Ideas)
(on Cecil Beaton's garden and conservatory)
180.1   29 March 1968   *Daily Telegraph Magazine*, London, 182,
                              pp (36), 37, (38)

C181 Jungle Rarities in Norfolk (Gardens of Ideas)
(on Maurice Marsh's garden)
181.1   10 April 1968   *Daily Telegraph Magazine*, London, 184, pp 42-5

C182 Round the library bush
182.1   22 March 1969   *The Times*, London

C183 Awakening extracts from *The Vanished World* (A 107)
183.1   23 August 1969   *The Times Saturday Review*, London, pp i and iv (with one illustration by Pauline Ellison)

C184 My Father and I extracts from *The Vanished World* (A 107)
184.1   January 1970   *Argosy*, London: xxxi, 1, pp 58-61

C185 From My Garden - The Scents of Summer
185.1   June 1971   *Living*, London, v, 6, p 12

C186 From My Garden - All Seeds Bright and Beautiful
186.1   October 1971   *Living*, London, v, 10, p 12

C187 All the Milkiness of May-Time
187.1   Summer 1972   *The Countryman*, lxxvii, 2, pp 41-5

C188 The Moment that Changed my Life
188.1   16 September 1972 *Woman*, London. lxxi, 1839, p 42

C189 A Countryman Remembers - Where Once I Walked
189.1   November 1973   *Living*, London, iii, 11, p 132 (illustrated by Rodney Shackell)

C190   A Countryman Remembers - God's Little Acres
190.1   January 1974   *Living*, London, viii, 1, p 80
                             (illustrated by Rodney Shackell)

C191   H.E. Bates - by himself
191.1   5 April 1974   *Daily Telegraph Magazine*, London, pp 27-33

C192   A Countryman Remembers - Trees and Foxes
192.1   June 1974   *Living*. London, viii 6, p 88 (illustrated
                             by Rodney Shackell)
An excerpt taken from *Through the Woods* (A 27)

C193   Foreword (published posthumously)
193.1   1984   *Higham Ferrers - A Pictorial History*,
                             The Rotary Club of Rushden, p 5.

C194   Peter Hebdon: An Appreciation
194.1   1986   *At the Sign of the Mermaid – Fifty Years
                             of Michael Joseph*, London: Michael Joseph,
                             pp 95-6

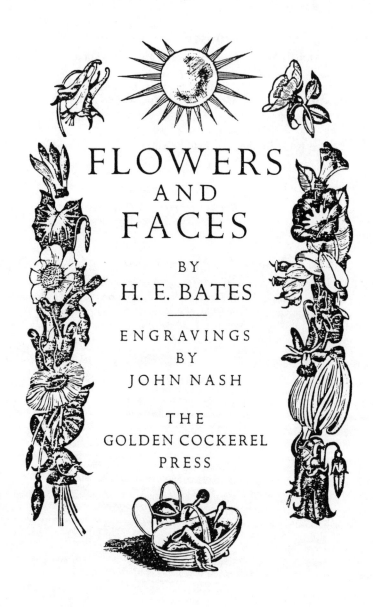

FLOWERS
AND
FACES

BY

H. E. BATES

———

ENGRAVINGS
BY
JOHN NASH

THE
GOLDEN COCKEREL
PRESS

D

Poems and Christmas cards

D1 ARMISTICE DAY, NOVEMBER 11th, 1920

Kettering Grammar School Magazine,
5, December 1920, p 2

ARMISTICE DAY, NOVEMBER 11th, 1920

I lingered long in that last resting-place,
I lingered and I then did dream awhile.
Methought I saw a lustrous wingéd host,
Come down from Heav'n, drest all in purest white.
They hovered gently o'er that dark and lonely grave
And from it took, in shrouded linen wrapt,
The body of a man. And then forthwith
With loving arms they bore it up, as though
Of precious gold it were. So up and up
They bore it, through a dreary pall of dark
Then through a blaze of light, and up and up
So seeméd they to go. The Abbey then did fade
And melt away, but in its place there came
A ring of light, and in that ring there stood
A Warrior, clad in white, and Known to God.

D2   EVENING

Kettering Grammar School Magazine,
6, December 1921, p 13

EVENING

Let the sun set, the summer sun,
   Let the pines grow dark
   Against the crimson sky;
Let the moon shine against the white birch bark,
   Let the day die.

Let the purple of even fade away,
   White grows the road
   Beneath the moonlit sky;
Home goes the wanderer to his own abode,
   Dear day, goodbye.

D3   SUNDAY

3.1   December 1923   *Poetry*, London, p 309
3.2   January 1924   *Kettering Grammar School* Magazine, 8, p 25

SUNDAY

I love the Sunday cool of trees;
My mother's fine blue dress
That is a loveliness.

I love the old sweet hymn that's sung;
The lovely tale of Him
Who breathed in Bethlehem ....

And wonder now if Christ my Lord
In all His holiness
Loved once his mother's dress.

D4   THE FIFTH SONG

Kettering & District Reminder, T. Beaty Hart Ltd,
Kettering, 26 March 1924, i, 4, p 10

THE FIFTH SONG

Five songs will I make to-day,
Five fine fairy songs for you,
One of silver, one of blue,
With five tunes for you to play.

They shall cheer you as you go,
Fairy songs men have not seen,
One of gold and one of green
With sweet notes for you to blow.

This shall be the last for you
Full of sounds that sweetest ring,
Coloured like an hour of spring:
Silver, green and white and blue.

D5   "TWO HOUSES"

Kettering & District Reminder T. Beaty Hart Ltd,
Kettering, 9 April 1924, i, 6, p 5

"TWO HOUSES"

In my father's garden, a house
Of finches in a tree is knit.
Alone, alone, at peace it blows,
For not a boy or cuckoo knows
The hermit site of it.

Give me a house, as idly rare,
A garden where a thought may flit,
And trees that finchs' nests may share
And God, inestimably there
In every part of it.

D6   THE PASSING

Kettering & District Reminder, T. Beaty Hart Ltd, Kettering, i, 8, p 7

THE PASSING

Blooms the yellow primrose now,
Lovliest I ever knew;
Leaves are green upon the bough,
Blooms the yellow primrose now.
Skies are lovelier than I knew,
Every face is gay and glad,
But my heart is only sad,
For beneath the green-leaf bough,
Dies the yellow primrose now.

D7   THE SPRING SHEPHERD

Kettering & District Reminder, T. Beaty Hart Ltd, Kettering. 23 April 1924, i, 8, p 20

THE SPRING SHEPHERD

Upon the quiet hills of day
His lambs are lovely things;
He tends them in his own sweet way
Upon the quiet hills of day,
For he's a shepherd kinder than
All shepherds since the world began.

Within the dusky fold of night
He scarcely hears them breathe,
Yet every one is his delight;
Within the dusky fold of night
Surrounded by his lambs and sheep
I wonder if he goes to sleep?

For ever with the quiet things
He will not tell his name;
Instead, it is his heart that sings
For ever of the quiet things,
And shows the thoughts he guards to keep
Are lovlier than his lambs and sheep.

D8   IF I WERE QUEEN

The Reminder, Kettering, 28 May 1924,
T. Beaty Hart Ltd, i, 13, p 4.

IF I WERE QUEEN

I'd have a garden,
    If I were queen;
With so many flowers,
    You couldn't see between.

Peacocks should walk there,
    Slow ... stately ... and blue,
While sparrows should come,
    And shy linnets too.

There should be blossoms
    of silver in Spring;
And God should be there
    To love everything.

A house should there be,
    With shutters of green;
And you should be King,
    If I were the Queen.

D9   THE WATCHERS

The Reminder, Kettering, 18 June 1924.
T. Beaty Hart Ltd, i, 16, p 20

THE WATCHERS

We envied him so,
We other children,
Because his mother let him go
To gather rushes by the broad river;
We thought him lucky then,
But we envy him no
Longer now ... for we think he must have gone
to gather rushes, all alone,
For ever ... .

D10 WE WHO NOW WAIT

The New Leader Book, Edited by
H.N. Brailsford. Office of The New
Leader, London. 1926, 4to, paper wrappers.

WE WHO NOW WAIT

We who now wait so sadly for the peace,
We who were born only a frail child-span
Before the shout began
That war had red release!–
We whose young blood had scarce in freedom run
Before Hill Sixty and Verdun! . . .

And you!
You who have known what dear ways peace has had,
Why do you wonder at us who wait
And watch, far-leaden-eyed and late?
Why need you wonder thus that we are sad,
So old in youth and so untimely sad?

D11 SONG IN WINTER

The New Coterie, E. Archer, London.
6, Summer-Autumn 1927, p 9.

SONG IN WINTER

Your hands have trembled under mine,
Your breast has surged: a summer sea,
And those impatient smears of wine,
Your lips, have set their mark on me.

And singing is so chaste a thing
And chastity so green a song,
I have no need to ache for spring
Nor go ungarlanded for long.

And have no turbulence but this:
What devil' else distracted me
Before your hands, and breast, and kiss
Reiterated constancy.

D12 CLAMOUR

The Nation & Athenaeum, London,
3 March 1928, p 813

CLAMOUR

Over the yellow arm of down
I lay and watched the teeth of tide
Wounding the sea-scarred shore again,
While at my beating side,
Sweet Unimpressionable,
Colossal by your tongue — you lay!
Prattling about the shipping in the bay.

And from your mouth, mouth-pressed a hundred times,
I knew that men were fools, clamouring and getting not,
Kissing to cover up their groans.
And suddenly at your side, hot
With your pulsed companionship, I lay
And shut you out, and kissed dark earth,
Passionately bleak against your voice and ships and bay.

D13   Song for December   Christmas card 1928

| [GREETINGS] |

8vo, 5 x 8 ins; (4) pp, consisting of front cover as above, with the word Greetings, verso blank, pp (1-2); 16-line verse, Song for December dated Christmas 1928 from H.E. Bates, with the author's signature, verso blank, pp (3-4).
    Produced on a deckle-edged white card; all text printed in green.
    A Christmas card for presentation only. 150 copies printed for Charles Lahr, 68 Red Lion Street, Holborn, London.

D14   CHRISTMAS 1930

CHRISTMAS | 1930 | (device) | H.E. BATES

8vo, $4\frac{1}{2}$ x 7 ins; (4) pp, consisting of front cover as above, verso blank, pp (1-2); 13-line verse, printed in italics, with author's signature at foot, verso blank, pp (3-4).
    All wording lettered in black with the exception of the initial letter of 'Christmas' printed in blue; the wording on the front cover contained within a decorated and rule border printed in blue.
    The card was produced simultaneously in four forms: (a) on Japanese vellum paper; all edges trimmed; (b) on a stiff white card with deckle edges; (c) uniform with (b) with complimentary inscription of good wishes from the bookshop of Esther and Charles Lahr on p (2); (d) faulty proof copies of issue (b) with H.E. BATES. lacking from front cover, filled in at foot of poem in ink, in the holograph of Charles Lahr. This issue unsigned by H.E. Bates.

D15   Holly and Sallow   Christmas 1931

(single rule) | Holly and Sallow | (single rule) | BY H.E. BATES

8vo, 3⅘ x 8⅗ ins; (6) pp, consisting of front cover as above, verso blank, pp (1-2); 8-line verse printed in italics, with headpiece design by Frederick Carter, signed at foot by the author, verso blank, pp (3-4); blank page, certificate of issue on verso, pp (5-6).

All lettering and design printed in black. Folded from one sheet in the form of a folder, from left to right.

100 copies of this verse, each signed by the author, were issued for sale in a portfolio of 18 Christmas cards, and not sold separately.

D16   Give them their Life ...

16.1   1944   *Air Force Poetry*, Edited by John Pudney and Henry Treece, John Lane, The Bodley Head, London, p 13.

16.2   1964   *A Moment in Time* (A 100), p (5)

In *A Moment in Time* (A 100), p (5)

In *A Moment in Time* line 4 reads 'Young-eyed', changed from 'Young-winged' as printed in *Air Force Poetry*.

> *GIVE THEM THEIR LIFE ...*
>
> *Give them their life:*
> *They do not know how short it grows;*
> *So let them go*
> *Young-winged, steel-fledged, gun-furious,*
> *For if they live they'll live,*
> *As well you know,*
> *Upon the bitter kernels of their sweet ideals.*
>
> *Give them their wings:*
> *They cannot fly too high or far*
> *To fly above*
> *The dirty-moted, bomb-soured, word-tired world.*
> *And if they die they'll die,*
> *As you should know,*
> *More swiftly, cleanly, star-defined, than you will ever feel.*

D17 1940-1945

The Spectator, London, 14 September 1945, p 241

1940-1945

You hardly knew him, girl, before he went,
Whipped into world's bedammed recriminations
From youth's examinations:
To give the firmament
And make the air his sacrament.

This bread you eat, this air you breathe:
Ah! no, they do not taste the same.
Is it for something else you grieve?
Is it the hunger, hunger for the dead?
Do not hunger, girl, again.
Your bread is grief's compounded kernel:
Free as the air, and sacrament eternal.

D18 Christmas Card 1949

Privately published for presentation only

8vo, 5½ x 4¾ ins. (4) pp, consisting of front cover, origin of the drawing by John Minton on verso, pp (1-2); Christmas greetings from Madge and H.E. Bates, verso blank, pp (3-4).

Cream card with illustration, border and lettering all in red.

Notes: The drawing by John Minton is to be found at p (109) in *The Country Heart* by H.E. Bates (A 62)

Let us drink and be merry, dance, joke, and rejoice,
With claret and sherry, theorbo and voice!
The changeable world to our joy is unjust,
All treasure's uncertain,
Then down with your dust!
In frolics dispose your pounds, shillings and pence,
For we shall be nothing a hundred years hence.

D18

Index

of book titles (in italics), stories,
articles and poems